PREACHING AND PREACHERS

PREACHING AND PREACHERS

by

D. MARTYN LLOYD-JONES

ZONDERVAN
PUBLISHING HOUSE

OF THE ZONDERVAN CORPORATION | GRAND RAPIDS, MICHIGAN 49506

To all the members of the Westminster
Fellowship of preachers – past and
present

Contents

Preface

When I was asked to deliver a series of lectures to the students of the Westminster Theological Seminary on any aspect of the ministry I might like to choose, I decided that I must speak on 'Preaching and Preachers'. Many times I had been asked to give a lecture, or two or three lectures, on 'Expository Preaching'. I always replied that that was impossible – that such a subject demanded a whole series of lectures because there was no magical formula that one could pass on to others.

I felt very diffident also to tackle such a great theme, and I have always been amazed at the readiness of certain young ministers to advise their brethren on preaching and pastoral matters. 'Who is sufficient for these things?'

Even now I am reluctant to put these lectures into print. Perhaps the one justification for doing so is that I speak out of an experience of some forty-four years. During that time in addition to preaching regularly in the two churches of which I have been the pastor – eleven and a half years in South Wales, and thirty years at Westminster Chapel, London – I have always travelled a great deal between the Sundays and preached elsewhere. While in South Wales I generally preached twice on Tuesdays and Thursdays, and during most of my time in London I would be away on Tuesdays and Wednesdays, trying to get home, if possible on Wednesday night in order to prepare for the three sermons I would have to deliver at Westminster Chapel during the week-end.

I should have learned something as the result of that; and that is my sole title to attempt this task.

Throughout the years I have read many books on preaching. I cannot say that I have learned much from them, but I have enjoyed them greatly, and have often been entertained by them – as far as I am concerned the more anecdotal they were the better.

I did not consult any of them again while preparing these lectures. I felt that the best plan would be for me to state my attitude and my practice for what they are worth.

I have aimed at being practical, and I have tried to deal with the various detailed problems and questions that men have often put to me privately, and which have also often been discussed in ministers' meetings. In any case, as appears in many of the lectures, I thoroughly dislike any theoretical or abstract treatment of this subject.

This consideration has also determined the style. I was talking to – in a sense thinking aloud with – ministerial students and some ordained preachers, and this book is addressed to preachers and all those interested in preaching. I have therefore not attempted to change the conversational and intimate style; and apart from minor corrections what is now in print is what I actually said.

While preaching I rarely refer to myself; but here I felt that to be impersonal would be quite wrong. So there is a good deal of the personal and anecdotal element, I trust that this will be found to be helpful by way of illustration of the principles which I have tried to inculcate.

Some may object to my dogmatic assertions; but I do not apologise for them. Every preacher should believe strongly in his own method; and if I cannot persuade all of the rightness of mine, I can at least stimulate them to think and to consider other possibilities. I can say quite honestly that I would not cross the road to listen to myself preaching, and the preachers whom I have enjoyed most have been very different indeed in their method and style. But my business is not to describe them but to state what I believe to be right, however imperfectly I have put my own precepts into practice. I can only hope

Preface

that the result will be of some help, and especially to young preachers called to this greatest of all tasks, and especially in these sad and evil times. With many others I pray that 'The Lord of the harvest may thrust forth' many mighty preachers to proclaim 'the unsearchable riches of Christ'.

I would like to thank Professor Clowney and the members of the faculty of Westminster Seminary, and all the students, for their most kindly reception, and for the stimulating atmosphere in which I delivered these lectures during six weeks in the spring of 1969.

My thanks are due to Mrs. E. Burney for transcribing the tape-recordings of these lectures and preparing the typescript, and also, as ever, to my wife who has had to endure my preaching throughout the years, and with whom I have constantly discussed the various aspects of this enthralling and vital subject.

JULY 1971   D. M. LLOYD-JONES

PREACHING AND PREACHERS

CHAPTER ONE

The Primacy of Preaching

WHY AM I prepared to speak and to lecture on preaching? There are a number of reasons. It has been my life's work. I have been forty-two years in the ministry, and the main part of my work has been preaching; not exclusively, but the main part of it has been preaching. In addition it is something that I have been constantly studying. I am conscious of my inadequacies and my failures as I have been trying to preach for all these years; and that has led inevitably to a good deal of study and of discussion and of general interest in the whole matter. But, ultimately, my reason for being very ready to give these lectures is that to me the work of preaching is the highest and the greatest and the most glorious calling to which anyone can ever be called. If you want something in addition to that I would say without any hesitation that the most urgent need in the Christian Church today is true preaching; and as it is the greatest and the most urgent need in the Church, it is obviously the greatest need of the world also.

The statement about its being the most urgent need leads to the first matter that we must discuss together—Is there any need of preaching? Is there any place for preaching in the modern Church and in the modern world, or has preaching become quite outmoded? The very fact that one has to pose such a question, and to consider it, is, it seems to me, the most illuminating commentary on the state of the Church at the present time. I feel that that is the chief explanation of the present more or less parlous condition and ineffectiveness of the Christian Church in the world today. This whole question of the need of preaching, and the place of preaching in the ministry of the Church, is in question at the present time, so we have to start with that. So often when people are asked to lecture or to speak on preaching they rush immediately to consider methods and ways and means and the mechanics. I believe that is quite wrong. We must start with the presuppositions and with the background, and with general principles; for, unless I am very greatly mistaken, the main trouble arises from the fact that people are not clear in their minds as to what preaching really is. So I am going to deal with the matter in general before I come down to particulars of any type.

Here is the great question therefore: Can we justify preaching? Is there need of preaching at all in the modern world? This, as you know, is a part of a larger question. We are living in an age when not only preaching but the very Church herself is being questioned. You are familiar with the talk of 'religionless Christianity', with the idea that many have that the Church herself is perhaps the greatest hindrance to the Christian faith, and that if we really want to see people becoming Christians, and the world being 'Christianised', as they put it, we have to get rid of the Church, because the Church has become an obstacle standing between people and the truth that is in Christ Jesus.

With much of this criticism of the Church one has, of course, to agree. There is so much that is wrong with the Church—traditionalism, formality and lifelessness and so on—and it would be idle and utterly foolish to deny this. Often one really has to ask about certain gatherings and communities of people whether they are entitled to the name Church at all. The Church so easily can degenerate into an organisation, or even, perhaps, into a social club or something of that kind; so that it is often necessary to raise the whole question of the Church herself. However, that is not our object in these lectures, and we are not going to deal with the nature of the Church as such; but, as part of the general attitude to the Church, this matter of preaching must obviously arise acutely; and that is the theme with which I have to deal.

The Primacy of Preaching

What is the cause of the present reaction against preaching? Why has preaching fallen from the position it once occupied in the life of the Church and in the esteem of people? You cannot read the history of the Church, even in a cursory manner, without seeing that preaching has always occupied a central and a predominating position in the life of the Church, particularly in Protestantism. Why then this decline in the place and power of preaching; and why this questioning of the necessity for any preaching at all?

I would divide my answer to that question under two general headings. First of all there are certain general reasons which account for this, and then there are certain particular reasons in the Church herself. When I say 'general' I mean certain common ideas current in the world outside the Church. Let me illustrate what I mean. When making this point, for instance, in Great Britain I generally refer to it as Baldwinism. For those not familiar with that term let me explain what it means. There was a prime minister in Britain in the twenties and in the thirties named Stanley Baldwin. This man, who was of such little significance that his name means nothing even today, had a considerable effect upon people's thinking concerning the value of speaking and oratory in the life of peoples. He came into power and into office after the era of a coalition government in England led and dominated by men such as Lloyd George, Winston Churchill, Lord Birkenhead and others of that type. Now these men were orators, great speakers. Stanley Baldwin did not have that gift, so he saw that if he was to succeed it was essential that he should discount the value and the importance of speech and oratory. He was competing with brilliant men who were at the same time great orators; so he posed as the simple, honest, ordinary Englishman. He said that he was not a great speaker, and conveyed the suggestion that if a man is a great speaker he is a man whom you cannot trust, and is not quite honest. He put up these things as antitheses; and his line was to adopt the pose of the plain Englishman who could not indulge in great flights of oratory and imagination, but who made simple and plain and honest statements.

This attitude to oratory and the power of speech has quite definitely become a vogue, especially amongst the politicians, in Britain. But, alas, I maintain that it has had an influence also upon the Church. There has been a new attitude towards oratory and eloquence and speaking worthy of the name. It is one of distrust of the orator. And, of course, accompanying this, and enforcing this whole attitude, there has been a new emphasis on the place of reading. The argument is that nowadays we are a more cultured and educated people; that in the past people did not read for themselves and were dependent upon great speakers, great orators; but that that is no longer necessary because we have books and libraries and so on. Then in addition, we now have the radio and the television with knowledge and information concerning truth coming directly into the home. All these, I believe, in a general way have influenced the Church, and the outlook of the Church and of Christian people, upon the spoken word, and upon preaching as such.

Now I do not want to take too much time in refuting this general atmosphere which is inimical to preaching; I would simply content myself by saying this—that it is a very interesting thing to note that some of the greatest men of action that the world has ever known have also been great speakers and great orators. It is not an accident, I think, that in Great Britain for instance, during the two World Wars in this present century, the two great leaders that were thrown up happened to be great orators; and these other men who tend to give the impression that if a man can speak he is a mere talker who does nothing, have been refuted by the sheer facts of history. The greatest men of action have been great speakers; and, of course, it is a part of the function of, and an essential desideratum in, a leader that he can enthuse people, and rouse them, and get them to take action. One thinks of Pericles and Demosthenes and others. The general history of the world surely demonstrates quite plainly that the men who truly made history have been men who could speak, who could deliver a message, and who could get people to act as the result of the effect they produced upon them.

There it is then, in general. But we are more concerned about certain attitudes in the Church herself, or certain reasons in the Church herself which account for the decline in the place of preaching. I suggest that here are some of the main and the leading factors under this heading. I would not hesitate to put in the first position: the loss of belief in the authority of the Scriptures, and a diminution in the belief of the Truth. I put this first because I am sure it is the main factor. If you have not got authority, you cannot speak well, you cannot preach. Great preaching always depends upon great themes. Great themes always produce great speaking in any realm, and this is particularly true, of course, in the realm of the Church. While men believed in the Scriptures as the authoritative Word of God and spoke on the basis of that authority you had great preaching. But once that went, and men began to speculate, and to theorise, and to put up hypotheses and so on, the eloquence and the greatness of the spoken word inevitably declined and began to wane. You cannot really deal with speculations and conjectures in the same way as preaching had formerly dealt with the great themes of the Scriptures. But as belief in the great doctrines of the Bible began to go out, and sermons were replaced by ethical addresses and homilies, and moral uplift and socio-political talk, it is not surprising that preaching declined. I suggest that that is the first and the greatest cause of this decline.

But there is a second; and we have got to be fair in these matters. I believe that there has been a reaction against what were called 'the great pulpiteers', especially of the second half of the last century. They were to be found in great numbers in England and also in the U.S.A. I always feel that the man who was most typical in this respect in the U.S.A. was Henry Ward Beecher. He illustrates perfectly the chief characteristics of the pulpiteer. The term itself is very interesting, and I believe it is a very accurate one. These men were pulpiteers rather than preachers. I mean that they were men who could occupy a pulpit and dominate it, and dominate the people. They were professionals. There was a good deal of the element of showmanship in them, and they were experts at handling congregations and playing on their emotions. In the end they could do almost what they liked with them.

Now this, I am sure, has produced a reaction; and that is a very good thing. These pulpiteers were to me—with my view of preaching —an abomination; and it is they who are in many ways largely responsible for this present reaction. It is very interesting to notice that this has happened in times past, not only with regard to the preaching of the Gospel, the Word of God, but in other realms also. There is an interesting statement in a book by Edwin Hatch on the influence of Greek ideas upon the Christian Church which seems to me to put this very well. He says that it is a fact that philosophy fell into disrepute and waned in the life of Greece as the result of rhetoric and the increasing use of rhetoric. Let me quote the words of Hatch. He says:

If you look more closely into history you will find that rhetoric killed philosophy. Philosophy died because for all but a small minority it ceased to be real, it passed from the sphere of thought and conduct to that of exposition and literature. Its preachers preached not because they were bursting with truths which could not help finding expression, but because they were masters of fine phrases and lived in an age in which fine phrases had a value. It died, in short, because it had become sophistry, but sophistry is of no special age or country, it is indigenous to all soils upon which literature grows. No sooner is any special form of literature created by the genius of a great writer than there arises a class of men who cultivate the style of it for the style's sake. No sooner is any new impulse given either to philosophy or to religion than there arises a class of men who copy the form without the substance, and try to make the echo of the past sound like the voice of the present. So it has been with Christianity.

That is a most important point, and I think it has very real relevance to this point I am making about the pernicious influence of pulpiteerism upon true preaching. You see, the form became more important than the substance, the oratory and the eloquence became things in and of themselves, and ultimately preaching became a form of entertainment. The Truth was noticed, they paid a passing respect to it, but the great thing was the form. I believe we are living in an age which is experiencing a reaction against that. And this has been continued in the present century when there has often been a form of popular preaching, in evangelism particularly, that has brought true preaching into disrepute because of a lack of substance and too much attention being paid to the form and to the presentation. It degenerates ultimately into what I have described as professionalism, not to say showmanship.

Finally, I would suggest that another factor has been the wrong conception of what a sermon really is, and therefore of what preaching really is. It is that same point concerning the form again, not in the crude way to which I have been referring, but I believe that the printing and publication of sermons has had a bad effect upon preaching. I refer particularly to the publication of sermons, speaking roughly, since somewhere about 1890, and—dare I say it—I have a feeling that the Scottish school of preachers have been the greatest offenders in this respect. I believe it happened in this way. These men were endowed with a real literary gift, and the emphasis passed, unconsciously again, from the truth of the message to the literary expression. They paid great attention to literary and historical allusions and quotations and so on. In other words, these men, as I shall suggest in a later lecture, were essayists rather than preachers; but as they published these essays as sermons, they were accepted as sermons. That has undoubtedly had a controlling effect upon the thinking of many in the Church as to what a sermon should be, and also as to what preaching really is. So I would attribute a good deal of the decline in preaching at the present time to those literary effusions which have passed under the name of sermons and of preaching.

The result of all these things has been that a new idea has crept in with regard to preaching, and it has taken various forms. A most significant one was that people began to talk about the 'address' in the service instead of the sermon. That in itself was indicative of a subtle change. An 'address'. No longer the sermon, but an 'address' or perhaps even a lecture. I shall be dealing with these distinctions later. There was a man in the U.S.A. who published a series of books under the significant title of *Quiet Talks*. *Quiet Talks*, you see, as against the 'ranting' of the preachers! *Quiet Talks on Prayer; Quiet Talks on Power*, etc. In other words the very title announces that the man is not going to preach. Preaching, of course, is something carnal lacking in spirituality, what is needed is a chat, a fireside chat, quiet talks, and so on! That idea came in.

Then on top of this a new emphasis was placed upon 'the service', what is often called, 'the element of worship'. Now these terms are very misleading. I remember a man once in a conference saying, 'Of course we in the Episcopal Churches pay greater attention to worship than you do in the Free Churches'. I was able to point out that what he really meant was that they had a liturgical form of service and we did not. But he equated the reading of the Liturgy with worship. So the confusion grows.

However, there has been this tendency; as preaching has waned, there has been an increase in the formal element in the service. It is interesting to observe how Free-Church men, non-Episcopalians, whatever you may call them, have been increasingly borrowing these ideas from the Episcopal type of service as preaching has waned. They have argued that the people should have a greater part in the service and so they have introduced 'responsive reading', and more and more music and singing and chanting. The manner of receiving the people's offerings has been elaborated, and the minister and the choir often enter the building as a procession. It has been illuminating to observe these things; as preaching has declined, these other things have been emphasised; and it has all been done quite deliberately. It is a part of this reaction against preaching; and people have felt that it is more dignified to pay this greater attention to ceremonial, and form, and ritual.

Still worse has been the increase in the element of entertainment in public worship—the use of films and the introduction of more and more singing; the reading of the Word and prayer shortened drastically, but more and more time given to singing. You have a 'song leader' as a new kind of official in the church, and he conducts the singing and is supposed to produce the atmosphere. But he often takes so much time in producing the atmosphere that there is no time for preaching in the atmosphere! This is a part of this whole depreciation of the message.

Then on top of this, there is the giving of testimonies. It has been interesting to observe that as preaching as such has been on the decline, preachers have more and more used people to give their testimonies; and particularly if they are important people in any realm. This is said to attract people to the Gospel and to persuade them to listen to it. If you can find an admiral or a general or anyone who has some special title, or a baseball player, or an actor or actress or film-star, or pop-singer, or somebody well-known to the public, get them to give their testimony. This is deemed to be of much greater value than the preaching and the exposition of the Gospel. Have you noticed that I have put all this under the term 'entertainment'? That is where I believe it truly belongs. But this is what the Church has been turning to as she has turned her back upon preaching.

Another whole section in this connection has been the increasing emphasis upon 'personal work', as it is called, or 'counselling'. Again it would be very interesting to draw a graph here as with those other things. You would find exactly the same thing—as preaching goes down personal counselling goes up. This has had a great vogue in this present century, particularly since the end of the First World War. The argument has been that owing to the new stresses and strains, and difficulties in living life in the modern world, that people need much more personal attention, that you have got to get to know their particular difficulty, and that you must deal with this in private. We are told that it is only as you deal with them one at a time that you can give people the needed psychological help and so enable them to resolve these problems, to get over their difficulties, and so live their life in an effective and efficient manner. I hope to take up some of these things more in detail later on, but I am giving a general picture now of the things that are responsible for the decline of, and the subordinate place given to, preaching in the Christian Church.

To make the list complete I must add tape-recording—as I see it, the peculiar and special abomination at this present time.

There, then, are certain general changes which have happened in the Church herself. So far I have been speaking about people who believe in the Church, and who attend the Church. Among them there has been this shift in the place and the position of preaching. Sometimes it has been expressed even in a purely physical manner. I have noticed that most of the new chapels that have been built in our country no longer have a central pulpit; it is pushed to one side. The pulpit used to be central, but that is so no longer, and you now find yourself looking at something that corresponds to an altar instead of looking at the pulpit which generally dominated the entire building. All this is most significant.

*   *   *

But now, turning from what has happened in that way amongst those who still believe in the Church, let us look at those who are more or less suggesting that the Church herself may be the hindrance, and that we have got to abandon the Church if we really are to propagate the Gospel. I am thinking here of those who say that we must, in a sense, make a clean break with all this tradition which we have inherited, and that if we really want to make people Christians, the way to do so is to mix with them, to live amongst them, to share our lives with them, to show the love of God to them by just bearing one another's burdens and being one of them.

I have heard this put in this way even by preachers. They have faced the fact of the decline in Church attendance, particularly in Britain. They say that this is not surprising, that while the preachers preach the Bible and Christian doctrines they have no right to expect any other result. The people, they say, are not interested; the people are interested in politics, they are interested in social conditions, they are interested in the various injustices from which people suffer in various parts of the world, and in war and peace. So, they argue, if you really want to influence people in the Christian direction you must not only talk politics and deal with social conditions in speech, you must take an active part in them. If only these men who have been set aside as preachers, and others who are prominent in the Church, were to go out and take part in politics and in social activities and philanthropic works they would do much more good than by standing in pulpits and preaching according to the traditional manner. A very well-known preacher in Britain actually put it like this some ten years ago. He said that the idea of sending out foreign missionaries to North Africa—he was dealing with that area in particular on that occasion— and training them to preach to these people was quite ridiculous, and it was time we stopped it. He suggested that instead we should send Christian people out to those places, and they should take on ordinary jobs, mix among the people, and more especially, enter into their political and social affairs. If you did that as Christians, he said, then there would be some hope perhaps that the grandchildren of this present generation might become Christian. But that was the way, you see, to do it. Not preaching, not the old method, but getting among the people, showing an interest, showing your sympathy, being one of them, sitting down among them, and discussing their affairs and problems.

This is being advocated a great deal in many countries at the present time, either as a means of bringing people to places of worship to listen to the Gospel, or else as not only a substitute for that, but as a very much better method of propagating the Christian faith.

Well now the great question is—what is our answer to all this? I am going to suggest, and this will be the burden of what I hope to say, that all this at best is secondary, very often not even secondary, often not worthy of a place at all, but at best, secondary, and that the primary task of the Church and of the Christian minister is the preaching of the Word of God.

I must substantiate that statement, and I do so in the following way and for these reasons. First of all, what is the answer of the Bible itself? Here, and confining ourselves only to the New Testament— though we could give evidence also from the Old Testament in the prophets—we start with our Lord Himself. Surely nothing is more interesting in His story than to notice these two sides, or these two parts, to His ministry. Our Lord performed miracles, but the interesting thing is that the miracles were not His primary work, they were secondary. John, as you know, refers to them always as 'signs', and that is what they were. He did not come into the world to heal the sick, and the lame, and the blind, or to quell storms on the sea. He could do such things and did so frequently; but these are all secondary, they are not primary. What was His primary object? The very terms He uses answer the question. He says He is 'The light of the world'. He says, 'Seek ye first the kingdom of God and His righteousness, and all these things shall be added unto you'. Those things are legitimate but they are not primary; they are secondary, they are consequences, they are effects, they are results. Or take His famous reply to the people who came to Him putting the question whether they should pay tribute money to Caesar or not? 'Render unto Caesar the things that are Caesar's, and [or but] unto God the things that are God's.' This was His special emphasis. Most people are concerned about the first thing, 'rendering unto Caesar'; the thing that is forgotten, He suggests, is that you 'render unto God the things that are God's'.

Then there are some very interesting side-lights on this whole matter, it seems to me, in what He did. You remember how after the miracle of the feeding of the five thousand we are told that the people were so impressed that they came and they tried to take Him by force to make Him a King (John 6:15). They felt, 'Now this is just what we want. He is dealing with a practical problem, hunger, the need of food. This is the one to be made King, He has got the power, He can do this.' But what we are told is that He pushed them away, as it were, 'and went up into a mountain Himself alone'. He regarded that as a temptation, as something that would side-track Him. It was precisely the same in the case of the temptations in the wilderness that we read of in Luke 4. The devil offered Him all the kingdoms of this world and so on. He rejects this deliberately, specifically. These are all secondary, they are not the primary function, not the primary task.

Or take another very interesting example of this found in Luke 12:14, where we are told that on one occasion our Lord had been speaking as He was sending out the disciples to preach and to teach, and telling them about their relationship to God and how they were to deal with opposition. He seems to have paused for a moment and immediately a man blurted out a question, saying, 'Speak to my brother that he divide the inheritance with me.' Our Lord's reply to that man surely gives us a great insight into this whole matter. He turned to him and said, 'Man, who made me a judge or a divider over you?' In other words He made it clear that He had not come into the world to do such things. It is not that these things do not need to be done; they do need to be done; justice and fair play and righteousness have their place; but He had not come to do these things. He said in effect, 'I have not left heaven and come on earth in order to do something like that, that is not my primary task'. So He rebuked this man. Indeed we find that many times when He had worked some striking and notable miracle and the people were trying to hold Him, hoping He would work still more, He deliberately left them and would go on to another place; and there He would proceed to teach and to preach. He is 'The light of the world'—this is the primary thing. 'I am the way, the truth, and the life: no man cometh unto the Father but by me'. All these other things are secondary. And you notice that when He sent out His disciples, He sent them out 'to teach, and to cast out devils'. The teaching is the first thing, and He reminded them that the Christian is the light of the world. As He is the light of the world so the Christian becomes the light of the world. 'A city that is set upon a hill cannot be hid,' and so on. I suggest that in the Gospels, and in the life and ministry of our Lord Himself, you have this clear indication of the primacy of preaching and of teaching.

Then after the Resurrection, and in the remainder of the New

Testament, you get exactly the same thing. He tells these chosen men that they are primarily to be 'witnesses unto Me'. That is to be their first great task. He is going to give them other powers, but their main business is to be witnesses unto Him. And it is therefore interesting to observe that immediately these men are filled with the Holy Spirit on the Day of Pentecost they begin to preach. Peter preaches and expounds and explains the Truth to the people at Jerusalem. What is this phenomenon that had just happened and had produced such a change in the disciples? That question can only be answered by preaching; so you get the sermon recorded in the latter portion of the second chapter of the Acts of the Apostles.

And when you go to the third chapter of Acts you find the same thing again. Peter and John heal this man at the Beautiful Gate of the Temple, and that creates excitement and interest. The people think these are miracle workers and that they are going to get great benefits out of them; but Peter again preaches and corrects them, and immediately draws their attention, as it were, from the miracle that he and John had just worked to the great truth concerning Christ and His salvation, which is so infinitely more important. The Apostles always bring out this emphasis.

And again in the fourth chapter of Acts—I am taking this in detail because this is the origin of the Church, this was what she actually did at the beginning. She was commissioned, sent out to preach and teach, and this is the thing that she proceeded to do. 'They spoke with boldness'. What the authorities were anxious to do above everything else was to stop these men teaching and preaching. They always criticise that much more than they do the miracles; it was the preaching and the teaching in this 'Name' that annoyed them. And the reply of the Apostles is, 'We cannot but speak of the things which we have seen and heard'. This was the thing that made them speak, they could not help themselves; they were conscious of the great constraint that was upon them.

But, and in many ways the most interesting statement of all, I sometimes think in this connection, is one that is found in the sixth chapter of the book of the Acts of the Apostles where we are told that a great crisis arose in the life of the early Church. I know of nothing that speaks more directly upon the present state and condition of the Church, and what is her primary task, than this sixth chapter of the book of the Acts of the Apostles. The essential message is in the first two verses: 'And in those days, when the number of the disciples was multiplied, there arose a murmuring of the Grecians against the Hebrews, because their widows were neglected in the daily ministration. Then the twelve called the multitude of the disciples unto them, and said, It is not reason that we should leave the Word of God, and serve tables.'

This is surely a most interesting and important statement, a crucial one. What was the Church to do? Here is a problem, here are these widows of the Grecians, and they are not only widows but they are in need and in need of food. It was a social problem, perhaps partly a political problem, but certainly a very acute and urgent social problem. Surely the business of the Christian Church, and the leaders particularly, is to deal with this crying need? Why go on preaching when people are starving and in need and are suffering? That was the great temptation that came to the Church immediately; but the Apostles under the leading and the guidance of the Holy Spirit, and the teaching they had already received, and the commission they had had from their Master, saw the danger and they said, 'It is not reason that we should leave the Word of God, and serve tables'. This is wrong. We shall be failing in our commission if we do this. We are here to preach this Word, this is the first thing, 'We will give ourselves continually to prayer and the ministry of the Word.'

Now there the priorities are laid down once and for ever. This is the primary task of the Church, the primary task of the leaders of the Church, the people who are set in this position of authority; and we must not allow anything to deflect us from this, however good the cause, however great the need. This is surely the direct answer to much of the false thinking and reasoning concerning these matters at the present time.

And as you go through the book of the Acts of the Apostles you find the same thing everywhere. I could take you through almost chapter by chapter and show you the same thing. Let me content myself with just one more example. In chapter 8 we are told of a great persecution that arose in Jerusalem, and how all the members of the Church were scattered abroad except the Apostles. What did they do? We are told in verses 4 and 5: 'Therefore they that were scattered abroad went everywhere preaching the Word.' That does not mean preaching from a pulpit. Someone has suggested that it should be translated 'gossiping' the Word. Their chief desire and concern was to tell people about this Word. 'Then Philip went down to the city of Samaria, and preached Christ unto them'. There, in verse 5 a different word is used. This means heralding, it is more a picture of a preacher in the pulpit or at any rate standing in a public place and addressing people. And so it goes on right through that book.

In the Epistles, in the same way, the Apostle Paul reminds Timothy that the Church is 'the pillar and ground of the truth'. She is not a social organisation or institution, not a political society, not a cultural society, but 'the pillar and the ground of the truth'.

Paul in writing to Timothy in the Second Epistle in the second chapter and the second verse puts it like this: 'The things that thou hast heard of me among many witnesses, the same commit thou to faithful men, who shall be able to teach others also.' His last word to him in a sense is this: 'Preach the word; be instant in season, out of season; reprove, rebuke, exhort with all longsuffering and doctrine.' There it is, surely, quite plainly.

I have simply skimmed the argument, the statement of it, in the New Testament. All this is fully confirmed in Church history. Is it not clear, as you take a bird's-eye view of Church history, that the decadent periods and eras in the history of the Church have always been those periods when preaching had declined? What is it that always heralds the dawn of a Reformation or of a Revival? It is renewed preaching. Not only a new interest in preaching but a new kind of preaching. A revival of true preaching has always heralded these great movements in the history of the Church. And, of course, when the Reformation and the Revival come they have always led to great and notable periods of the greatest preaching that the Church has ever known. As that was true in the beginning as described in the book of Acts, it was also after the Protestant Reformation. Luther, Calvin, Knox, Latimer, Ridley—all these men were great preachers. In the seventeenth century you had exactly the same thing—the great Puritan preachers and others. And in the eighteenth century, Jonathan Edwards, Whitefield, the Wesleys, Rowlands and Harris were all great preachers. It was an era of great preaching. Whenever you get Reformation and Revival this is always and inevitably the result.

So my answer so far, my justification of my statement that preaching is the primary task of the Church, is based in that way on the evidence of the Scriptures, and the supporting and confirming evidence of the history of the Church.

We shall go on to reason and to argue it out yet further.

CHAPTER TWO

No Substitute

IN OUR FIRST lecture I laid down a proposition that preaching is the primary task of the Church and therefore of the minister of the Church, that everything else is subsidiary to this, and can be represented as the outworking or the carrying out of this in daily practice. What I am doing is to justify this proposition, and I am doing so, particularly, in view of the tendency today to depreciate preaching at the expense of various other forms of activity. Having laid down the proposition, I have tried to substantiate it by evidence from the New Testament and also from the history of the Church.

I now want to go a step further and to suggest that this evidence from the New Testament itself, supported and exemplified by the history of the Church, leads us to the conclusion that the ultimate justification for asserting the primacy of preaching is theological. In other words I argue that the whole message of the Bible asserts this and drives us to this conclusion. What do I mean by that? Essentially I mean that the moment you consider man's real need, and also the nature of the salvation announced and proclaimed in the Scriptures, you are driven to the conclusion that the primary task of the Church is to preach and to proclaim this, to show man's real need, and to show the only remedy, the only cure for it.

Let me elaborate that a little. This is of the very essence of my argument. I am suggesting that it is because there are false views current with regard to these matters that people no longer see the importance of preaching. Take the question of the need, man's need.

What is it? Well, negatively, it is not a mere sickness. There is a tendency to regard man's essential trouble as being a sickness. I do not mean physical sickness only. That comes in; but I mean a kind of mental and moral and spiritual sickness. It is not that; that is not man's real need, not his real trouble. I would say the same about his misery and his unhappiness, and also about his being a victim of circumstances.

These are the things that are given prominence today. There are so many people trying to diagnose the human situation; and they come to the conclusion that man is sick, man is unhappy, man is the victim of circumstances. They believe therefore that his primary need is to have these things dealt with, that he must be delivered from them. But I suggest that that is too superficial a diagnosis of the condition of man, and that man's real trouble is that he is a rebel against God and consequently under the wrath of God.

Now this is the biblical statement concerning him, this is the biblical view of man as he is by nature. He is 'dead in trespasses and sins', that means, spiritually dead. He is dead to the life of God, to the spiritual realm and to all the beneficent influences of that realm upon him. We are also told that he is 'blind'. 'If our gospel be hid,' says Paul in 2 Corinthians 4:3–4, 'it is hid to them that are lost: In whom the god of this world hath blinded the minds of them which believe not'. Or as Paul puts it again in Ephesians 4:17ff., man's trouble is that 'his understanding is darkened, because he is alienated from the life of God through the sin that is in him'. Another very common biblical term to describe this condition of man is the term 'darkness'. You have it in John 3:19: 'This is the condemnation, that light is come into the world, but men loved darkness rather than light, because their deeds were evil'. And in the First Epistle of John you find the same idea worked out. Writing to Christians he says that 'the darkness is past and the true light now shineth.' The Apostle Paul uses the same idea exactly in Ephesians 5. He says, 'Ye were sometimes darkness, but now are ye light in the Lord.' These are the terms that express the biblical diagnosis of man's essential trouble. In other words we can sum it up in one word by saying that it is ignorance. All the terms such as 'blindness' and 'darkness' are indicative of ignorance. And according to this biblical view of man all these other things, such as unhappiness and misery, even physical illness, and all the other things which torment and trouble us so much are the results and the consequences of original sin and the Fall of Adam. They are not the main problem, they are consequences, or symptoms if you like, and manifestations of this primary, this ultimate disease.

That being the picture of man's need it is not surprising that when you turn to the biblical account of salvation you find that it is put in terms which correspond to this expression of the need. The Apostle describes salvation in these words: it means, 'coming to a knowledge of the truth' (1 Timothy 2:4). It is the will of God that all men should be saved, and come to the knowledge of the truth. Salvation is a knowledge of the truth. In 2 Corinthians 5:19 and 20 he says that the message which has been committed to the preacher, who is an 'ambassador for Christ' is to say to men 'be ye reconciled to God.' You find it again in the practice of the Apostle. We read of him preaching in Athens, in Acts 17, and saying, 'Whom ye ignorantly worship, him declare I unto you.' They were ignorant though they were philosophers, and he is the one who can teach them and give them light in this matter.

I am simply showing that the biblical teaching concerning salvation is that it is the result of bringing men to this 'knowledge' which they lack, it is dealing with this ignorance. Paul talks about 'preaching the whole counsel of God', and Peter had the same idea when he says that Christians are people who have been 'called out of darkness into God's marvellous light'. Now these are the biblical terms, and they all, it seems to me, indicate that preaching always comes first and is given priority. If this is the greatest need of man, if his ultimate need is something that arises out of this ignorance of his which, in turn, is the result of rebellion against God, well then, what he needs first and foremost is to be told about this, to be told the truth about himself, and to be told of the only way in which this can be dealt with. So I assert that it is the peculiar task of the Church, and of the preacher, to make all this known.

I would emphasise the word 'peculiar'—you can use the word 'exceptional' if you like, or 'special'. The preacher alone is the one who can do this. He is the only one who is in a position to deal with the greatest need of the world. Paul puts it in 1 Corinthians 4:17 ff.: He says of himself that 'a dispensation of the Gospel has been committed unto me'. That is what he was called for—this dispensation of the Gospel, this message had been given to him. And you have the same thing expressed in a very glorious statement in the third chapter of the Epistle to the Ephesians, verses 8–10: 'Unto me,' he says, 'who am less than the least of all saints, is this grace given, that I should preach among the Gentiles the unsearchable riches of Christ.' This is his calling, this is his task. He has said before that 'all this in other ages was not made known unto the sons of men, as it is now revealed unto his holy apostles and prophets by the Spirit'. This is the message —'And to make all men see, what is the fellowship of the mystery, which from the beginning of the world hath been hid in God, who created all things by Jesus Christ: To the intent that now unto the principalities and powers in heavenly places might be made known by the church the manifold wisdom of God.'

My whole contention is that it is the Church alone that can do this, and it is the preacher therefore who alone can make it known. He is set apart by the Church, as I am going to show, to serve this particular function, to perform this particular task. This is the thing that is given primacy and is emphasised, and it must surely of necessity be the case. The moment we realise man's true need and see the only answer, it becomes clear that only those who are in possession of this understanding can impart this message to those who lack it.

Let me work this out a little. There are other agencies in the world which can deal with many of the problems of mankind. I mean by that, things like medicine, the State, even other religions, and cults, and psychology and various other teachings and political agencies. These are all designed to help, and to relieve somewhat, the human condition, to ease the pain and the problem of life and to enable men to live more harmoniously and to enjoy life in a greater measure. They set out to do that, and it is no part of our case to say that they are of no value. We must observe the facts and grant that they can do good, and do much good. They are capable in a measure of dealing with these things. But none of them can deal with this fundamental, this primary trouble at which we have been looking.

Not only that, when they have done their all, or when even the Church coming down to that level and operating on that level alone, has done her all, the primary trouble still remains. So I would lay it down as a basic proposition that the primary task of the Church is not to educate man, is not to heal him physically or psychologically, it is not to make him happy. I will go further; it is not even to make him good. These are things that accompany salvation; and when the Church performs her true task she does incidentally educate men and give them knowledge and information, she does bring them happiness, she does make them good and better than they were. But my point is that those are not her primary objectives. Her primary purpose is not any of these; it is rather to put man into the right relationship with God, to reconcile man to God. This really does need to be emphasised at the present time, because this, it seems to me, is the essence of the modern fallacy. It has come into the Church and it is influencing the thinking of many in the Church—this notion that the business of the Church is to make people happy, or to integrate their lives, or to relieve their circumstances and improve their conditions. My whole case is that to do that is just to palliate the symptoms, to give temporary ease, and that it does not get beyond that.

I am not saying that it is a bad thing to palliate symptoms; it is not, and it is obviously right and good to do so. But I am constrained to say this, that though to palliate symptoms, or to relieve them, is not bad in and of itself, it can be bad, it can have a bad influence, and a bad effect, from the standpoint of the biblical understanding of man and his needs. It can become harmful in this way, that by palliating the symptoms you can conceal the real disease. Here is something that we have to bear in mind at the present time because, unless I am greatly mistaken, this is a vital part of our problem today.

Let me use a medical illustration. Take a man who is lying on a bed and writhing in agony with abdominal pain. Now a doctor may come along who happens to be a very nice and a very sympathetic man. He does not like to see people suffering, he does not like to see people in pain; so he feels that the one thing to do is to relieve this man of his pain. He is able to do so. He can give him an injection of morphia or various other drugs which would give the man almost immediate relief. 'Well,' you say, 'surely there is nothing wrong in doing that; it is a kind action, it is a good action, the patient is made more comfortable, he is made happier and is no longer suffering.' The answer to that is that it is well-nigh a criminal act on the part of this doctor. It is criminal because merely to remove a symptom without discovering the cause of the symptom is to do a dis-service to the patient. A symptom after all is a manifestation of a disease, and symptoms are very valuable. It is through tracking the symptoms and following the lead that they give that you should arrive at the disease which has given rise to the symptoms. So if you just remove the symptoms before you have discovered the cause of the symptoms you are actually doing your patient real harm because you are giving him this temporary ease which makes him think that all is well. But all is not well, it is only a temporary relief, and the disease is there, is still continuing. If this happened to have been an acute appendix, or something like that, the sooner it is taken out the better; and if you have merely given the patient ease and relief without dealing with it you are asking for an abscess or something even worse.

That, surely, gives us a picture of a great deal that is happening at the present time. This is one of the problems confronting the Christian Church today. This 'affluent society' in which we are living is drugging people and making them feel that all is well with them. They have better wages, better houses, better cars, every gadget desirable in the home; life is satisfactory and all seems to be well; and because of that people have ceased to think and to face the real problems. They are content with this superficial ease and satisfaction, and that militates against a true and a radical understanding of their actual condition. And, of course, this is aggravated at the present time by many other agencies. There is the pleasure mania, and television and radio bringing their influence right into the home. All these things persuade man that all is well; they give him temporary feelings of happiness; and so he assumes that all is well and stops thinking. The result is that he does not realise his true position and then face it.

Then you have to add to that the giving of tranquillising drugs and the taking of so-called pep pills and hypnotics. People live on these, and all this, very often, not only has the effect of concealing the physical problem, but also, and still more serious, the spiritual problem. As man is content with this temporary relief, he tends to go on assuming that all is well, and eventually ends in a crash. The form which the crash is taking so often today is drug addiction and so on; and there are many who cannot continue to do their work without this alternation of pep pills and hypnotics, tranquillisers and stimulants. I suggest that many of these agencies to which the Church seems to be turning today, instead of carrying out her primary task of preaching, are ultimately having that same kind of effect. While they are not bad in and of themselves, they can become bad, and truly harmful, by concealing the real need.

The business of the Church, and the business of preaching—and she alone can do this—is to isolate the radical problems and to deal with them in a radical manner. This is specialist work, it is the peculiar task of the Church. The Church is not one of a number of agencies, she is not in competition with the cults, she is not in competition with other religions, she is not in competition with the psychologists or any other agency, political or social or whatever it may chance to be. The Church is a special and a specialist institution and this is a work that she alone can perform.

I want to support this contention by certain other statements. Here for instance is one, which, to me, has an almost amusing aspect to it.

These proposals that we should preach less, and do various other things more, are of course not new at all. People seem to think that all this is quite new, and that it is the hallmark of modernity to decry or to depreciate preaching, and to put your emphasis on these other things. The simple answer to that is that there is nothing new about it. The actual form may be new, but the principle is certainly not a new one at all; indeed it has been the particular emphasis of this present century.

Take all this new interest in the social application of the Gospel, and the idea of going to live amongst the people and to talk politics and to enter into their social affairs and so on. The simple answer to that is that until the First World War in this present century that was the real vogue in most Western countries. It was then called the 'social gospel', but it was precisely the same thing. The argument was that the old evangelical preaching of the Gospel was too personal, too simple, that it did not deal with the social problems and conditions. It was a part, of course, of the liberal, modernist, higher-critical view of the Scriptures and of our Lord. He was just a perfect man and a great teacher, a political agitator and reformer, and the great exemplar. He had come to do good, and the Sermon on the Mount was something that you could put into Acts of Parliament and turn into legislation. So you were going to make a perfect world. That was the old liberalism of the pre-1914 period. The very thing that is regarded as so new today, and what is regarded as the primary task of the Church, is something that has already been tried, and tried with great thoroughness in the early part of this century.

The same is true of various other agencies that are coming into the life and activity of the Church. What is advocated today as a new approach was practised by what was then called the Institutional Church; and this, once more, was done with considerable thoroughness. There were all sorts of cultural clubs in the churches, and the Church became the centre of social life. There were organised games and clubs of various descriptions. All this was given a most thorough trial in the pre-1914 period.

33

But we are entitled to ask, surely, whether they worked, how effective they were, and what they led to. The answer is that they were failures, they were proved to be failures. I am not so aware in a detailed way of the position in the U.S.A., which I know is somewhat different from that in Great Britain, but I have no hesitation in asserting that what was largely responsible for emptying the churches in Great Britain was that 'social gospel' preaching and the institutional church. It was more responsible for doing so than anything else. The people rightly argued in this way, that if the business of the Church was really just to preach a form of political and social reform and pacifism then the Church was not really necessary, for all that could be done through the political agencies. So they left the churches and went and did it, or tried to do it, through their political parties. That was perfectly logical, but its effect upon the churches was most harmful.

That can be illustrated and shown equally well at the present time. There are two preachers in London who are great advocates of this politico-social interest of the Church in the man of the world, and who contend that this is the way to win him, and to help him, and to make him a Christian. It is most interesting to notice that these two men who are most given to this teaching in Britain have small congregations on Sundays in their churches in the very heart and most accessible part of London. These are facts that can be verified, and that this should be the case is not at all surprising. People say to themselves that there is no need to go to church to hear that kind of thing. You can get it daily in the newspapers, and in the political and social institutions which are designed to do this very thing. One of these two men who gets great publicity because of this interest of his has recently even ceased to have a Sunday evening service at all in his own building. He has had to join his evening service with that of another church in the same street.

Now this is most interesting and most important. When you depart from the primary task of the Church and do something else, though your motive may be pure and excellent, that is the result. I am not

34

disputing or criticising the motives, I am simply showing that actually this theory in practice has the reverse effect from that which it sets out to achieve. I argue that in many ways it is the departure of the Church from preaching that is responsible in a large measure for the state of modern society. The Church has been trying to preach morality and ethics without the Gospel as a basis; it has been preaching morality without godliness; and it simply does not work. It never has done, and it never will. And the result is that the Church, having abandoned her real task, has left humanity more or less to its own devices.

Another argument that I would adduce at this point is that the moment you begin to turn from preaching to these other expedients you will find yourself undergoing a constant series of changes. One of the advantages of being old is that you have experience, so when something new comes up, and you see people getting very excited about it, you happen to be in the position of being able to remember a similar excitement perhaps forty years ago. And so one has seen fashions and vogues and stunts coming one after another in the Church. Each one creates great excitement and enthusiasm and is loudly advertised as *the* thing that is going to fill the churches, *the* thing that is going to solve the problem. They have said that about every single one of them. But in a few years they have forgotten all about it, and another stunt comes along, or another new idea; somebody has hit upon the one thing needful or he has a psychological understanding of modern man. Here is the thing, and everybody rushes after it; but soon it wanes and disappears and something else takes its place.

This is, surely, a very sad and regrettable state for the Christian Church to be in, that like the world she should exhibit these constant changes of fashion. In that state she lacks the stability and the solidity and the continuing message that has ever been the glory of the Christtian Church.

But my objection to the substitution of a socio-political interest for the preaching of the Gospel can be stated more positively. This concern about the social and political conditions, and about the happiness of the individual and so on, has always been dealt with most effectively when you have had reformation and revival and true preaching in the Christian Church. I would go further and suggest that it is the Christian Church that has made the greatest contribution throughout the centuries to the solution of these very problems. The modern man is very ignorant of history; he does not know that the hospitals originally came through the Church. It was Christian people who first, out of a sense of compassion for suffering and illness, began to do something about even physical diseases and illnesses. The first hospitals were founded by Christian people. The same thing is true of education; it was the Church that first saw this need and proceeded to do something about it. The same is true of Poor Law Relief and the mitigation of the sufferings of people who were enduring poverty. I argue that it is the Church that really has done this. Your trades unions and other such movements, you will find, if you go back to their beginnings, have almost invariably had Christian origins.

My argument is that when the Church performs her primary task these other things invariably result from it. In other words, the Protestant Reformation, for instance, gave a stimulus to the whole of man's outlook on, and activity in, life. It can be demonstrated quite satisfactorily that the Protestant Reformation gave the greatest possible stimulus to science and scientific enquiry and study, and it certainly did the same to literature and many other activities of man. In other words when man truly becomes what he is meant to be under God he then begins to realise what faculties and propensities he has, and he begins to use them. And so you will find that the greatest periods and epochs in the history of countries have always been those eras that have followed in the wake of great religious reformations and revivals. The other people talk a great deal about the political and social conditions but do very little about them. It is this activity of the Church that really deals with the situation and produces enduring and permanent results. So I argue that even from the pragmatic stand-point it can be demonstrated that you must keep preaching in the primary and central position.

We turn now to the realm of personal problems. This is a familiar argument today as I have already indicated. People say that the preachers stand in their pulpits and preach their sermons, but that there before them are individuals with their individual problems and sufferings. So the argument runs, you ought to preach less and spend more time in doing personal work and counselling and interviewing· My reply to this argument is to suggest, once more, that the answer is to put preaching into the primary position. Why? For the reason that true preaching does deal with personal problems, so much so that true preaching saves a great deal of time for the pastor. I am speaking out of forty years of experience. What do I mean? Let me explain. The Puritans are justly famous for their pastoral preaching. They would take up what they called 'cases of conscience' and deal with them in their sermons; and as they dealt with these problems they were solving the personal individual problems of those who were listening to them. That has constantly been my experience. The preaching of the Gospel from the pulpit, applied by the Holy Spirit to the individuals who are listening, has been the means of dealing with personal problems of which I as the preacher knew nothing until people came to me at the end of the service saying, 'I want to thank you for that sermon because if you had known I was there and the exact nature of my problem, you could not have answered my various questions more perfectly. I have often thought of bringing them to you but you have now answered them without my doing so.' The preaching had already dealt with the personal problems. Do not misunderstand me, I am not saying that the preacher should never do any personal work; far from it. But I do contend that preaching must always come first, and that it must not be replaced by anything else.

I have often told a story of a remarkable case which illustrates this point. Many years ago I was asked to see, with a doctor and a pastor, a young lady who was said to have been paralysed in both legs for eight years. I went to see her with them and I found to my amazement that she was capable of making most extraordinary movements with her legs. This led me at once to diagnose her as a case of hysteria; and so it turned out to be. This supposed paralysis, this functional condition, had come on as the result of a disappointment in her emotional life. She lay there on the bed, and I was not able to help her because she just would not keep sufficiently quiet for the doctor or myself to examine her properly. However, this is what happened afterwards. She had two sisters; and her older sister, as the result of this visit of mine, began to attend our church; and after a number of months was converted and became a very fine Christian. After a while the second sister began to attend our services, and she in turn became a Christian. Then eventually one Sunday night I saw the so-called paralytic being half-carried into the church by her two sisters. She continued to attend, and in due course she became a Christian. Now the point I want to emphasise is this: I never had another conversation with her about her so-called paralysis; it was never mentioned, it was never discussed, but it completely disappeared. Why? How? As the result of the preaching of the Gospel. As she became a Christian this matter was dealt with by the application of the Truth by the Holy Spirit without any personal counselling or psychological analysis or treatment.

Now I am not arguing that this will happen every time. My contention is that if the Gospel is truly preached, in a most astonishing manner it can be so applied by the Spirit to these individual cases and problems that they are dealt with without the preacher knowing it at all. I could tell you numerous stories to illustrate this very thing and how, sometimes, even a mere aside by the preacher has been the means of dealing with some person's problem:

In any case I have often found that the preaching of the Gospel brings people to talk to the preacher, and gives him an opportunity of dealing with their particular condition. It is the best means of introducing them to one another, it forms the link. Something that the preacher has said either gives them the impression that he will be sympathetic and understanding, or that he has got an insight into their particular difficulty. It is the preaching that brings them for this personal help to the preacher.

Moreover by doing it in this way you are able to deal with dozens, and perhaps hundreds, of people at one and the same time. It is quite astonishing to find that in expounding the Scriptures you are able to deal with a variety of differing conditions all together in one service. That is what I meant by saying that it saves the pastor a lot of time. If he had to see all these people one by one his life would be impossible, he could not do it; but in one sermon he can cover quite a number of problems at one and the same time.

But in any case—and this to me is a very important argument—it is preaching that lays down the essential principles by which alone personal help can be given. Let me illustrate briefly. Someone comes into your room, into your vestry, and wants to consult you about a problem. The first thing you have to do is to discover the nature of the problem. You have to discover whether this person is a Christian or whether he is not a Christian, because that will determine what you are going to do. If a man is not a Christian you cannot give him spiritual help. If he is not a Christian the first thing you have to do is to help him to become a Christian. That is essential first; and it is only then that you can apply your spiritual teaching to the particular problem. If he is not a Christian it is idle for you to try to apply spiritual teaching. You are wasting your time as a minister of the Gospel in dealing with such a man's particular problems and difficulties. I suggest that your duty in that case is to hand him over to someone else whose professional work is to deal with such problems. Your business as a Christian minister is this specialist business of dealing with spiritual problems, so this is the first question you have to decide. It is no use talking to people in a spiritual way unless they have spiritual understanding, and such understanding is the result of a spiritual re-birth, which is generally produced by the preaching of the Gospel (1 Cor. 2:10-16; 1 Pet. 1:23). If in your preaching you have brought these people to see that they are not Christians they will come to you about that, and you will be able to show them that the particular symptom which had worried them was due to the fact that they were not Christian, that they were in the wrong relationship to God. So they come to you, and you can then counsel them and help them and show them the way of salvation. If that does not in and of itself deal with the particular problem, you are now in a position to reason it out with them in a spiritual manner. I maintain that ultimately the only true basis for personal work, unless it is to degenerate into purely psychological treatment, is the true and sound preaching of the Gospel.

My contention, then, is that personal counselling and all these other activities are meant to supplement the preaching, not to supplant it; that they are the 'carrying on', 'follow up' work if you like, but must never be thought of as the primary work. The moment you get these into the wrong relationship you are not only asking for trouble in a personal sense, I suggest also that you are not interpreting the mandate of the Church in a true and right manner. So I would sum up by saying that it is preaching alone that can convey the Truth to people, and bring them to the realisation of their need, and to the only satisfaction for their need. Ceremonies and ritual, singing and entertainment, and all your interest in political and social affairs, and all else cannot do this. I am not denying that they can produce effects, I have granted that they can, and that this is where the danger sometimes comes in. What men and women need is to be brought to 'a knowledge of the truth'; and if this is not done you are simply palliating symptoms, and patching up the problem for the time being. In any case you are not carrying out the great mandate given to the Church and her ministers.

But let me deal with a few objections to this contention and point of view. Someone may say, 'Have not the times changed? All you have been saying might have been correct, say, even twenty years ago, still more so, perhaps, a hundred years ago; but have not times changed? Is your method right now in the light of our new conditions?' Or some perhaps, in the U.S.A. may say, 'Well, all you are saying may be all right for London and in Britain, but it does not work in America. Conditions are different here; there is a different background, different cultures, different circumstances and so on.' What is the answer to that? It is quite simple. God has not changed, and man has not changed. I know that there are superficial changes--we may dress differently, we may travel at four hundred miles an hour instead of four miles an hour—but man as man has not changed at all, and man's needs are exactly and precisely what they have always been. Not only that, there have been dead and lifeless times in the history of the Church before in past ages, as we saw in the first lecture.

There is nothing new about this condition of ours; one of the central fallacies of today is to think that because we are living in the mid-twentieth century we have an entirely new problem. This creeps even into the life and the thinking of the Church with all the talk about postwar world, scientific age, atomic age, post-Christian era etc. It is just nonsense; it is not new at all. God does not change. As someone put it, 'Time writes no wrinkle on the brow of the Eternal.' And man does not change; he is exactly what he has always been ever since he fell and has the same problems. Indeed I would go so far as to say that never has there been a greater opportunity for preaching than there is today, because we are living in an age of disillusionment. The Victorian age, last century, was an age of optimism. People were carried away by the theory of evolution and development, and the poets sang about the coming of 'the parliament of man and the federation of the world'. We would banish war and all would be well, and the world would be one great nation. They really believed that sort of thing. Nobody believes it by now apart from an odd representative here and there of the old 'social gospel' of the pre-1914 era. We have lived to see the fallacy of that old optimistic liberalism, and we are living in an age of disillusionment when men are desperate. That is why we are witnessing this student protest and every other kind of protest; that is why people are taking drugs. It is the end of all the optimism of the liberals. It was bound to lead to this because it was wrong in its basic conceptions, its origin, in its very thinking. We are seeing the end of all that. Is not this then the very time when the door is wide open for the preaching of the Gospel? The age in which we are living is so similar to the first century in many respects. The old world was exhausted then. The flowering period of Greek philosophy had come and had gone, Rome in a sense had passed her zenith, and there was the same kind of tiredness and weariness, with consequent turning to pleasure and amusement. The same is so true today; and so far from saying that we must have less preaching and turn more and more to other devices and expedients, I say that we have a heaven-sent opportunity for preaching.

Then let us look at a second objection. People may say, 'Surely with man as he is now, educated and sophisticated and so on, cannot all you want to do be done equally well by reading—reading books and journals? Cannot it be done by television or radio, through discussions particularly?' Of course reading can help and is a great help, as are these other agencies; but I do suggest that it is time we asked the question as to what extent they are really helping and dealing with the situation? I suggest that the result is a disappointing one, and I think I can give the reasons for this. The first is that this is a wrong approach because it is too individualistic. The man sits on his own reading his book. That is too purely intellectual in its approach, it is a matter of intellectual interest. Another thing, which I find very difficult to put into words, but which to me is most important is that the man himself is too much in control. What I mean is that if you do not agree with the book you put it down, if you do not like what you are hearing on the television you switch it off. You are an isolated individual and you are in control of the situation. Or, to put it more positively, that whole approach lacks the vital element of the Church.

Now the Church is a missionary body, and we must recapture this notion that the whole Church is a part of this witness to the Gospel and its truth and its message. It is therefore most important that people should come together and listen in companies in the realm of the Church. That has an impact in and of itself. I have often been told this. The preacher after all is not speaking for himself, he is speaking for the Church, he is explaining what the Church is and what these people are, and why they are what they are. You remember that the Apostle Paul in the First Epistle to the Thessalonians makes quite a point of this. It is something which we tend to neglect at the present time. He tells those Thessalonians that they as a Church had been a great help to him in his preaching; he puts it like this in 1 Thessalonians 1:6 ff:

Ye became followers of us, and of the Lord, having received the word in much affliction, with joy of the Holy Ghost: So that ye were ensamples to all that believe in Macedonia and Achaia. For from you sounded out the word of the Lord not only in Macedonia and Achaia, but also in every place your faith to God-ward is spread abroad; so that we need not to speak anything; For they themselves show of us what manner of entering in we had unto you . . .

The very presence of a body of people in itself is a part of the preaching, and these influences begin to act immediately upon anyone who comes into a service. These influences, I suggest, are very often more potent in a spiritual sense than pure intellectual argumentation.

Not only that, when a man comes into a church to a body of people he begins to get some idea of the fact that they are the people of God, and that they are the modern representatives of something that has been known in every age and generation throughout the centuries. This makes an impact on him, in and of itself. He is not simply considering a new theory or a new teaching or a new idea. Here he is visiting or entering into something that has this long history and tradition.

But let me put it in this form; the man who thinks that all this can be done by reading, or by just looking at a television set, is missing the mysterious element in the life of the Church. What is this? It is what our Lord was suggesting, I think, when He said, 'Where two or three are gathered together in My name, there am I in the midst.' It is not a mere gathering of people; Christ is present. This is the great mystery of the Church. There is something in the very atmosphere of Christian people meeting together to worship God and to listen to the preaching of the Gospel.

Let me tell you one story to illustrate what I mean. I remember a woman who was a spiritist, and even a medium, a paid medium employed by a spiritist society. She used to go every Sunday evening to a spiritist meeting and was paid three guineas for acting as a medium. This was during the thirties, and that was quite a large sum of money for a lower middle-class woman. She was ill one Sunday and could not go to keep her appointment. She was sitting in her house and she saw people passing by on their way to the church where I happened to be ministering in South Wales. Something made her feel a desire to know what those people had, and so she decided to go to the service, and did so. She came ever afterwards until she died, and became a very fine Christian. One day I asked her what she had felt on that first visit, and this is what she said to me; and this is the point I am illustrating. She said, 'The moment I entered your chapel and sat down on a seat amongst the people I was conscious of a power. I was conscious of the same sort of power as I was accustomed to in our spiritist meetings, but there was one big difference; I had a feeling that the power in your chapel was a clean power.' The point I am making is simply this, that she was aware of a power. This is this mysterious element. It is the presence of the Spirit in the heart of God's children, God's people, and an outsider becomes aware of this. This is something you can never get if you just sit and read a book on your own. The Spirit can use a book, I know, but because of the very constitution of man's nature—our gregarious character, and the way in which we lean on one another, and are helped by one another even unconsciously—this is a most important factor. That is so in a natural sense, but when the Spirit is present, it is still more so. I am not advocating a mob or a mass psychology which I regard as extremely dangerous, particularly when it is worked up. All I am contending for is that when you enter a church, a society, a company of God's people, there is a factor which immediately comes into operation, which is reinforced still more by the preacher expounding the Word in the pulpit; and that is why preaching can never be replaced by either reading or by watching television or any one of these other activities.

CHAPTER THREE

The Sermon and the Preaching

WE ARE STILL trying to establish the proposition that preaching is the primary task of the Church, and of the minister in the Church. We have adduced scriptural proofs of this and further proofs from Church history; and then we have tried to develop the theological argument showing how our very theology insists upon this because of the subject with which we are dealing. Having done so we began to consider some objections to all this. The first is, 'Have not times changed?' And the second is, 'Cannot all this be done now by means of reading, or by means of watching television or listening to the radio and so on?'

That brings us to a third objection which asks, 'Cannot all this be done better by means of group discussions? Why must it be preaching? Why this particular form? Cannot this be replaced by a kind of "dialogue", as it is now called, or exchange of views? Should we not rather encourage more questions at the end of sermons, and a dialogue between the minister and the people who have come to listen, all, of course, within the realm of the Church?' Furthermore it is suggested that this can also be done on television by means of discussion; that you have a panel of people, some of them Christians and some of them not Christians, and that they engage in a discussion together. The suggestion is that this is not only a good way of evangelising, and making known the message of the Bible, but that it is, in the present age, a superior one to preaching.

As this is gaining a good deal of support and gaining, certainly, a great deal of publicity at the present time in most countries, we have got to address ourselves to it. I would answer it in the form of a personal reminiscence again, and I put it in that form in order that the principles involved may stand out more clearly. I remember back about 1942 I received an invitation to have a public debate on the question of religion with a man who was very famous at that time namely the late Dr. C. E. M. Joad. He had gained a good deal of publicity, not to say notoriety by taking part in what was called a Brains' Trust on the radio, and he was a very popular speaker who held more or less atheistical views at that time. I was asked to debate religion with him at the Union Debating Society in the University of Oxford. I need not trouble you with the background to that, nor the reasons why I was asked to do that, but it really did arise out of my preaching. That is one of my reasons for mentioning it. I was taking part in a mission in the University and it was directly as the result of my preaching on a Sunday night that this invitation came to me. I turned down that invitation, and refused to take part in the debate. Was I right in refusing this? There were many who took the view that I was wrong, that it was a wonderful opportunity for preaching and presenting the Gospel, that the very fame of Dr. Joad in itself would attract a wonderful house to listen to the debate, that it might very well obtain publicity in the Press and so on. So, many felt that I was rejecting and missing a wonderful evangelistic opportunity.

But I maintained then, and I still maintain, that my decision was the correct one. Quite apart from any detailed reasons which I am going to give, I think it is wrong as a total approach. My impression is that experience of that kind of thing shows clearly that it very rarely succeeds, or leads to anything. It provides entertainment, but as far as I am aware, and in my experience and knowledge of it, it has very rarely been fruitful or effective as a means of winning people to the Christian faith.

But more important still are my detailed reasons. The first is, and to me this was an all-sufficient reason in itself, that God is not to be discussed or debated. God is not a subject for debate, because He is Who He is and What He is. We are told that the unbeliever, of course, does not agree with that; and that is perfectly true; but that makes no difference. We believe it, and it is a part of our very case to assert it. Holding the view that we do, believing what we do about God, we cannot in any circumstances allow Him to become a subject for discussion or of debate or investigation. I base my argument at this point on the word addressed by God Himself to Moses at the burning bush (Exod. 3:1-6). Moses had suddenly seen this remarkable phenomenon of the burning bush, and was proposing to turn aside and to examine this astonishing phenomenon. But, immediately, he is rebuked by the voice which came to him saying, 'Draw not nigh hither: put off thy shoes from off thy feet, for the place whereon thou standest is holy ground.' That seems to me to be the governing principle in this whole matter. Our attitude is more important than anything that we do in detail, and as we are reminded in the Epistle to the Hebrews, God is always to be approached 'with reverence and with godly fear: for our God is a consuming fire' (Heb. 12:28 and 29).

To me this is a very vital matter. To discuss the being of God in a casual manner, lounging in an armchair, smoking a pipe or a cigarette or a cigar, is to me something that we should never allow, because God, as I say, is not a kind of philosophic X or a concept. We believe in the almighty, the glorious, the living God; and whatever may be true of others we must never put ourselves, or allow ourselves to be put, into a position in which we are debating about God as if He were but a philosophical proposition. To me this is an overriding consideration which is enough in and of itself.

There are further supporting reasons which arise inevitably out of that. The second argument I adduce would be that in discussing these matters we are dealing with the most serious and the most solemn matter in life. We are dealing with something which we believe is not only going to affect the lives of these people with whom we are concerned while they are in this world, but also with their eternal destiny. In other words, the very character and nature of the subject is such that it cannot possibly be placed in any context except that of the most thoughtful and serious atmosphere that we know, or can create. Certainly it should never be approached in a light spirit, or in a mere debating spirit; still less should it ever be regarded as a matter of entertainment.

It seems to me that these supposed discussions and dialogues on religion that we have on the television and radio are generally nothing but sheer entertainment. Equal time is given to the unbeliever as to the believer, and there is the cut and thrust of debate and jocularity and fun. The programme is so arranged that the subject cannot be dealt with in depth. I protest that the matter with which we are concerned is so desperately serious and vital and urgent that we should never allow it to be approached in this way.

I can give a very good and sound reason for saying that in the form of a comparison. Any one of us might develop or be suddenly stricken with, a very serious illness. Not only are you in great pain, and running a temperature, but you are feeling desperately ill. Your doctor takes a most serious view of your case and calls in another and a higher opinion. Would anyone like to put up the suggestion that in such a condition, in such a state, that what you would really like is a discussion and a debate concerning the rival possibilities, a discussion conducted in a light-hearted manner with one proposition put up and criticised and valuated, and then another, and so on? All of us would resent that. We would point out that our life is in jeopardy, that this is no time for debate and discussion and levity and light-heartedness. In that state and condition we look for certainty, for serious dealing, for hope, and the possibility of being cured, and of being put right. You would resent jocularity and a detached attitude because of the urgency; and of course you would be perfectly right. If that is the case with regard to physical health and well-being how much more so should it be the case when we are discussing the ills and diseases of the soul and a man's eternal destiny.

I cannot emphasise this matter too strongly. This should come as a rebuke to all of us, and we who are Christians need to be reminded of this quite as much, I fear, as those who are not Christians. So often we discuss theology in a light manner, as we debate many other subjects, and as if we were handling something quite apart from our lives and our well-being and eternal destiny. But that is obviously wrong. We are always involved personally and vitally in this if we really believe what we claim to believe and say that we believe. These matters should never be dealt with in terms of a debate or in the atmosphere of debate and discussion; they are too serious and too solemn, our true living in this world and our eternal destiny are involved.

Then, thirdly, there is a sense in which such a debate or discussion or dialogue is impossible because of the spiritual ignorance of the natural man, the non-Christian. I maintain that the man who is not a Christian is incapable of entering into a discussion about these matters. That is so, of course, for the good reason that he is blind to spiritual things and in a state of darkness. The Apostle Paul tells us in 1 Corinthians 2:14 that 'The natural man receiveth not the things of the Spirit of God: for they are foolishness unto him: neither can he know them, because they are spiritually discerned.' He is entirely lacking in spiritual understanding. The whole argument of 1 Corinthians 2 is that these things are 'spiritually discerned'. They belong to the realm of spiritual truth, they are stated in spiritual terminology and language, and they can only be understood by the mind that is already spiritual. The 'natural man', the non-Christian says Paul, is incapable of doing this. Clearly then, if he is incapable of doing this you cannot have a discussion with him. In other words there is no neutral point at which the Christian and the non-Christian can meet, there is no common starting point as it were. Our whole position as Christians is the very opposite and antithesis of the other, and is a complete condemnation of it. That makes a discussion or a debate on these matters quite impossible.

I go on to a fourth point which enforces that by saying that what the natural man needs above everything else is to be humbled. This is essential before we can do anything with him. The ultimate trouble with the natural man is his pride. This point is worked out in the second half of the first chapter of Paul's First Epistle to the Corinthians: 'Where is the wise? where is the scribe? where is the disputer of this world?' And the Apostle's argument is that what God does to this man is not to have a discussion with him but to make him look foolish. He has to be humbled because he glories in himself, whereas the Christian position is that 'he that glorieth, let him glory in the Lord'. The first thing that has to be done with the man who does not accept the Christian faith is to humble him. That is the first essential. 'Hath not God made foolish the wisdom of this world?' Or as our Lord Himself put it: 'Except ye be converted, and become as little children, ye shall not enter into the kingdom of heaven' (Matt. 18:3). That is a vital statement, a controlling statement, and it applies to all men. All men have to be converted and 'become as little children'. All they know, and all they are, and all they have, and all they have done, is utterly useless in this realm. There is no hope for them until they become aware of their utter bankruptcy and 'become as little children'. You obviously, therefore, do not, and must not, debate or discuss these matters with them on an equal standing. To do so is to deny the initial Christian postulate. Indeed our Lord went further when He uttered these words:

> At that time Jesus answered and said, I thank thee, O Father, Lord of heaven and earth, because thou hast hid these things from the wise and prudent, and hast revealed them unto babes. Even so, Father: for so it seemed good in thy sight. All things are delivered unto me of my Father: and no man knoweth the Son, but the Father; neither knoweth any man the Father, save the Son, and he to whomsoever the Son will reveal him (Matt. 11:25–27).

Truth is revealed to us in the Scriptures and by the illumination that the Holy Spirit alone can produce. I argue therefore that this whole notion of having a debate or a discussion or exchange of views concerning these matters is something that is contrary to the very character and nature of the Gospel itself.

I reject all these modern substitutes for preaching therefore and say that there is only one way; it is the way that was adopted by the Apostle Paul himself in Athens. I have already quoted it: 'Whom ye ignorantly worship, him declare I unto you.' This declaration is essential; it must come first. There can be no profitable exchange until this declaration has been made and people have been given a certain amount of information. This 'declaration' is something that we, the Church, the preacher alone, can make, and this is the first and the primary thing that we must do.

That leaves just one further argument or objection, namely that that may be all right in theory but that people will not come to listen. So what do you do then? It is all very well to put up this wonderful case, it is said, but people will not listen to this sort of thing these days, they are not interested, and they insist upon having their say and putting forward their views and so on. I shall be dealing with this point later when I come to consider 'the congregation that listens to the preacher'; but let me say just this at this point. The answer is that they will come, and that they do come when it is true preaching. I have already adduced evidence from history that people have always done so in the past; and I claim that it is still the same today. The reason for that we have seen already—that God is still the same, and man is still the same. Still more important, not to believe this is indicative, ultimately, of the fact that we have very little place for the Holy Spirit and His work in our outlook upon this whole matter.

This may be slow work; it often is; it is a long-term policy. But my whole contention is that it works, that it pays, and that it is honoured, and must be, because it is God's own method. This is the thing to which He calls us, it is the thing into which He thrusts us forth, and therefore He will honour it. He has always honoured it, and still honours it in this modern world, and after you have tried these other methods and schemes, and found that they will come to nothing, you will be driven back to this ultimately. This is the method by which churches have always come into being. You see it in the New Testament, and you see it in the subsequent history of the Church, and you can see it in this modern world.

*   *   *

But all that has led us repeatedly to the same question, What is preaching? I assert that when there is true preaching people will come and listen to it; so that immediately involves us in a discussion of the question, What is preaching? This, of course, is the vital question for us, and I now address myself to it. My position is that most of these problems with which we have been dealing, and most of these situations and difficulties that have arisen, and which are causing such concern, and rightly so, to those who are in the Church, are all ultimately due to the fact that there has been a defective view of preaching, and therefore defective preaching. I do not think that the pulpit itself can escape responsibility for this. If the people are not attending places of worship I hold the pulpit to be primarily responsible. The tendency is, of course, to blame other factors. The commonest excuse is the two world wars. Then at one time we were told that poverty was the explanation, and that you could not expect people who had insufficient food and inadequate clothing to come to listen to preaching; poverty, we were told, was the great obstacle. But by today we are being told that affluence is the great problem, and that the difficulty now is that the people are so well off, and have so much of everything, that they do not see the need of the Gospel. The moment you begin to try to explain these things in terms of circumstances you always land yourself ultimately in some such ridiculous position.

My contention is that it is the pulpit itself that is ultimately responsible, and that when the pulpit is right, and the preaching is true, that it will attract and draw the people to listen to its message. Once more I would say that in my opinion there has scarcely ever been an era in the history of the world when the opportunity for, and the need for, preaching has been greater than it is in this present troubled modern world.

What then is preaching? What do I mean by preaching? Let us look at it like this. There, is a man standing in a pulpit and speaking, and there, are people sitting in pews or seats and listening. What is happening? What is this? Why does that man stand in that pulpit? What is his object? Why does the Church put him there to do this? Why do these other people come to listen? What is this man meant to be doing? What is he trying to do? What ought he to be doing? These it seems to me are the great questions. We must not rush to consider techniques and methods and 'the problem of communication'. It is because these preliminary questions have not been asked, and faced, that people get bogged down in all the details and discussions. This is the big question and the controlling consideration—what is this man doing there?

Any true definition of preaching must say that that man is there to deliver the message of God, a message from God to those people. If you prefer the language of Paul, he is 'an ambassador for Christ'. That is what he is. He has been sent, he is a commissioned person, and he is standing there as the mouthpiece of God and of Christ to address these people. In other words he is not there merely to talk to them, he is not there to entertain them. He is there—and I want to emphasise this—to do something to those people; he is there to produce results of various kinds, he is there to influence people. He is not merely to influence a part of them; he is not only to influence their minds, or only their emotions, or merely to bring pressure to bear upon their wills and to induce them to some kind of activity. He is there to deal with the whole person; and his preaching is meant to affect the whole person at the very centre of life. Preaching should make such a difference to a man who is listening that he is never the same again. Preaching, in other words, is a transaction between the preacher and the listener. It does something for the soul of man, for the whole of the person, the entire man; it deals with him in a vital and radical manner.

I remember a remark made to me a few years back about some studies of mine on The Sermon on the Mount. I had deliberately published them in sermonic form. There were many who advised me not to do that on the grounds that people no longer like sermons. The days for sermons, I was told, were past, and I was pressed to turn my sermons into essays and to give them a different form. I was most interested therefore when this man to whom I was talking, and he is a very well-known Christian layman in Britain, said, "I like these Studies of yours on The Sermon on the Mount because they speak to me.' Then he went on to say, 'I have been recommended many books by learned preachers and professors but,' he said, 'what I feel about those books is that it always seems to be professors writing to professors; they do not speak to me. But,' he said, 'your stuff speaks to me.'

Now he was an able man, and a man in a prominent position, but that is how he put it. I think there is a great deal of truth in this. He felt that so much that he had been recommended to read was very learned and very clever and scholarly, but as he put it, it was 'professors writing to professors.' This is, I believe, a most important point for us to bear in mind when we read sermons. I have referred already to the danger of giving the literary style too much prominence. I remember reading an article in a literary journal some five or six years ago which I thought was most illuminating because the writer was making the selfsame point in his own field. His case was that the trouble today is that far too often instead of getting true literature we tend to get 'reviewers writing books for reviewers'. These men review one another's books, with the result that when they write, what they have in their mind too often is the reviewer and not the reading public to whom the book should be addressed, at any rate in the first instance. The same thing tends to happen in connection with preaching. This ruins preaching, which should always be a transaction between preacher and listener with something vital and living taking place. It is not the mere imparting of knowledge, there is something much bigger involved. The total person is engaged on both sides; and if we fail to realise this our preaching will be a failure.

Let me enforce this particular point by quoting from a pagan philosopher who certainly saw this point very clearly with regard to philosophy. A young philosopher went one day to Epictetus to ask him for advice. The reply Epictetus gave him is very good advice also for preachers. He said, 'The philosopher's lecture room is a surgery. When you go away you ought to have felt not pleasure but pain, for when you come in something is wrong with you. One man has put his shoulder out, another has an abscess, another a headache. Am I the surgeon then to sit down and give you a string of fine sentences that you may praise me and then go away—the man with the dislocated arm, the man with the abscess, the man with the headache—just as you came? Is it for this that young men come away from home and leave their parents and their kinsmen and their property to say, "Bravo to you for your fine moral conclusions"? Is this what Socrates did or Zeno or Cleanthes?'

That is most important for the preacher. Epictetus says that this is true even of the philosopher for he is not discussing abstract problems and questions. Even philosophy should be concerned with men, with living themes and with problems and with conditions. That is the situation, he says; these people come because there is something wrong with them. One man, metaphorically, has put his shoulder out, another has an abscess, another a headache. That is true; and it is always true of every congregation. These people do not come just as minds or as intellects, they come as total persons in the midst of life, with all its attendant circumstances and its problems, and its difficulties and its trials; and the business of the preacher is not only to remember that but to preach accordingly. He is dealing with living persons, people who are in need and in trouble, sometimes not consciously; and he is to make them aware of that, and to deal with it. It is this living transaction.

Or take another statement by the same Epictetus: 'Tell me,' he says in a challenge to the philosopher—and an equally good challenge to the preacher—'Tell me, who after hearing your lecture or discourse became anxious about or reflected upon himself?' That is the test. If people can listen to us without becoming anxious about themselves or reflecting on themselves we have not been preaching. 'Or who,' asks Epictetus, 'as he went out of the room said, "The philosopher put his finger upon my faults. I must not behave in that way again"?'

That is an excellent statement of my view of preaching; that is what preaching is meant to do. It addresses us in such a manner as to bring us under judgment; and it deals with us in such a way that we feel our whole life is involved, and we go out saying, 'I can never go back and live just as I did before. This has done something to me, it has made a difference to me. I am a different person as the result of listening to this.' Epictetus adds that if you do not do this, the utmost praise you get is when one man says to another, 'That was a beautiful passage about Xerxes.' And the other says, 'No, I like that best about the Battle of Thermopylae.' In that case, you see, nothing has been done to them at all, but they were just sitting in a detached manner and estimating and judging the speaker. One liked this quotation, the other liked that historical allusion. It had been an entertainment—very interesting, very attractive, very stimulating perhaps for the intellect. But it had done nothing to them, and they went out just praising this or that aspect of the preacher's performance.

To me that is not what preaching is meant to be. Preaching is that which deals with the total person, the hearer becomes involved and knows that he has been dealt with and addressed by God through this preacher. Something has taken place in him and in his experience, and it is going to affect the whole of his life.

There, then, is a general definition of preaching. But what exactly is this man doing in that pulpit? That is the object, that is the purpose; but what exactly is he doing? Here I believe that we have to draw a distinction between two elements in preaching. There is first of all the sermon or the message—the content of that which is being delivered. But secondly, there is the act of preaching, the delivery, if you like, or what is commonly called 'preaching'. It is a great pity that this word 'preaching' is not confined to this second aspect which we may describe as the act of delivering the message.

I am concerned to emphasise this very real distinction between the message and the imparting of the message, or the delivery of the message. Let me try to show what I mean by this distinction. I remember being told of a statement once made by the late Dr. J. D. Jones of Bournemouth in England. He was preaching in a certain place and a number of the local ministers were invited to meet him after the evening service. One of them put to him the question that is so often put to older preachers, 'Who is the greatest preacher you have ever heard?' His reply was most discriminating. He said, 'I do not know that I can tell you who is the greatest preacher I have ever heard, but I can tell you this quite certainly; the greatest preaching I have ever heard is the preaching of John Hutton.'

That brings out very well this vital distinction. You see, when he was asked who is the greatest preacher, he felt that it was too inclusive a term. It included the person of the preacher, his character, his sermon, and so on. There, he found it difficult to be definite and certain and to say that one man was superior to all the others. But with regard to the preaching, as he put it, this act of communicating the message, he had no doubt at all; it was this particular man Dr. John A. Hutton, one-time minister of Westminster Chapel, London.

Now that is the kind of distinction I would draw between the message and the act of delivering it. Or take another illustration. I remember reading a statement by a great preacher of the end of the eighteenth century in Wales. He was drawing a distinction between the two greatest evangelical preachers of that century. One was George Whitefield, who was as famous in the U.S.A. as in Britain, and was beyond any question one of the greatest preachers of all time. The other was a preacher in Wales called Daniel Rowlands. He was a contemporary of Whitefield and out-lived Whitefield by some twenty years. Here was another great preacher, another great orator. This man to whom I am referring, David Jones, Llangan in South Wales, was being asked to evaluate the difference between Whitefield and

57

Daniel Rowland as preachers. In his reply he said, 'As regards the oratory, as regards the delivery, as regards the act of preaching, as regards the soaring to the heights and the lifting up of the congregation to the heavens I really could detect very little difference between them; the one was as good as the other. The one big difference between them,' he continued, 'was this, that you could always be certain of getting a good sermon from Rowland, but not always from Whitefield.'

There we have exactly this same distinction. You can have good preaching even with a poor sermon; it is a real possibility. I shall be referring to this in another connection later. All I am concerned to do now is to show that there is an essential distinction between these two elements in what this man is doing in the pulpit. There is the sermon, a sermon which he has prepared; and then there is the 'act' of delivering this sermon. Another way of stating it is this. A man came—I think it was actually in Philadelphia—on one occasion to the great George Whitefield and asked if he might print his sermons. Whitefield gave this reply; he said, 'Well, I have no inherent objection, if you like, but you will never be able to put on the printed page the lightning and the thunder.' That is the distinction—the sermon, and the 'lightning and the thunder'. To Whitefield this was of very great importance, and it should be of very great importance to all preachers, as I hope to show. You can put the sermon into print, but not the lightning and the thunder. That comes into the act of preaching and cannot be conveyed by cold print. Indeed it almost baffles the descriptive powers of the best reporters.

*   *   *

That then is our basic division of the matter. So we start with the sermon. Once more I have to divide the subject into two sections. With regard to the sermon itself you have first of all the content, the message; and secondly, you have the form given to that content or message. Here, again, is a most important distinction.

We start with the content. What is it that determines the content of our message, of our sermon? I suggest that a very good text of Scripture which focuses our attention on this particular point is the famous statement made by Peter as he and John were walking into the Temple one afternoon at the hour of prayer. Suddenly they were confronted by an impotent man at the Beautiful Gate of the Temple. This man looked at them, expecting to receive a gift from them. He had received alms from many people. That was all the world could do for him. It could not heal him, but it could help him to live and to exist, and to improve his lot somewhat, and to give him a certain amount of comfort. So he looked at these two men expecting to receive something of them. But he did not receive what he expected. Peter spoke to him like this, saying, 'Silver and gold have I none; but such as I have give I thee: In the name of Jesus Christ of Nazareth rise up and walk' (Acts 3:1–6)

What is this message? That statement of Peter's reminds us that there is a negative aspect to it. There are certain things we are not to do, certain things we are not equipped to do. But then there is that special task that we are equipped to do, which we are called to do, and which we are enabled to do.

I use that illustration simply because it will help us to remember the point, because it puts it in a dramatic form. What then are our principles? First and foremost the message or the sermon is not to consist merely of topical comments. In other words we are not to talk to people about the events of the week, things that have happened, things that have caught the headlines in the newspapers, political matters, or anything you like. There is the type of preacher who obviously depends upon what he reads in the newspapers for his message on Sunday; and he just makes comments on this. That is what is called topical preaching. Other men seem to rely almost entirely upon their reading, in some cases their reading of novels. They tell the people about the last novel they have read, about its story and its message, and try to give a moral application or a moral twist at the end. In this connection I remember a woman journalist, who used to write to a certain weekly religious paper in England, writing about the

man she described as her favourite preacher. In the article she told us
why he was her favourite preacher. The reason she gave was this—
'He always shares his reading with us.'

Then there are others who seem to think that a sermon is a moral
essay or some kind of disquisition on ethical principles, with an
appeal, and a call, and an urging to a certain type of ethical behaviour.

To others the message is to be one of general uplift, a kind of
psychological treatment. It may use Christian terminology, but it
evacuates it of its real meaning. The terms are used to do something
psychologically to people, to make them feel happy, to make them feel
better, to teach them how to face the problems of life—'Positive
thinking' and so on. It has had a great vogue during the present
century.

Then, and coming to a more intellectual type under this negative
heading, we have speculative thought, philosophising and playing
with ideas, trying to meet the modern man at his own level, and
trying to get a message that is 'adequate for men in this atomic age'
and so on.

I suggest that all this is entirely wrong, that this is not the business
of the man who stands in the pulpit. Why not? Because the world can
do that; there is nothing special about it. I have put that under the
category of 'silver and gold'; the world does that, the world can do
that. But this is not the message that has been committed to us. Let
me make it clear that I am not saying that the effect of preaching
should not be to make people happier, it should; because, as I have
emphasised, it effects the whole person. But all the effects and results
which arise in that way are incidentals, they are results or consequences of the message preached, and not the message itself.

When I come to consider the actual construction of the sermon I
shall go out of my way to show that we must always show that the
sermon is relevant. But there is all the difference in the world between
showing the relevance of the message of God's Word and preaching a
topical sermon. The topical application is incidental, and consequen-
tial; it is not primary. That is the sort of thing that the world in its

ethical and philosophical and social and political clubs and societies can do; but it is not the thing which the preacher is called upon to do.

Well what is that? Turning then to the positive side, and using this analogy of Peter and John with the man at the Beautiful Gate of the Temple, what is the message? It is, 'such as I have'. I have not got the other, that is not my province, it is not my business; I am not competent to do that. But 'such as I have'. I have got something; something has been given to me, something has been committed to me, I have a commission—'such as I have give I thee'.

The way in which the Apostle Paul puts that is, 'I delivered unto you first of all that which I also received.' That is what determines the message or the sermon as such; it is that which the preacher has received. The other term used by Paul—'ambassador'—brings it out very clearly. An ambassador is not a man who voices his own thoughts or his own opinions or views, or his own desires. The very essence of the position of the ambassador is that he is a man who has been 'sent' to speak for somebody else. He is the speaker for his Government or his President or his King or Emperor, or whatever form of government his country may have. He is not a man who speculates and gives his own views and ideas. He is the bearer of a message, he is commissioned to do this, he is sent to do this; and that is what he must do.

In other words, the content of the sermon is what is called in the New Testament 'The Word'. 'Preach the word', or 'preach the Gospel', or 'the whole counsel of God.' That being interpreted means the message of the Bible, the message of the Scriptures.

What is the message? It is that 'such as I have', it is limited to that. This is what I have received, this is what I possess—'such as I have'. I have received this, it has been handed to me. I do not bring my own thoughts and ideas, I do not just tell people what I think or surmise: I deliver to them what has been given to me. I have been given it, and I give it to them. I am a vehicle, I am a channel, I am an instrument, I am a representative.

That then is the essential message. But obviously this is something that must be divided into two main sections. It is very important that we should recognise these two main sections in the message of the Bible. The first is what you may call the message of salvation, the *kerygma*, that is what determines evangelistic preaching. The second is the teaching aspect, the *didache*, that which builds up those who have already believed—the edification of the saints. Here is a major division which we must always draw, and this must always be a controlling factor in our preparation of our sermons and messages.

What do I mean by this first message of salvation, or evangelistic preaching? There is a very perfect summary of this in just two verses in the First Epistle of Paul to the Thessalonians. Paul reminds the Thessalonians of what it was that he had actually preached to them when he first came among them. This is what brought the Church at Thessalonica into being. He says, 'They themselves shew of us what manner of entering we had unto you, and how ye turned to God from idols to serve the living and true God; And to wait for his Son from heaven, whom he raised from the dead, even Jesus, which delivered us from the wrath to come' (1 Thes. 1:9-10). That is a perfect summary of the evangelistic message.

He gives another summary of it in his farewell address to the elders of the Church at Ephesus when they came down to meet him at the near-by seashore as he was going up to Jerusalem. There is a wonderful account of it in Acts 20. He reminds them of the character of his preaching. He had preached and taught 'publickly and from house to house', 'with many tears'. What was the message? He says it was, 'repentance toward God, and faith toward our Lord Jesus Christ' (vs. 17-21). That is the Apostle's summary of his own message.

For our purposes we can put it like this. This type of preaching is first of all a proclamation of the being of God—' . . . how ye turned to God from idols to serve the living and the true God.' Evangelistic preaching worthy of the name starts with God and with a declaration concerning His being and power and glory. You find that everywhere in the New Testament. That was precisely what Paul did in Athens— 'Him declare I unto you'. 'Him'! Preaching about God, and contrasting Him with the idols, exposing the emptiness and the vacuity and uselessness of idols.

That, in turn, leads on to preaching the Law. The character of God leads to the Law of God—God's whole relationship to the world and to man. All this is designed to bring people to a conviction of sin, and to lead them to repentance. And that in turn should lead them to faith in the Lord Jesus Christ as the One and only Saviour. That is the message of salvation, that is what is called evangelistic preaching. It is found perfectly in John 3:16—'God so loved the world, that he gave his only begotten Son, that whosoever believeth in him should not perish, but have everlasting life.'

But then there is the other side, which is teaching, the 'building up of the saints'. This, again, I would subdivide into two sections; that which is more primarily experimental, and that which is instructional. I do not elaborate on this now; I shall do so when we come to the more practical parts of our treatment of the subject. But fundamentally I suggest that this man in the pulpit should have that main two-fold division in his mind, and that he must sub-divide the second into these two sections—the experimental and the instructional.

In other words every preacher should be, as it were, at least three types or kinds of preacher. There is the preaching which is primarily evangelistic. This should take place at least once each week. There is the preaching which is instructional teaching but mainly experimental. That I generally did on a Sunday morning. There is a more purely instructional type of preaching which I personally did on a week-night.

I would emphasise that these distinctions should not be pressed in too absolute a sense. But for the general guidance of the preacher in his preparation of his message it is good to think of it in that three-fold way—preaching to those who are unbelievers, then preaching to a believer in an experimental manner, and, thirdly, in a more directly didactic instructional manner.

We shall have to go on from there and see how this man relates the total message of the Bible to these particular types of presentation.

CHAPTER FOUR

The Form of the Sermon

WE HAVE SEEN that there are three main types of messages which the preacher has to prepare.

I would emphasise that while I regard these divisions or distinctions as important I must stress the fact that they are not absolute distinctions or divisions. What really matters is that we should have this kind of division of the matter in our minds, and it is also, of course, good for the people. Preaching which is nothing but evangelistic is obviously inadequate. Preaching, on the other hand, which is never evangelistic is equally inadequate, and so on. This, then, is a good practical kind of division and distinction to hold in one's mind. But I must emphasise that these differing types are always interrelated and inter-dependent.

A most important question arises here. How is this inter-relationship between these three types of preaching to be preserved? I suggest that the way to answer that question is to realise the relationship between theology and preaching. I would lay down a general proposition that preaching must always be theological, always based on a theological foundation. We should be particularly careful when we preach on isolated texts and deal with each one separately. The reason for that, of course, is that we may well find ourselves becoming guilty of contradictions. We deliver a message on the basis of one text, but because it is not related to others, and to the whole truth, when we come to deal with another text we may say something that contradicts what we have said in the first sermon. The way to avoid that, and to maintain and preserve the interrelationship between these types of preaching, is to be always theological. There is no type of preaching that should be non-theological.

A type of preaching that is sometimes, indeed very frequently today, regarded as non-theological is evangelistic preaching. I well remember how when an evangelistic campaign was being held in London a few years ago, one of the liberal religious weeklies supporting the campaign said, 'Let us have a theological truce while the campaign is on.' It went on to say that after the campaign we must then think things out and become theological. The idea was that evangelism is non-theological, and to introduce theology at that stage is wrong. You 'bring people to Christ' as they put it; and then you teach them the truth. It is only subsequently that theology comes in.

That, to me, is quite wrong, and indeed monstrous. I would be prepared to argue that in many ways evangelistic preaching should be more, rather than less theological, than any other, and for this good reason. Why is it that you call people to repent? Why do you call them to believe the gospel? You cannot deal properly with repentance without dealing with the doctrine of man, the doctrine of the Fall, the doctrine of sin and the wrath of God against sin. Then when you call men to come to Christ and to give themselves to Him, how can you do so without knowing who He is, and on what grounds you invite them to come to Him, and so on. In other words it is all highly theological. Evangelism which is not theological is not evangelism at all in any true sense. It may be a calling for decisions, it may be a calling on people to come to religion, or to live a better kind of life, or the offering of some psychological benefits; but it cannot by any definition be regarded as Christian evangelism, because there is no true reason for what you are doing apart from these great theological principles. I assert therefore that every type of preaching must be theological, including evangelistic preaching.

At the same time it is vital that we should realise that preaching is not lecturing on theology, or on any aspect of theology. I hope to take this up later on; I am dealing only with general definitions at the moment.

If then I say that preaching must be theological and yet that it is not lecturing on theology, what is the relationship between preaching and theology? I would put it like this, that the preacher must have a grasp, and a good grasp, of the whole biblical message, which is of course a unity. In other words the preacher should be well versed in biblical theology which in turn leads on to a systematic theology. To me there is nothing more important in a preacher than that he should have a systematic theology, that he should know it and be well grounded in it. This systematic theology, this body of truth which is derived from the Scripture, should always be present as a background and as a controlling influence in his preaching. Each message, which arises out of a particular text or statement of the Scripture, must always be a part or an aspect of this total body of truth. It is never something in isolation, never something separate or apart. The doctrine in a particular text, we must always remember, is a part of this greater whole—the Truth or the Faith. That is the meaning of the phrase 'comparing Scripture with Scripture'. We must not deal with any text in isolation; all our preparation of a sermon should be controlled by this background of systematic theology.

It is necessary to issue a warning at this point. It is wrong for a man to impose his system violently on any particular text; but at the same time it is vital that his interpretation of any particular text should be checked and controlled by this system, this body of doctrine and of truth which is found in the Bible. The tendency of some men who have a systematic theology, which they hold very rigidly, is to impose this wrongly upon particular texts and so to do violence to those texts. In other words they do not actually derive that particular doctrine from the text with which they are dealing at that point. The doctrine may be true but it does not arise from that particular text; and we must always be textual. That is what I mean by not 'imposing' your system upon a particular text or statement. The right use of systematic theology is, that when you discover a particular doctrine in your text

66

you check it, and control it, by making sure that it fits into this whole body of biblical doctrine which is vital and essential.

In other words I am contending that our primary call is to deliver this whole message, this 'whole counsel of God', and that this is always more important than the particulars, the particular parts and portions.

Perhaps I can clarify this by reminding you that it is obvious that in New Testament times, and in the early days of the Christian Church, they did not preach in the manner that has become customary with us. They did not take a text out of the New Testament and analyse it and expound it and then apply it, because they did not have the New Testament. Well, what did they preach? They preached the great message that had been committed to them, this great body of truth, this whole doctrine of salvation. My argument is that this is what we should always be doing, though we do it through individual expositions of particular texts. That is, to me, in general the relationship between theology and preaching.

There is one other general point I would emphasise here before we leave this matter of the content of the sermon; and that is that we are to preach the Gospel, and not to preach about the Gospel. That is a very vital distinction, which one cannot easily put into words, but which is nevertheless really important. There are men who think that they are preaching the Gospel when actually in fact they are simply saying things about the Gospel. I have always felt that this is the particular characteristic, and indeed the snare, of the Barthians. They talk constantly about 'the Word', and say things about 'the Word'. But that is not what we are called to do; we are called to preach the Word and to present the Word, and to bring the Word directly to people. We are not simply to say things about it, we are actually to convey it itself. We are the channels and the vehicles through which this Word is to pass to the people.

Another way I can put that is to say that we are not called just to say things about the Gospel. I remember a type of preaching fifty years ago and more, which was often described as 'praising the Gospel'. The comment on the sermon and the preacher was, that he had praised the Gospel. He had been saying wonderful things about it, or showing how wonderful it was. I suggest that that is wrong. The Gospel is wonderful, the Gospel is to be praised, but that is not the preacher's primary task. He is to 'present', to declare the Gospel.

Or let me put it like this. The business of the preacher is not to present the Gospel academically. This again is done frequently. The preacher can analyse it and show its parts and portions, and show how excellent it is; but still he is saying things about the Gospel, whereas we are called to preach the Gospel, to convey it, and to bring it directly to the individuals who are listening to us, and to bring it to the whole man. So let us be clear that we are not to talk about the Gospel as if it were something outside us. We are involved in it; we are not to look at it just as a subject, and to say things about it; it itself is being directly presented and conveyed to the congregation through us.

Here, it is important for us to emphasise once more that we must present the total Gospel. There is a personal side to it; we must deal with that, and we must start with that. But we do not stop with that; there is a social side, indeed a cosmic side as well. We must present the whole plan of salvation as it is revealed in the Scriptures. We must show that the ultimate object, as the Apostle Paul puts it in Ephesians 1:10, is to head up in Christ all things, 'both which are in heaven, and which are on earth; even in Him'. That is what we have to do, and that is why I advocate that we should divide our preaching and our ministering of the Word into the three divisions I have suggested. It is, of course, in that third type of preaching, which I said should be more instructional, that this element comes out. There, you are not preaching evangelistically, nor are you dealing with the problems of the people, but you want them to see that they are part of this greater whole. You are emphasising that salvation is not merely something subjective, a nice feeling, or peace, or whatever it is they are seeking. All that is very important, and is a part of it; but there is something much more important, namely that the whole universe is involved. We must give the people a conception of this, of the scope and the ambit and the greatness of the Gospel in this all-inclusive aspect.

Every part, in other words, is a part of this whole, and it is important that we should always convey that impression. I am always fascinated by the way in which this particular characteristic of preaching comes out so clearly in the Epistles of the Apostle Paul everywhere. Let me use them to bring home my point. You know how, in general, his Epistles can be divided into two main sections. Having started with his preliminary salutation he goes on to remind his readers of the great doctrines which they have believed. Having done that, about halfway through the letter he then introduces his great word 'therefore'. Now he is going to apply the doctrine. He says in effect, 'In the light of all this which you claim to have believed, this is what follows.' He reasons with them as to how they should live and so on. In other words, the first half, speaking very roughly, of every Epistle 'is doctrinal, and the second part is practical or application. Yet, having said that, what is always so fascinating, and to me thrilling and moving, is to observe the way in which even in the practical section he keeps on bringing in the doctrine again. There is the general division, but you must not press it too far, you must not make these divisions too absolute. You cannot do this with Paul's Epistles; all these aspects are so intimately related that you have got to keep them going together always.

In other words, while there is an aspect of preaching which is concerned to inculcate moral and ethical principles, and the application of them to life, this must never be done in isolation. Take, for instance, the way in which Paul opens out in the twelfth chapter of the Epistle to the Romans: 'I beseech you therefore brethren by the mercies of God, that ye present your bodies . . .' That is the appeal. It is not simply morality; this element comes in 'because of' what we have already known and believed. So while you must recognise this kind of distinction you must not press it. It is good for practical purposes, but you must never isolate these things. The preacher must always be saying the 'whole thing' as it were, even while he is putting particular stress and emphasis on certain individual matters for the moment.

Indeed, you will discover that though you set out with these ideas in your mind you will sometimes find that what you have proposed is not what really happens. I mean this; you will find that people who have listened to your more evangelistic preaching without having come under its power, without having been converted, may well be converted when you are preaching to the saints, as it were, and edifying the believers. These are the surprises that one gets, and later on I hope to show that we ought to thank God for this. It is a part of the great romance of preaching. You set out rightly by saying to yourself, in one type of service, Now this is to be an evangelistic service, whereas in another I shall be setting out to edify the saints and to build them up in the faith. But to your surprise you will find that someone will be converted by the second type of sermon and not by the first, and so on. 'The wind bloweth where it listeth . . .' Though we do not control these matters it is right and good that we should have this kind of system in our minds.

So far I have been dealing with the content of the sermon in a general way. We come now to the form of the sermon. I am ready to confess that this is undoubtedly, in my opinion, the most difficult matter that we shall have to deal with. It is the most difficult, but at the same time I would emphasise that it is also one of the most important.

Let us start with some negatives. A sermon is not an essay. That is something that needs to be said, and said constantly, because there are so many who clearly draw no distinction between a sermon and an essay. This is one of the points to which I was referring earlier when pointing out the danger of printing sermons and reading them. On what grounds do I say that a sermon is not an essay? I would say that by definition the style is entirely different. An essay is written to read, a sermon is primarily meant to be spoken and to be listened to. In an essay you look for literary elegance and a particular form, whereas that is not one of the primary desiderata in a sermon. A further difference is seen in this; repetition in an essay is bad, but I would stress that repetition in a sermon is good. It is a part of the very essence of teaching and preaching that there should be repetition; it helps to drive the point home and to make it clear. But when you are reading an essay that is unnecessary and therefore bad. Furthermore, an essay generally deals with a particular idea or thought or concept. It plays with it and looks at it from different aspects. The danger, therefore, for a preacher who does not recognise the distinction is to go to a text just to get an idea; then, having got this idea, to say farewell to the text and the context, and to proceed to write an essay on the idea that has been suggested by the reading of that verse or passage. He proceeds to write an essay, and then enters a pulpit and either reads or recites this essay which he has so prepared. But I suggest that that is not preaching at all; that really it has very little, if anything, to do with preaching. This is so, very largely, because there is no element of attack in it. If there is an element of attack in an essay it is correspondingly a bad essay. The essential character of an essay is that it should play with ideas, and on the whole handle them lightly. An essay should have charm and elegance. It is a form of literature which should make interesting, entertaining and enjoyable reading; but it is not preaching.

Secondly, I assert that preaching a sermon is not to be confused with giving a lecture. This, again, is something quite different, and for these reasons. A lecture starts with a subject, and what it is concerned to do is to give knowledge and information concerning this particular subject. Its appeal is primarily and almost exclusively to the mind; its object is to give instruction and state facts. That is its primary purpose and function. So a lecture, again, lacks, and should lack, the element of attack, the concern to do something to the listener, which is a vital element in preaching. But the big difference, I would say, between a lecture and a sermon is that a sermon does not start with a subject; a sermon should always be expository. In a sermon the theme or the doctrine is something that arises out of the text and its context, it is something which is illustrated by that text and context.

So a sermon should not start with the subject as such; it should start with the Scripture which has in it a doctrine or a theme. That doctrine should then be dealt with in terms of this particular setting.

I therefore lay down this proposition that a sermon should always be expository. But, immediately, that leads me to say something which I regard as very important indeed in this whole matter. A sermon is not a running commentary on, or a mere exposition of, the meaning of a verse or a passage or a paragraph. I emphasise this because there are many today who have become interested in what they regard as expository preaching but who show very clearly that they do not know what is meant by expository preaching. They think that it just means making a series of comments, or a running commentary, on a paragraph or a passage or a statement. They take a passage verse by verse; and they make their comments on the first, then they go on to the next verse, and do the same with that, then the next, and so on. When they have gone through the passage in this way they imagine they have preached a sermon. But they have not; all they have done is to make a series of comments on a passage. I would suggest that far from having preached a sermon such preachers have only preached the introduction to a sermon!

This, in other words, raises the whole question of the relationship of exposition to the sermon. My basic contention is that the essential characteristic of a sermon is that it has a definite form, and that it is this form that makes it a sermon. It is based upon exposition, but it is this exposition turned or moulded into a message which has this characteristic form. A phrase that helps to bring out this point is one which is to be found in the Old Testament in the Prophets where we read about 'the burden of the Lord'. The message has come to the prophet as a burden, it has come to him as an entire message, and he delivers this. That is something, I argue, which is never true of an essay or of a lecture, and indeed it is not true of a mere series of comments upon a number of verses. I maintain that a sermon should have form in the sense that a musical symphony has form. A symphony always has form, it has its parts and its portions. The divisions are clear, and are recognised, and can be described; and yet a symphony is a whole. You can divide it into parts, and yet you always realise that they are parts of a whole, and that the whole is more than the mere summation or aggregate of the parts. One should always think of a sermon as a construction, a work which is in that way comparable to a symphony. In other words a sermon is not a mere meandering through a number of verses; it is not a mere collection or series of excellent and true statements and remarks. All those should be found in the sermon, but they do not constitute a sermon. What makes a sermon a sermon is that it has this particular 'form' which differentiates it from everything else.

*   *   *

I have to turn aside for a moment here to raise a question, or to deal with a position; and I frankly confess that I have often been very troubled by what I am about to say. Edwin Hatch in his Hibbert Lectures in 1888—I have quoted from them already—makes a great point of the fact that the earliest Christian preaching was entirely prophetic. He says that Christian men received messages through the Holy Spirit and got up and delivered them without premeditation, thought, or preparation. They had no form, no sermonic form, about them, but were isolated statements. 'Men spoke as they were moved by the Holy Spirit,' a message suddenly came to them and they gave utterance to it. There are indications of this in 1 Corinthians 14 and in other places. Hatch goes so far as to suggest not only that that was the original Christian preaching, but, further, that our idea of preaching, and in particular, this idea of a sermon which I am putting forward is something that is foreign to the New Testament. He argues that it came into the Christian Church and her preaching as the result of Greek influence upon the early Church, and especially during the second century. The Greeks, of course, were interested in form, they were interested in form in everything—the human body, buildings, etc—so they had become interested in the form of their addresses or speeches. They laid great emphasis upon this. A man did not just get up and speak; the way in which he presented his matter was very important if he wanted to influence people. So they had developed this method, or this form, and this form has characterised the sermon, according to general acceptance, in the long history of the Christian Church.

I want to deal with this very briefly. I admit at once that there is a great element of truth in what Hatch says. One can see this pneumatic, this prophetic element clearly in the New Testament. But I still dissent from his ultimate verdict, and I believe that his contention is not quite true to the New Testament evidence. I agree that we must always be careful—and this was the thrust of Hatch's teaching—lest we impose this form upon the matter and become more interested in the form than in the content. There is a very real danger at that point. The moment you have any kind of form, literary or any other, there is the danger of our becoming slaves to the form, and of becoming more interested in the way in which we say something rather than in what we are saying. Very well, I accept that, but still I argue that, even on the New Testament evidence itself, Hatch goes too far. I would say that in the report of Peter's sermon on the Day of Pentecost, as found in Acts 2, that there is distinct form, that he did not get up and make a series of isolated remarks, but that there was a definite form in his sermon or speech. In the case of Stephen's self-defence before the Sanhedrin, as recorded in Acts 7, there is again a most definite form, what I would call the form of a sermon. There is a distinct plan which he works out as he proceeds from step to step. Stephen knew exactly where he was going to end before he began, and he leads on to that. You cannot read Acts 7 without being impressed by the form, the architecture, the construction, of that famous address. And surely in Paul's address in Antioch in Pisidia, as recorded in Acts 13, you find exactly the same thing. He was speaking to a plan, or if you prefer it, he had a kind of skeleton, or outline; there was certainly form to that address.

Having made those remarks in passing in defence of the sermon as I conceive it, as against the criticisms of Hatch, I nevertheless urge that we must keep ourselves fluid on these matters. We must not become hardened. The history of the Church, and the history of preaching, show very clearly how these things can be carried to extremes which, in turn, always lead to reactions. The history of the Church in this respect, as in many others, has been excess and then over-reaction against that instead of holding to the pattern of the New Testament itself.

What, then, is this form that should characterise a sermon? I suggest it is something like this. As you start preparing your sermon you must begin with the exposition of your passage or single verse. This is essential, this is vital; as I have said, all preaching must be expository. You do not start with a thought, even though it be a right thought, a good thought; you do not start with that, and then work out an address on that. You must not do that, because, if you do, you will find that you will be tending to say the same thing each time; you will be repeating yourself endlessly. If there were no other argument for expository preaching this, to me, would be sufficient in and of itself; it will preserve and guarantee variety and variation in your preaching. It will save you from repetition; and that will be a good thing for your people as well as for yourself!

So you must be expository; and in any case my whole argument is that it should be clear to people that what we are saying is something that comes out of the Bible. We are presenting the Bible and its message. That is why I am one of those who like to have a pulpit Bible. It should always be there and it should always be open, to emphasise the fact that the preacher is preaching out of it. I have known men who have just opened the Bible to read the text. They then shut the Bible and put it on one side and go on talking. I think that is wrong from the standpoint of true preaching. We are always to give the impression, and it may be more important than anything we say, that what we are saying comes out of the Bible, and always comes out of it. That is the origin of our message, this is where we have received it.

So you start with exposition; not only in your own preparation, but

75

you are going to give this to the people as well. What you are going to say, the burden of your message arises from this exposition. If you have truly understood the verse or passage you will arrive at a doctrine, a particular doctrine, which is a part of the whole message of the Bible. It is your business to search for this and to seek it diligently. You have to question your text, to put questions to it, and especially this question—What is this saying? What is the particular doctrine here, the special message? In the preparation of a sermon nothing is more important than that.

Having isolated your doctrine in this way and, having got it quite clear in your own mind, you then proceed to consider the relevance of this particular doctrine to the people who are listening to you. This question of relevance must never be forgotten. As I have said, you are not lecturing, you are not reading an essay; you are setting out to do something definite and particular, to influence these people and the whole of their lives and outlook. Obviously, therefore, you have got to show the relevance of all this. You are not an antiquary lecturing on ancient history or on ancient civilisations, or something like that. The preacher is a man who is speaking to people who are alive today and confronted by the problems of life; and therefore you have to show that this is not some academic or theoretical matter which may be of interest to people who take up that particular hobby, as others take up crossword puzzles or something of that type. You are to show that this message is vitally important for them, and that they must listen with the whole of their being, because this really is going to help them to live.

Having done that you now come to the division of this matter into propositions or headings, or heads—whatever you may like to call them. The object of these headings or divisions is to make clear this central doctrine or proposition. But there is a definite form to all this. As the musical composer in the introduction to his symphony, or in the overture to his opera, generally lets us into the secret of the various motifs he is going to take up, so the preacher should indicate the main theme and its various divisions in his general introduction. He must then work these out in detail and in order in his sermon. So the matter is to be divided up in this way into a number of subordinate propositions.

The arrangement of these propositions or heads is a very important matter. Having divided up the theme, and having seen its respective elements, you do not now place these haphazardly in any sort of order. You have a doctrine, an argument, a case which you want to argue out, and to reason, and to develop with the people. So, obviously, you must arrange your headings and your divisions in such a way that point number one leads to point number two, and point number two leads to point number three, etc. Each one should lead to the next, and work ultimately to a definite conclusion. Everything is to be so arranged as to bring out the main thrust of this particular doctrine.

The point I am emphasising is that there must be progression in the thought, that each one of these points is not independent, and is not, in a sense, of equal value with all the others. Each is a part of the whole, and in each you must be advancing and taking the matter further on. You are not simply saying the same thing a number of times, you are aiming at an ultimate conclusion. So in this matter of the form of a sermon, the progression, and the advance, and the development of the argument and the case is absolutely vital. You must end on a climax, and everything should lead up to it in such a way that the great truth stands out dominating everything that has been said, and the listeners go away with this in their minds.

But as you have presented your message in this way it is important that you should have been applying what you have been saying as you go along. There are many ways of doing this. You can do so by asking questions and answering them, or in various other ways; but you must apply the message as you go along. This again shows that you are not just lecturing, that you are not dealing with an abstract or academic or theoretical matter; but that this is a living matter which is of real concern to the people in the whole of their life and being. So you must keep on applying what you are saying. Then to make absolutely certain of this, when you have ended the reason and the argument, and have arrived at this climax, you apply it all again. This can be done in the form of an exhortation which again may take the form of a series of questions, or a series of terse statements. But it is vital to the sermon that it should always end on this note of application or of exhortation.

That is my idea of a sermon, and that is what I mean when I stress this idea of the form. You do not stop at mere exposition or explanation of the meaning of the text. You do that, you have got to do that, but what you are concerned to do is to convey its message. In other words a sermon is an entity, it is a complete whole. This must always be true of a sermon; it must always have this completeness, this form. This is particularly important if you should be preaching a series of sermons. You may preach a series of sermons on the same text, or on a particular passage; and the danger is that finding that you cannot say all that you desired to say in the one sermon, you will say—'Well there it is, that is all we can do this time'; and then stop abruptly at that.

To me, that is bad. We are to see that every single sermon is rounded off, is complete, has this element of wholeness in it. When you continue the same subject in a subsequent sermon you must in a few sentences at the beginning sum up what you have already said, and then develop it. But again you must make sure that this sermon also is an entity and a whole, and is complete in and of itself.

I am very concerned about this, and for many reasons. One is, obviously, that there may be people listening who will not be present on the following Sunday, and who will therefore go away disappointed and wondering what you are going to say further. Or there may be people present who were not there on the previous Sunday, and they will feel that because they were not present then that they cannot grasp what you are saying now. That is one reason why it is important that every sermon should be a complete entity and should always have this form.

In other words I assert that there is an artistic element in a sermon. This is where the labour of preparing sermons comes in. The matter has to be given form, it must be moulded into shape. I imagine

78

that the musical composer or the poet has to do this very thing. The poet has certain general ideas, certain themes suggest themselves to him; but if he is to produce a poem, he has to take all these ideas that have come to him, and to mould them into shape, and put them into a particular form. This involves considerable effort and labour. I hope to dwell in detail, when I come to the actual practical preparation of a sermon, on the variable character of this toil, and on some of the difficulties, and also on the way in which the problems are sometimes resolved in strange and unexpected manners. All I am saying now is that it is our business as preachers to hammer out our subject matter in order to get it into the form of a sermon.

But someone may ask why all this is necessary. The answer is, because of the people who are going to listen. This is what the Greeks had discovered, and I believe rightly. They had found that when truth is presented in this particular way it is more easily assimilated by the people, it is easier for them to take it in, to remember it, to understand it, and to benefit from it. So you do not take this trouble with the form merely because you believe in 'Art for Art's sake'; the artistic element comes in for the sake of the people, because it helps in the propagation of the Truth and the honour of the Gospel. I believe that what I have been trying to say can be substantiated very clearly from the long history of the Christian Church. The preaching which God through the Spirit has been most pleased to honour throughout the centuries has been preaching which has been based on great sermons; the great preachers have been men who prepared great sermons.

Should someone cite some particular preacher and say, 'But what about So-and-so, who rarely prepared a sermon but who was clearly greatly used of God?' I reply saying, Exactly! That is the exception that proves the rule. You do not legislate for hard cases, you do not build your theory on exceptions. God can use anyone and in any way. God can even use a man's silence. But we are called to be preachers who are to convey the Truth. My contention is, that if you read about the great preaching of the past, or the great sermons, you will find that these are the ones that have been most honoured by the Spirit, and used of God in the conversion of sinners and in the upbuilding and edification of the saints.

So it comes to this. The preparation of sermons involves sweat and labour. It can be extremely difficult at times to get all this matter that you have found in the Scriptures into this particular form. It is like a potter fashioning something out of the clay, or like a blacksmith making shoes for a horse; you have to keep on putting the material into the fire and on to the anvil and hit it again and again with the hammer. Each time it is a bit better, but not quite right; so you put it back again and again until you are satisfied with it or can do no better. This is the most gruelling part of the preparation of a sermon; but at the same time it is a most fascinating and a most glorious occupation. It can be at times most difficult, most exhausting, most trying. But at the same time I can assure you that when you have finally succeeded you will experience one of the most glorious feelings that ever comes to a man on the face of this earth. To borrow the title of a book by Arthur Koestler, you will be conscious of having performed an 'Act of Creation', and you will have some dim understanding of what the Scripture means which tells us that when God looked at the world He had created He saw that 'it was good'. Very well; the preacher must always start by preparing a sermon. I have not yet dealt with how he prepares it; I shall come to that. There are various ways of doing so. But he has to prepare a sermon, and it must be a true entity however he does so. This is where he begins. But let me remind you that this is only the first half, this is only the beginning. There is another side. What is that? Well, that is the actual preaching of this sermon which he has so prepared; and, as I hope to be able to show, though you may go into the pulpit with what you regard as an almost perfect sermon, you never know what is going to happen to it when you start preaching, if it is preaching worthy of the name!

CHAPTER FIVE

The Act of Preaching

WE TURN NOW to what is called the 'delivery' of the sermon, or the 'act' of preaching, what may be called preaching itself as distinct from the sermon. This is the second great aspect of our subject.

I would like to make it clear again that at this stage I am only going to deal with this in general. I am trying to give first of all a general picture of what preaching really is, and we shall then go on to more detailed considerations. It is good to have a clear general picture first before we begin to discuss the details.

Now this matter of the delivery, or what is sometimes called preaching is, once more, something very difficult to define. It is certainly not a matter of rules or regulations; and much of the trouble I think arises because people do regard it as a matter of instructions and rules and regulations, of dos and don'ts. It is not that. The difficulty is that of actually putting our definition into words. Preaching is something that one recognises when one hears it. So the best we can do is to say certain things about it. We cannot get nearer to it than that. The position is such as the Apostle Paul seems to have felt in 1 Corinthians 13 when he tried to define love; it baffles description. All you can do is to say a number of things about it, that it is this, and not that. However, certain things are true, and must be present when you get authentic preaching.

The first is that the whole personality of the preacher must be involved. That is the point, of course, that was brought out in the well-known definition of preaching by Phillips Brookes, that it is 'truth mediated through personality'. I believe that is right, that in preaching all one's faculties should be engaged, the whole man should be involved. I go so far as to suggest that even the body is involved. I am reminded as I say this of something once said by one of my predecessors at Westminster Chapel in London, Dr. John A. Hutton. In his case the preaching could always be differentiated from the matter of his sermon. His predecessor at Westminster was a well-known preacher in the U.S.A. as well as in Britain, Dr. John Henry Jowett. Jowett was rather a quiet, nervous kind of man, and he found the particularly large rostrum in Westminster Chapel very trying. He used to say that when he stood in that rostrum on his own, with the whole of his body visible to the congregation from various angles, that he felt as if he were standing naked in a field. He became so self-conscious about this that he asked for the railings round the rostrum to be draped with a curtain so that at any rate most of his body should be concealed. Well then he, as I say, was succeeded by Dr. John Hutton. I happened to be present in a service about the third Sunday after the arrival of Dr. Hutton. I noticed, as everyone else noticed, that all the drapery round the rostrum had been removed and that the whole body of the preacher was visible as in former times. Dr. Hutton gave us the explanation of this and told us that the drapery had been removed at his request because he believed that a preacher should preach with the whole of his body—and that this was certainly true of him. He told us that he preached as much with his legs as with his head, and that if we watched him we would discover that this was true. Watching him one found that it was true! I am not sure that that was always to the advantage of the preaching, because he went through all kinds of contortions. He would stand on his toes and wind one foot round the other leg and so on. The point I am making is that there was something in what he said, the whole man was involved. He did not stand like a statue and just utter words through his lips; the entire person was engaged—gestures, activity and so on.

I do not want to make too much of this, but you will remember that when Demosthenes was asked what is the first great essential in oratory, his reply was 'Action'. Then he was asked, 'Well, what is the second greatest desideratum?' He replied again, 'Action'. 'Well', they said, 'what is the third most important point?' Still the reply was, 'Action'. There is no doubt about this; effective speaking involves action; and that is why I stress that the whole personality must be involved in preaching.

The second element I would emphasise is a sense of authority and control over the congregation and the proceedings. The preacher should never be apologetic, he should never give the impression that he is speaking by their leave as it were; he should not be tentatively putting forward certain suggestions and ideas. That is not to be his attitude at all. He is a man, who is there to 'declare'certain things; he is a man under commission and under authority. He is an ambassador, and he should be aware of his authority. He should always know that he comes to the congregation as a sent messenger. Obviously this is not a matter of self-confidence; that is always deplorable in a preacher. We have the word of the Apostle Paul himself, that when he went to Corinth he went 'in weakness, and in fear, and in much trembling'. We also should always be conscious of that. But that does not mean that you are apologetic; it means that you are aware of the solemnity and the seriousness and the importance of what you are doing. You have no self-confidence, but you are a man under authority, and you have authority; and this should be evident and obvious. I put this very high up on the list, and, say that, far from being controlled by the congregation the preacher is in charge and in control of the congregation. I shall take up some of these points in great detail later in this series.

The next quality in this general view of the preacher, and of this 'act' of preaching, is the element of freedom. I attach very great importance to this. Though the sermon has been prepared in the way we have indicated, and prepared carefully, yet the preacher must be free in the act of preaching, in the delivery of the sermon. He must not be too tied to his preparation and by it. This is a crucial point; this is of the very essence of this act of preaching. I am not thinking merely in terms of having a manuscript with him in the pulpit, for he can be tied without having a manuscript. All I am saying is that he must be free; free in the sense that he must be open to the inspiration of the moment. Regarding preaching as I do as an activity under the influence and power of the Holy Spirit, we have to emphasise this point because the preparation is not finished just when a man has finished his preparation of the sermon. One of the remarkable things about preaching is that often one finds that the best things one says are things that have not been premeditated, and were not even thought of in the preparation of the sermon, but are given while one is actually speaking and preaching.

Another element to which I attach importance is that the preacher while speaking should in a sense be deriving something from his congregation. There are those present in the congregation who are spiritually-minded people, and filled with the Spirit, and they make their contribution to the occasion. There is always an element of exchange in true preaching. This is another way of showing the vita distinction between an essay and a lecture on the one hand, and a preached sermon on the other hand. The man who reads his essay gets nothing from his audience, he has it all there before him in what he has written; there is nothing new or creative taking place, no exchange. But the preacher—though he has prepared, and prepared carefully—because of this element of spiritual freedom is still able to receive something from the congregation, and does so. There is an interplay, action and response, and this often makes a very vital difference.

Any preacher worth his salt can testify to this. Indeed, any man worthy to be called a speaker even on secular matters—politics and so on—knows something about this, and has often experienced that a meeting has been made by the responsiveness of the audience he has been addressing. This should happen much more in the case of the preacher. Thank God, it often occurs that when the preacher, poor fellow, is at his worst for various reasons—perhaps has not had time to prepare as he should have done, or various physical factors and

84

other things may be operating to militate against the success of the occasion—the responsiveness and eagerness of his congregation lifts him up and enlivens him. But the preacher must be open to this; if he is not, he is going to miss one of the most glorious experiences that ever comes to a preacher. So this element of freedom is tremendously important.

That is what I meant in my last remark in the previous lecture that though you have prepared your sermon carefully and thoroughly, you never know what is going to happen to it until you get into the pulpit and start preaching it. You may find yourself amazed and astonished at what has happened. New elements may have entered, there may be loose ends, and there may be incomplete sentences. There may well be many such things which the pedants would condemn, and which a literary critic would utterly and rightly censure in an essay; but this is of the very essence of preaching. Because preaching is designed to do something to people. And as long as you keep that in the forefront, and do not attach too much significance to these other elements, you will be able to succeed.

This element of freedom is all important. Preaching should be always under the Spirit—His power and control—and you do not know what is going to happen. So always be free. It may sound contradictory to say 'prepare, and prepare carefully', and yet 'be free'. But there is no contradiction, as there is no contradiction when Paul says, 'Work out your own salvation with fear and trembling, for it is God that worketh in you both to will and to do of his good pleasure' (Phil. 2:12–13). You will find that the Spirit Who has helped you in your preparation may now help you, while you are speaking, in an entirely new way, and open things out to you which you had not seen while you were preparing your sermon.

*　　*　　*

The next element is that of seriousness. The preacher must be a serious man; he must never give the impression that preaching is something light or superficial or trivial. I merely mention this now because I propose to deal with it later at greater length. I simply make the general statement now that a preacher of necessity must give the impression that he is dealing with the most serious matter that men and women can ever consider together.

What is happening? What is happening is that he is speaking to them from God, he is speaking to them about God, he is speaking about their condition, the state of their souls. He is telling them that they are, by nature, under the wrath of God—'the children of wrath even as others'—that the character of the life they are living is offensive to God and under the judgment of God, and warning them of the dread eternal possibility that lies ahead of them. In any case the preacher, of all men, should realise the fleeting nature of life in this world. The men of the world are so immersed in its business and affairs, its pleasures and all its vain show, that the one thing they never stop to consider is the fleeting character of life. All this means that the preacher should always create and convey the impression of the seriousness of what is happening the moment he even appears in the pulpit. You remember the famous lines of Richard Baxter:

> I preached as never sure to preach again
> And as a dying man to dying men.

I do not think that can be bettered. You remember what was said of the saintly Robert Murray McCheyne of Scotland in the last century. It is said that when he appeared in the pulpit, even before he had uttered a single word, people would begin to weep silently. Why? Because of this very element of seriousness. The very sight of the man gave the impression that he had come from the presence of God and that he was to deliver a message from God to them. That is what had such an effect upon people even before he had opened his mouth. We forget this element at our peril, and at great cost to our listeners.

I put next something which is meant partly to correct, or perhaps not so much to correct, as to safeguard, what I have been saying, from misunderstanding. I refer to the element of 'liveliness'. This underlines the fact that seriousness does not mean solemnity, does not mean sadness, does not mean morbidity. These are all very important distinctions. The preacher must be lively; and you can be lively and serious at the same time.

Let me put this in other words. The preacher must never be dull, he must never be boring; he should never be what is called 'heavy'. I am emphasising these points because of something I am often told and which worries me a great deal. I belong to the Reformed tradition, and may have had perhaps a little to do in Britain with the restoration of this emphasis during the last forty years or so. I am disturbed therefore when I am often told by members of churches that many of the younger Reformed men are very good men, who have no doubt read a great deal, and are very learned men, but that they are very dull and boring preachers; and I am told this by people who themselves hold the Reformed position. This is to me a very serious matter; there is something radically wrong with dull and boring preachers. How can a man be dull when he is handling such themes? I would say that a 'dull preacher' is a contradiction in terms; if he is dull he is not a preacher. He may stand in a pulpit and talk, but he is certainly not a preacher. With the grand theme and message of the Bible dullness is impossible. This is the most interesting, the most thrilling, the most absorbing subject in the universe; and the idea that this can be presented in a dull manner makes me seriously doubt whether the men who are guilty of this dullness have ever really understood the doctrine they claim to believe, and which they advocate. We often betray ourselves by our manner.

But let us go on. We come next to zeal, and a sense of concern. These elements of course are all intimately related. When I say zeal I mean that a preacher must always convey the impression that he himself has been gripped by what he is saying. If he has not been gripped nobody else will be. So this is absolutely essential. He must impress the people by the fact that he is taken up and absorbed by what he is doing. He is full of matter, and he is anxious to impart this.

He is so moved and thrilled by it himself that he wants everybody else to share in this. He is concerned about them; that is why he is preaching to them. He is anxious about them; anxious to help them, anxious to tell them the truth of God. So he does it with energy, with zeal, and with this obvious concern for people. In other words a preacher who seems to be detached from the Truth, and who is just saying a number of things which may be very good and true and excellent in themselves, is not a preacher at all.

I came across a notable example of what I am condemning recently when I was convalescing after an illness. I was staying in a village in a certain part of England and went to the local church just across the road from where I was staying. I found that the preacher was preaching that evening on the prophet Jeremiah. He told us that he was starting a series of sermons on the prophet. So he was starting with that great text where Jeremiah said he could not refrain any longer, but that the Word of God was like a fire in his bones. That was the text he took. What happened? I left the service feeling that I had witnessed something quite extraordinary, for the one big thing that was entirely missing in that service was 'fire'. The good man was talking about fire as if he were sitting on an iceberg. He was actually dealing with the theme of fire in a detached and cold manner; he was a living denial of the very thing that he was saying, or perhaps I should say a dead denial. It was a good sermon from the standpoint of construction and preparation. He had obviously taken considerable care over this, and had obviously written it out every word, because he was reading it; but that one thing that was absent was fire. There was no zeal, no enthusiasm, no apparent concern for us as members of the congregation. His whole attitude seemed to be detached and academic and formal.

Let me put it in this way. I remember reading years ago an account by a well-known journalist in Scotland of a meeting which he had attended. He used a phrase which I have never forgotten; it has often upbraided me and often condemned me. He had been listening to two speakers speaking on the same subject. He went on to say that they were both very able and learned men. Then came the devastating phrase, 'The difference between the two speakers was this; the first spoke as an advocate, the second as a witness.' That crystallises this point perfectly. The preacher is never just an advocate. The task, the business of the advocate, the attorney, is to represent somebody in the Court of Law. He is not interested in this person, may not even know him, and has no personal interest in him; but he has been handed what we call a brief concerning this man's case. The brief has been prepared for him, all the facts and the details, the legal points and the salient matters in this particular case. He is handed his brief and what he does is to speak to his brief. He is not involved personally, he is not really concerned. He is in a position of detachment handling a matter right outside himself.

Now that must never be true of the preacher. This is, again, one of the differences between the preacher and the lecturer. The preacher is involved all along, and that is why there must be this element of zeal. He is not just 'handling' a case. To do just that is one of the greatest temptations of many preachers, and especially those of us who are combative by nature. We have an incomparable case, as we have seen; we have our systematic theology and this knowledge of the Truth. What a wonderful opportunity for arguing, reasoning, demonstrating and proving the case and refuting all objections and counter-arguments. But if the preacher gives the impression that he is only an advocate presenting a case he has failed completely. The preacher is a witness. That is the very word used by our Lord Himself, 'Ye shall be witnesses unto me'; and this is what the preacher must always be at all times. Nothing is so fatal in a preacher as that he should fail to give the impression of personal involvement.

That leads inevitably to the next element, which is Warmth. To use a term that is common today, the preacher must never be 'clinical'. So often the preacher is. Everything he does is right, is indeed almost perfect; but it is clinical, it is not living; it is cold, it is not moving, because the man has not been moved himself. But that should never be true of the preacher. If he really believes what he is saying he must

89

be moved by it; it is impossible for him not to be. That leads to warmth of necessity. The Apostle Paul tells us himself that he preached 'with tears'. He reminds the Ephesian elders of that in Acts 20. And as he refers to certain false preachers in Philippians 3 he does so with 'weeping'.

Now the Apostle Paul was a giant intellect, one of the master minds of the centuries; but he often wept as he spoke and preached. He was often moved to tears. Where has this notion come from that if you are a great intellect you show no emotion? How ridiculous and fatuous it is! A man who is not moved by these things, I maintain, has never really understood them. A man is not an intellect in a vacuum; he is a whole person. He has a heart as well as a head; and if his head truly understands, his heart will be moved. You remember how the Apostle puts it in Romans 6:17, 'God be thanked,' he says, 'that ye were the servants of sin, but ye have obeyed from the heart that form of sound doctrine which was delivered you.' If a man's heart is not engaged I take leave to query and to question whether he has really understood with his head, because of the very character of the Truth with which we are dealing. This has been true, of course, of all the great preachers of the ages. Whitefield, it seems, almost invariably as he was preaching would have tears streaming down his face. I feel we are all under condemnation here and need to be rebuked. I confess freely that I need to be rebuked myself. Where is the passion in preaching that has always characterised great preaching in the past? Why are not modern preachers moved and carried away as the great preachers of the past so often were? The Truth has not changed. Do we believe it, have we been gripped and humbled by it, and then exalted until we are 'lost in wonder love and praise'?

The preacher then is a man who for these reasons and in these ways makes contact with the people who are listening to him. Far from being detached, there is *rapport*. This comes out in his voice, in his manner, in his whole approach; everything about him shows that there is this intimacy of contact between the preacher and his congregation.

So I go on to the next point which is Urgency. I have already said this in a sense; but it deserves to be isolated and underlined in and of itself. The preacher must always be 'urgent in season and out of season' says Paul to Timothy; again for the same reason, because of the entire situation. That is what makes preaching such an astonishing act and such a responsible and overwhelming matter. It is not surprising that the Apostle Paul, looking at the ministry, asks 'Who is sufficient for these things?' A man who imagines that because he has a head full of knowledge that he is sufficient for these things had better start learning again. 'Who is sufficient for these things?' What are you doing? You are not simply imparting information, you are dealing with souls, you are dealing with pilgrims on the way to eternity, you are dealing with matters not only of life and death in this world, but with eternal destiny. Nothing can be so terribly urgent. I am reminded of the words spoken one afternoon by William Chalmers Burns who was greatly used in revivals in Scotland round about 1840, and, incidentally, in the church of Robert Murray McCheyne to whom I have already referred. He one day put his hand on the shoulder of a brother minister and said, 'Brother, we must hurry.' If we do not know something about this sense of urgency we do not know what true preaching is. You can give a lecture at any time, now, or in a year's time; it will not make much difference. The same is true of most other subjects. But the message of the Gospel is something that cannot be postponed, because you do not know whether you or the people will be alive even in a week's time or even in a day's time. 'In the midst of life we are in death.' If the preacher does not suggest this sense of urgency, that he is there between God and men, speaking between time and eternity he has no business to be in a pulpit. There is no place for calm, cool, scientific detachment in these matters. That may possibly be all right in a philosopher, but it is unthinkable in a preacher because of the whole situation in which he is involved.

For exactly the same reason preaching must always be characterised by persuasiveness. 'We beseech you in Christ's stead be ye reconciled to God.' Surely the whole object of this act is to persuade people. The preacher does not just say things with the attitude of 'take it or leave it'. He desires to persuade them of the truth of his message; he wants them to see it; he is trying to do something to them, to influence them. He is not giving a learned disquisition on a text, he is not giving a display of his own knowledge; he is dealing with these living souls and he wants to move them, to take them with him, to lead them to the Truth. That is his whole purpose. So if this element is not present, whatever else it may be, it is not preaching. All these points bring out the difference between delivering a lecture and preaching, or between an essay and a sermon.

A special word must be given also, though in a sense we have been covering it, to the element of pathos. If I had to plead guilty of one thing more than any other I would have to confess that this perhaps is what has been most lacking in my own ministry. This should arise partly from a love for the people. Richard Cecil, an Anglican preacher in London towards the end of the eighteenth century and the beginning of the nineteenth said something which should make us all think. 'To love to preach is one thing, to love those to whom we preach quite another.' The trouble with some of us is that we love preaching, but we are not always careful to make sure that we love the people to whom we are actually preaching. If you lack this element of compassion for the people you will also lack the pathos which is a very vital element in all true preaching. Our Lord looked out upon the multitude and 'saw them as sheep without a shepherd', and was 'filled with compassion'. And if you know nothing of this you should not be in a pulpit, for this is certain to come out in your preaching. We must not be purely intellectual or argumentative, this other element must be there. Not only will your love for the people produce this pathos, the matter itself is bound to do this in and of itself. What can possibly be more moving than a realisation of what God in Christ has done for us? Any attempt therefore to consider and to understand it should move us profoundly. Notice what happens to the great Apostle himself. He starts off with an argument designed to convince us of our sinfulness and lost condition and utter dependence on Christ. But the moment he mentions that Name he seems to forget his argument and bursts forth into one of his flights of great eloquence. He is moved to the depths of his being, and he writes some of those glowing passages that should move us also to tears. It is the contemplation of what God has done for us in Christ, and the suffering involved, and the greatness of the love of God toward us. 'God "so" loved the world . . .'

This element of pathos was a great characteristic of the preaching of Whitefield, one of the greatest master preachers of all the ages. It was David Garrick, the great actor of the eighteenth century who once said that he wished he could even utter the word 'Mesopotamia' as Whitefield uttered it! He also said that he would gladly give a hundred guineas if he could but utter the word 'Oh!' with the same pathos as Whitefield did. Modern sophisticated man may laugh at this, but it is only when we begin to know something of this melting quality that we shall be real preachers. Of course a man who tries to produce an effect becomes an actor, and is an abominable impostor. But the fact is that when 'the love of God is shed abroad' in a man's heart as it was in Whitefield's pathos is inevitable.

This element of pathos and of emotion is, to me, a very vital one. It is what has been so seriously lacking in the present century, and perhaps especially among Reformed people. We tend to lose our balance and to become over-intellectual, indeed almost to despise the element of feeling and emotion. We are such learned men, we have such a great grasp of the Truth, that we tend to despise feeling. The common herd, we feel, are emotional and sentimental, but they have no understanding!

Is not this the danger, is not this the tendency, to despise feeling which is an essential part of man put there by God? We do not know what it is to be carried away, we no longer know what it is to be moved profoundly. You remember Matthew Arnold's description of religion. He said that 'Religion is morality tinged with emotion'. How typical of Matthew Arnold, and how wrong; how completely blind! 'Morality "tinged" with emotion.' Just a 'tinge'. It would be rude and impolite to have anything more than a tinge. The 'little gentleman' never shows his emotion. Do not forget that Matthew Arnold was the son of Thomas Arnold, the headmaster of the well-known public school at Rugby. He taught that the real gentleman never shows his feelings but always keeps them under control. That outlook seems to have permeated the life of the Church and many Christians. Emotion is regarded as something almost indecent. My reply to all that, once more, is simply to say that if you contemplate these glorious truths that are committed to our charge as preachers without being moved by them there is something defective in your spiritual eyesight.

The Apostle Paul, as I say, could never look at these things without being moved to the depth of his great soul. Let me give one illustration of what I am saying. You remember how in Romans 9, 10 and 11 he has been working out the particular problem of the Jews. Where do they come in, what is their position in the light of what he has been saying about justification by faith, and so on? He has taken up this subject, and he has argued it, and has reasoned it out, and he has arrived at his great conclusion. But he does not leave it at that; he bursts forth,

O the depth of the riches both of the wisdom and the knowledge of God! How unsearchable are his judgments, and his ways past finding out! For who hath known the mind of the Lord? or who hath been his counsellor? Or who hath first given to him, and it shall be recompensed unto him again? For of him, and through him, and to him, are all things: to whom be glory for ever. Amen.

That is sheer grand emotion. Note that I say emotion not emotionalism. I reprobate that. There is nothing more hateful than a man who deliberately tries to play on the surface and superficial emotions of people. I have no interest in that except to denounce it. My contention is that when a man really understands this truth which he claims to believe he must be moved by it. If he is not, he does not belong to that company, that category which includes the great Apostle himself. But it has become the fashion to dislike emotion.

94

I remember how a few years back when there was a great evangelistic campaign in London, a man who was a leader in religious circles came to me one day and asked, 'Have you been to the campaign?' I said, 'No, not yet.' 'This is marvellous,' he said, 'marvellous.' He continued, 'People are going forward by the hundred. No emotion you know—marvellous.' He kept on repeating this 'No emotion.' What to him was so marvellous was that all these people who went forward in response to the appeal showed no emotion. This was something glorious. No emotion, wonderful! No emotion, marvellous!

What can one say about such an attitude? I content myself by asking a few questions. Can a man see himself as a damned sinner without emotion? Can a man look into hell without emotion? Can a man listen to the thunderings of the Law and feel nothing? Or conversely, can a man really contemplate the love of God in Christ Jesus and feel no emotion? The whole position is utterly ridiculous. I fear that many people today in their reaction against excesses and emotionalism put themselves into a position in which, in the end, they are virtually denying the Truth. The Gospel of Jesus Christ takes up the whole man, and if what purports to be the Gospel does not do so it is not the Gospel. The Gospel is meant to do that, and it does that. The whole man is involved because the Gospel leads to regeneration; and so I say that this element of pathos and emotion, this element of being moved, should always be very prominent in preaching.

Lastly I have to introduce the word Power. I am not going into this at length now because this is so important that it deserves a whole section to itself, not in the next lecture but some time later. But, if there is no power it is not preaching. True preaching, after all, is God acting. It is not just a man uttering words; it is God using him. He is being used of God. He is under the influence of the Holy Spirit; it is what Paul calls in 1 Corinthians 2 'preaching in demonstration of the Spirit of power'. Or as he puts it in 1 Thessalonians 1:5: 'Our gospel came not unto you in word only, but also in power, and in the Holy Ghost, and in much assurance . . .' There it is; and that is an essential element in true preaching.

To sum it up, true preaching, then, consists of both these elements combined in their right proportions—the sermon, and the act of preaching. This 'act', in addition to the sermon. That is true preaching. Both must be emphasised. The difference between the two I have already hinted at, but I must say a further word about it. If you do not know the difference between the sermon and the act of preaching, as a preacher you will very soon discover it. One of the ways in which you are most likely to discover it is the way I have discovered myself many a time. It happens like this. You are in your own church preaching on a Sunday. You preach a sermon, and for some reason this sermon seems to go easily, smoothly, and with a degree of power. You are moved yourself; you have what is called 'a good service', and the people are as aware of this as you are. Very well; you are due to preach somewhere else, either the next Sunday or on a week-night, and you say to yourself, 'I will preach that sermon which I preached last Sunday. We had a wonderful service with it.' So you go into this other pulpit and you take that same text, and you start preaching. But you suddenly find that you have got virtually nothing; it all seems to collapse in your hands. What is the explanation? One explanation is this. What happened on the previous Sunday when you were preaching that sermon in your own pulpit was that the Spirit came upon you, or perhaps upon the people, (it may well have been, as I have previously explained, that it was mainly the people, and you received it from them) and your little sermon was taken up, and you were given this special unction and authority in an unusual manner, and so you had that exceptional service. But you are in different circumstances with a different congregation, and you yourself may be feeling different. So you now have to rely upon your sermon; and you suddenly find that you haven't much of a sermon.

That helps to illustrate the difference between a sermon and the act of preaching the sermon. This is a great mystery. I hope to deal with it again. But I say this now to emphasise that the two things are different, and that true preaching means the combination of these two things. You must not rely on either the one or the other. You must not rely on your sermon only, you must not rely on the preaching act only; both are essential to true preaching.

Let me put this again in the form of a story, an anecdote. There was an old preacher whom I knew very well in Wales. He was a very able old man and a good theologian; but, I am sorry to say, he had a tendency to cynicism. But he was a very acute critic. On one occasion he was present at a synod in the final session of which two men were preaching. Both these men were professors of theology. The first man preached, and when he had finished this old preacher, this old critic turned to his neighbour and said, 'Light without heat.' Then the second professor preached—he was an older man and somewhat emotional. When he had finished the old cynic turned to his neighbour and said, 'Heat without light.' Now he was right in both cases. But the important point is that both preachers were defective. You must have light and heat, sermon plus preaching. Light without heat never affects anybody; heat without light is of no permanent value. It may have a passing temporary effect but it does not really help your people and build them up and really deal with them.

What is preaching? Logic on fire! Eloquent reason! Are these contradictions? Of course they are not. Reason concerning this Truth ought to be mightily eloquent, as you see it in the case of the Apostle Paul and others. It is theology on fire. And a theology which does not take fire, I maintain, is a defective theology; or at least the man's understanding of it is defective. Preaching is theology coming through a man who is on fire. A true understanding and experience of the Truth must lead to this. I say again that a man who can speak about these things dispassionately has no right whatsoever to be in a pulpit; and should never be allowed to enter one.

What is the chief end of preaching? I like to think it is this. It is to give men and women a sense of God and His presence. As I have said already, during this last year I have been ill, and so have had the opportunity, and the privilege, of listening to others, instead of preaching myself. As I have listened in physical weakness this is the thing I have looked for and longed for and desired. I can forgive a man for a bad sermon, I can forgive the preacher almost anything if he gives me a sense of God, if he gives me something for my soul, if he gives me the sense that, though he is inadequate himself, he is handling something which is very great and very glorious, if he gives me some dim glimpse of the majesty and the glory of God, the love of Christ my Saviour, and the magnificence of the Gospel. If he does that I am his debtor, and I am profoundly grateful to him. Preaching is the most amazing, and the most thrilling activity that one can ever be engaged in, because of all that it holds out for all of us in the present, and because of the glorious endless possibilities in an eternal future.

Let me close with two quotations. There was a very great preacher in the U.S.A. just over a hundred years ago, James Henry Thornwell. He was, possibly, the greatest theologian the Southern Presbyterian Church has ever produced; but he was also a great preacher and a most eloquent man. There are those who say that next to Samuel Davies he was the most eloquent preacher the American continent has ever produced. This is how his biographer tries to give us some impression of what it was to see and to hear Thornwell preaching. Notice that it confirms and illustrates my definition of true preaching as something to look at as well as to hear because the whole man is involved in the action. This is how he puts it:

> What invented symbols could convey that kindling eye, those trembling and varied tones, the expressive attitude, the foreshadowing and typical gesture, the whole quivering frame which made up in him the complement of the finished author! The lightning's flash, the fleecy clouds embroidered on the sky, and the white crest of the ocean wave, surpass the painter's skill. It was indescribable.

That was his impression of the preaching of Thornwell.

Then consider what Thornwell himself said about preaching, and about himself as a preacher.

The Act of Preaching

It is a great matter to understand what it is to be a preacher, and how preaching should be done. Effective sermons are the offspring of study, of discipline, of prayer, and especially of the unction of the Holy Ghost. They are to combine the characteristic excellencies of every other species of composition intended for delivery, and ought to be pronounced not merely with the earnestness of faith but the constraining influence of Heaven-born charity. They should be seen to come from the heart, and from the heart as filled with the love of Christ and the love of souls. Depend upon it that there is but little preaching in the world, and it is a mystery of grace and of divine power that God's cause is not ruined in the world when we consider the qualifications of many of its professed ministers to preach it. My own performances in this way fill me with disgust. I have never made, much less preached, a sermon in my life, and I am beginning to despair of ever being able to do it. May the Lord give you more knowledge and grace and singleness of purpose.

There is nothing to add to that. Any man who has had some glimpse of what it is to preach will inevitably feel that he has never preached. But he will go on trying, hoping that by the grace of God one day he may truly preach.

CHAPTER SIX

The Preacher

I WOULD REMIND you again of our method of approach to our subject. We are in a church service, and we are looking at a man standing in a pulpit and addressing people. Having shown the all-importance of preaching and that this is the primary business and task of the Church, we have gone on to consider the two aspects of preaching—the sermon and the actual act of preaching. I trust I have made it clear that, as I see things at any rate, the two aspects are vitally important; you must not have the one without the other. Both are essential, and true preaching consists in the right blending of these two elements.

Proceeding now with this same approach, and still looking at preaching in general, it seems to me that the next logical question to ask is: Who is to do this? Who is to preach? Or in scriptural terms, 'Who is sufficient for these things?', for the delivering of this message as we have defined it, and in the manner which we have indicated? Here is a most important question, and especially today when some say that we do not need the Church at all and talk about a 'religionless Christianity'. But even amongst those who still believe in the Church this question needs to be asked, Who is to do this preaching?

The first principle I would lay down is that all Christians are clearly not meant to do this, and that not even all Christian men are meant to preach, still less the women! In other words we must consider what is called 'lay-preaching'. This has been practised very commonly for a hundred years and more. Prior to that it was comparatively rare, but it has become very common. It would be interesting to go into the history of that, but time prohibits our doing so. The interesting thing to notice is that this change once more, was primarily due to theological causes. It was the shift in theology last century from a Reformed Calvinistic attitude to an essentially Arminian one that gave rise to the increase in lay-preaching. The explanation of that cause and effect is that Arminianism, ultimately, is non-theological. That is why most denominations today are generally non-theological. That being the case it is not surprising that the view gained currency that preaching was open to almost any man who had become a Christian, and later, any woman also.

My assertion is that this is an unscriptural view of preaching. There are of course exceptional circumstances where this may be necessary; but I would then query as to whether it is actually 'lay-preaching'. What I mean by exceptional circumstances is that it may well be the case, owing to the state and the condition of the Church—lack of means and so on—that the Church may not be in a position to support a man full-time in the work of the ministry, and particularly preaching. Definitions are important at this point. The modern view of lay-preaching, largely derived from the teaching of Methodism and Brethrenism, is that this should be the normal practice and not the exception, and that a preacher is a man who earns his living in a profession or business, and preaches, as it were, in his spare time.

The exceptional position which I am envisaging is that of a man who feels called to the ministry, and who would like to spend all his time in it, but who, because of the circumstances I have described, is unable to do so. He longs for the day when the Church will be sufficiently strong financially and in other respects to support him, that he may give the whole of his time to this work. So I would not call him, strictly speaking, a lay-preacher; he is a man who, for the time being, has to earn his livelihood, partly, by doing something else in order to make his preaching possible. What I am concerned to examine is the notion that any man who is a Christian can preach and should preach. There are some sections of the Christian Church who have taught this regularly. There has been the slogan, 'Give the new convert something to do; send him out to preach and to give his testimony'—and so on. There has been this tendency to thrust people out into preaching. Much of this can be attributed to the influence of Charles G. Finney and also D. L. Moody, who was very keen on that idea of giving the new converts something to do.

On what grounds are we critical of this attitude to preaching? I suggest that it is due to a failure to understand the difference between saying that every Christian should be ready, as Peter puts it in 1 Peter 3:15 '. . . to give . . . a reason of the hope that is in [him]', and saying that every Christian should preach the Gospel. That is the distinction. Every Christian should be able to give an account of why he is a Christian; but that does not mean that every Christian is meant to preach.

This distinction is brought out in a most interesting way in Acts 8 in verses 4 and 5. There we are told in the first verse that a great persecution of the Church arose in Jerusalem, and that all the members of the Church were scattered abroad except the Apostles. Then we are told in verses 4 and 5, 'Therefore they that were scattered abroad went everywhere preaching the Word. Then Philip went down to the city of Samaria, and preached Christ unto them.' That is the King James Version translation, and in both cases you have the word 'preached'. But in the original the same word was not used in the two verses; and this is the vital distinction. What 'the people' who went everywhere did was, as someone has suggested it might be translated, 'to gossip' the Word, to talk about it in conversation. Philip on the other hand did something different; he was 'heralding' the Gospel. This is, strictly speaking, what is meant by preaching in the sense that I have been using it. It is not accidental that such a distinction should be drawn there in the actual text.

That is the position then, that every Christian should be capable of doing what is indicated in the fourth verse, but that only some are called upon to do what is indicated in the fifth verse. In the New Testament this distinction is drawn very clearly; certain people only are set apart and called upon to deliver the message, as it were, on behalf of the Church in an official manner. That act is confined to the elders, and only to some of them—the teaching elders, the elder who has received the gift of teaching, the pastors and the teachers. It is clear that the preaching in the New Testament was confined to the Apostles and the prophets and the evangelists and these others.

Why do I suggest that this is important? What is the ultimate criticism of what is called 'lay-preaching'? The answer comes to this, that it seems to miss completely the whole notion of a 'call'. There are also other reasons which seem to me to militate against the idea. My main argument is that the picture I have already given of the preacher, and what he is doing, insists not only that this is something to which a man is called, but also something that should occupy the whole of his time apart from exceptional circumstances. It is not something that can be done as an aside, as it were; that is a wrong approach and a wrong attitude to it.

Let us first look at it in terms of this question of a call. What is the preacher? Well, obviously the preacher is a Christian like every other Christian. That is basic and an absolute essential. But he is something more than that, there is something further; and this is where this whole question of a call comes in. A preacher is not a Christian who decides to preach, he does not just decide to do it; he does not even decide to take up preaching as a calling. Now that has often happened. There have been men who have rather liked the idea of being a minister. It seems to be an ideal type of life, a life with a fair amount of leisure, giving ample opportunity for reading—reading philosophy, theology, or anything they may want to read. If they happen to be poets, well it is something that will give them ample time to write poetry. The same applies to essayists or novelists. This picture of the type of life lived by the minister has often appealed to young men, and there have been many who have gone into the ministry in that way.

I need scarcely say that this is entirely wrong and quite foreign to the picture one gets in the Scriptures, and also as one reads the lives of the great preachers throughout the centuries. The answer to that false view is that preaching is never something that a man decides to do. What happens rather is that he becomes conscious of a 'call'. This whole question of the call is not an easy matter; and all ministers have struggled with it because it is so vitally important for us.

'Am I called to be a preacher or not? How do you know?' I suggest that there are certain tests. A call generally starts in the form of a consciousness within one's own spirit, an awareness of a kind of pressure being brought to bear upon one's spirit, some disturbance in the realm of the spirit, then that your mind is being directed to the whole question of preaching. You have not thought of it deliberately, you have not sat down in cold blood to consider possibilities, and then, having looked at several have decided to take this up. It is not that. This is something that happens to you; it is God dealing with you, and God acting upon you by His Spirit; it is something you become aware of rather than what you do. It is thrust upon you, it is presented to you and almost forced upon you constantly in this way.

Then what has been happening in the realm of your spirit in that way is confirmed or accentuated through the influence of others who may talk to you and put questions to you. This has often been the way in which men have been called to be preachers. In many biographies you will read that a young man who had never thought of preaching was approached by an elder or spiritually-minded fellow-member of the Church who puts the question to him: 'Don't you think that perhaps you are called to be a preacher of this Gospel?' The questioner then gives his reasons for saying that. He has been watching you and observing you and has felt led to speak to you. It is through him perhaps that this initial move may come. My experience is that, generally, these two things go together.

Then this develops and leads to a concern about others. I am contrasting this with the far-too-common idea of entering the ministry as the taking up of a profession or 'a calling'. The true call always includes a concern about others, an interest in them, a realisation of their lost estate and condition, and a desire to do something about them, and to tell them the message and point them to the way of salvation. This is an essential part of the call; and it is important, particularly, as a means whereby we may check ourselves.

It has often happened that young men with certain gifts who listen to a great preacher are captivated by him and what he is doing. They are captivated by his personality or by his eloquence, they are moved by him, and, unconsciously, they begin to feel a desire to be like him and to do what he is doing. Now that may be right, or it may be quite wrong. They may only be fascinated by the glamour of preaching, and attracted by the idea of addressing audiences, and influencing them. All kinds of wrong and false motives may insinuate themselves. The way to check oneself against such a danger is to ask oneself the question, Why do I want to do this? Why am I concerned about this? And unless one can discover a genuine concern about others, and their state and condition, and a desire to help them, you are very right in querying your motives.

But we must go on to something yet deeper; there should also be a sense of constraint. This is surely the most crucial test. It means that you have the feeling that you can do nothing else. It was Mr. Spurgeon, I believe, who used to say to young men—'If you can do anything else do it. If you can stay out of the ministry, stay out of the ministry.' I would certainly say that without any hesitation whatsoever. I would say that the only man who is called to preach is the man who cannot do anything else, in the sense that he is not satisfied with anything else. This call to preach is so put upon him, and such pressure comes to bear upon him that he says, 'I can do nothing else, I must preach.'

Or let me put it like this—and I am speaking from personal experience. You are certain of the call when you are unable to keep it back and to resist it. You try your utmost to do so. You say, 'No, I shall go on with what I am doing; I am able to do it and it is good work.' You do your utmost to push back and to rid yourself of this disturbance in your spirit which comes in these various ways. But you reach the point when you cannot do so any longer. It almost becomes an obsession, and so overwhelming that in the end you say, 'I can do nothing else, I cannot resist any longer.'

That is, as I understand it, what is meant by a call to preaching. But let us check it yet further by something which is equally important. I have hinted at it already, and that is, that there is in you a sense of diffidence, a sense of unworthiness, a sense of inadequacy. No more perfect expression of this can be found anywhere than in 1 Corinthians 2, where Paul talks about 'weakness, fear, and much trembling'. He repeats the same idea in 2 Corinthians 2:16, where he asks, 'Who is sufficient for these things?' Paul's teaching concerning the call of God to this particular work, and which we have been expounding in detail, leads quite inevitably to that question. He puts it like this:

Thanks be unto God, which always causeth us to triumph in Christ, and maketh manifest the savour of his knowledge by us in every place. For we are unto God a sweet savour of Christ, in them we are saved, and in them that perish: To the one we are the savour of death unto death; and to the other the savour of life unto life. And who is sufficient for these things?

Realising that that is what is involved in preaching, it is inevitable that a man should feel unworthy, and inadequate. So he is not only hesitant, he questions his feeling and queries it, and examines it very carefully; he does his utmost to push it away.

I am emphasising all this because, for some strange reason, it is an aspect of the matter that is scarcely ever mentioned in our age and generation. It is also my final argument against the idea of lay-preaching. Take such a man who sets himself up as a preacher, and does not hesitate to rush into a pulpit and to preach, and who claims that he can do it as an aside in his spare time. What does he know about 'weakness, fear, and much trembling'? Sometimes, alas, it is the exact opposite, and in his self-confidence he is highly critical, and even contemptuous, of ordained preachers. Though they have nothing else to do they are miserable failures; but he can do it as an aside! That is just to contradict completely what we find to be true of the great Apostle, and what has also been true of all the greatest preachers in the Church in all the succeeding centuries. Indeed it seems to be the case that the greater the preacher the more hesitant he has generally been to preach. Oftentimes such men have had to be persuaded by ministers and elders and others to do this; they so shrank from the dread responsibility. This was true of George Whitefield, one of the greatest and most eloquent preachers ever to adorn a pulpit. And it has been true of many others. My argument is, therefore, that a man who feels that he is competent, and that he can do this easily, and so rushes to preach without any sense of fear or trembling, or any hesitation whatsoever, is a man who is proclaiming that he has never been 'called' to be a preacher. The man who is called by God is a man who realises what he is called to do, and he so realises the awefulness of the task that he shrinks from it. Nothing but this overwhelming sense of being called, and of compulsion, should ever lead anyone to preach.

* * *

That, then is the first thing that puts this man into a pulpit to preach. I must hasten to add that even this needs to be checked and to be confirmed; and this is something which is done by the Church. The first aspect is put again by the Apostle in the tenth chapter of the Epistle to the Romans: 'Whosoever shall call upon the name of the Lord shall be saved. How then shall they call upon him in whom they have not believed? and how shall they believe in him of whom they have not heard? and how shall they hear without a preacher? And how shall they preach except they be sent?' (Romans 10:13–15). The preacher is 'sent'. But how can we be sure that we are 'sent' in this sense and that we are not simply appointing ourselves? This is where the Church comes in. This is the teaching of the New Testament not only with regard to preaching and teaching but also with regard to the various offices in the Church. As early as the sixth chapter of the book of the Acts of the Apostles certain qualifications are laid down with respect to deacons. The Church selects these men in terms of given principles; she is taught what to look for, and she looks for such qualities. You find the same in the Pastoral Epistles where instructions are given with regard to the qualifications of elders and deacons. So before you can be quite sure that a man is called to be a preacher, his personal call must be confirmed by the Church, it must be attested by the Church.

Once more I must qualify this by saying that the history of the Church, and of preachers, shows quite plainly that sometimes the Church can make a mistake. She has done so many times, and has rejected men who have proved by their records as preachers that they were obviously called of God. For instance, Dr. G. Campbell Morgan was rejected by the Methodist Church in England. But that is the exception, the exception which proves the rule; and you do not legislate for exceptions and hard cases. I am speaking generally. When there is an exceptional and outstanding man God will make him known somehow, and in spite of men; but that does not happen very often.

The more common occurrence is that men feel called who are not called; and it is the business of the Church to see to this and to handle the situation. I could give many examples and illustrations of this. I have always felt when someone has come to me and told me that he has been called to be a preacher, that my main business is to put every conceivable obstacle that I can think of in his way. In addition to that I exercise what judgment I have in assessing his personality, intelligence, and ability to speak. The correspondence of what the man feels and what the Church must feel is most important. A well-known story about Spurgeon illustrates this well. A man came to him at the close of a service on a Sunday night and said, 'Mr Spurgeon, the Spirit tells me that I am to preach here, in this Tabernacle, next Thursday night.' 'Well, it is a very curious thing,' said Spurgeon, 'that the Spirit has not told me that.' So of course the man did not preach on the Thursday in the Tabernacle! That was very sound logic. If the Spirit had told this man to do this He would also have told Mr. Spurgeon. The Holy Spirit always acts in an orderly manner.

This is a most subtle matter. One's nature, or one's ambition, or one's liking for particular offices, or particular tasks, may create in one a desire to be a preacher, and we persuade ourselves that this is the Spirit of God leading us. I have known this happen many times; and one of the most painful tasks that ever confronts a minister is to discourage a man who comes to him in that way. On what grounds does he discourage him? There are certain tests which he must apply, and the same applies to the Church. What does the Church look for in a man who says that he is called to be a preacher? Obviously she must look for something exceptional in him. He must be a Christian of course, but there must be something more, there must be something additional.

What do you look for? Well, you remember how in Acts 6, even in the matter of appointing deacons, who were simply to handle a financial problem, a charitable matter of feeding widows, it was insisted upon that they should be men 'filled with the Spirit'. That is the first and the greatest qualification. You are entitled to look for an unusual degree of spirituality, and this must come first because of the nature of the task. In addition you are entitled to look for a degree of assurance with respect to his knowledge of the Truth and his relationship to it. It is surely clear that if he is a man who is always struggling with problems and difficulties and perplexities himself, and trying to discover truth, or if he is so uncertain that he is always influenced by the last book he reads, and is 'carried about by every wind of doctrine' and every new theological fashion, it is clear that he is *ipso facto* a man who is not called to the ministry. A man who has great problems himself and is in a state of perplexity is clearly not one who is fitted to be a preacher, because he will be preaching to people with problems and his primary function is to help them to deal with them. 'How can the blind lead the blind?' is our Lord's own question in such a situation. The preacher then must be a man who is characterised by spirituality in an unusual degree, and a man who has arrived at a settled assured

knowledge and understanding of the Truth, and feels that he is able
to preach it to others.

What else do you desiderate? You now proceed to look at what we
commonly call character. I would not describe 'being filled with the
Spirit' as character, which means that he is a man who is characterised
by a godly life. Again all this is put to us plainly in the Scriptures, for
instance in Paul's epistle to Titus: 'Young men likewise exhort to be
sober minded. In all things shewing thyself a pattern of good works;
in doctrine shewing uncorruptness, gravity, sincerity, Sound speech,
that cannot be condemned; that he that is of the contrary part may be
ashamed, having no evil thing to say of you' (Titus 2:6–8). The
preacher must be a godly man. But he must also have wisdom. And
not only that, he must also have patience and forbearance. This is
most important in a preacher. The Apostle puts it thus: 'The servant
of the Lord must not strive; but be gentle unto all men, apt to teach,
patient' (2 Timothy 2:24).

These are basic qualifications. A man may be a good Christian, and
he may be many other things; but if he is lacking in these qualities he
is not going to make a preacher. He must be, furthermore, a man who
has an understanding of people and of human nature. These are
general qualities and characteristics that should be looked for and on
which we must insist.

It is only after emphasising such qualities that we come to the
question of ability. It seems to me to be one of the tragedies of the
modern Church that we tend to put ability first. It should not come
first, but only at about this stage. It certainly does and must come in.
I remember a young man who came to me many years ago telling me
that he was quite sure that he was called to the ministry. Not only did
he tell me that, but also something else which worried me much more.
On the previous Sunday I happened to have been away from my own
church and a visiting preacher was taking my place. My young friend
had gone to the visiting preacher and told him that he felt called to
preach and to the ministry; and the visiting preacher, not knowing
anything at all about him, had encouraged him and praised him, and

urged him to go on. The actual fact was that the poor fellow lacked the mental ability necessary to the making of a preacher. It was as simple as that. He would never have been able to pass even the preliminary examinations; and even if he had scraped through them somehow, he lacked the mental capacity demanded by the work we have already described. So we have got to emphasise natural intelligence and ability. If a man is to 'rightly divide the word of truth' he must have ability. The Apostle Paul says that he must be 'apt to teach'. As preaching means delivering the message of God in the way which we have described, involving the relationship between systematic theology and the exact meaning of the particular text, it obviously demands a certain degree of intellect and ability. So if a man lacks a basic minimum in that respect he is clearly not called to be a preacher.

Then I would add to that 'the gift of speech'. Here again is something, surely, that we are tending to forget today. That is why I have put all that emphasis upon the act of preaching, upon the actual speaking part. What is a preacher? The first thing, obviously, is that he is a speaker. He is not primarily a writer of books, he is not an essayist or a literary man; the preacher is primarily a speaker. So if the candidate has not got the gift of speech, whatever else he may have, he is not going to make a preacher. He may be a great theologian, he can be an excellent man at giving private advice and counselling, and many other things, but by basic definition, if a man has not got the gift of speech he cannot be a preacher.

Once more I can illustrate this by an example. I remember the case of a young man who was a very good scientist and who had done well, and was doing well, in his own line. He came to me saying that he was sure that he was called to be a preacher. But immediately I knew that he was wrong. Why? Not because of any special insight on my part, but simply because he obviously could scarcely express himself even in private conversation leave alone in public. He was a very able man, but he obviously had not got the gift of communicating. He could not speak freely; he was hesitant and halting and doubtful, and diffident in his whole manner of speech. I did my utmost to prevent his going forward for training. However he would not listen to me because he was so certain of his call. He became a theological student, did very well at Oxford, and eventually was ordained. I think I am right in saying that altogether he had three different churches in about seven years. Then, and as the result of that experience, he came to see quite clearly himself that he had never been called to preach. He returned to scientific work and is doing well there. That is where he always should have been, because he lacked this essential particular gift of speech.

These particular points are of the greatest importance. I speak as one who has had to deal with this problem so often during the last forty years. Let me tell another story which illustrates what I am saying. Sometimes this mistake about a call has been made not so much by the man himself, as by some minister or elder who has taken it upon himself to suggest to the man that he should become a preacher, and indeed to urge him, and to put pressure on him to do so. I remember very well an incident on a Sunday night. I had got back into my vestry after preaching, and a young man came in to see me. He looked very agitated, and I said, 'Well, what is the matter, how can I help you?' He said that he did not want to take much of my time, that he only wanted to know one thing from me. Did I know of a Christian psychiatrist? 'Well,' I said, 'why do you need to see a Christian psychiatrist?' He replied saying, 'I am in great trouble, I am in great confusion.' I questioned him as to the cause of the confusion. Incidentally, you should not send a man to a psychiatrist unless you are quite sure that he needs such help; and my experience is that most of the people who come to ask for the name of a Christian psychiatrist need spiritual help rather than psychiatric treatment. However, I asked the young man, 'Why do you need to see a psychiatrist?' Again he replied, 'I am in great confusion.' 'What is the cause of your confusion?' I asked. He then told me his story. He had been for the previous fortnight at a certain college which had recently been set up to train evangelists. Until then he had been following his occupation as a baker in the west of England. He had been gifted with a good singing voice which he used to help the work of his local church. Recently there had been an evangelistic campaign in his little town, and he had been the soloist every night. At the end of the campaign the visiting evangelist had drawn this young man aside and had said to him, 'Don't you think you are meant for the ministry?' He had talked to him at length and eventually persuaded the young fellow that he really should be in the ministry. Both agreed that he, of course, needed a bit of training, and the evangelist was able to tell him that fortunately there was a college now available. So he had sent the young man to this new college and there he had been for two weeks. But he now came to me in great trouble. What has happened? I asked. 'Well,' he said, 'I cannot follow the lectures. I see the other students taking notes but I do not know how to take notes.' He had never been much of a reader and had never attended lectures, so here he was, utterly confused. The evangelist had told him that he was called to the ministry, and who was he to question such a man's verdict. Yet he felt that he could not go on. He had become so unhappy and so confused that he had gone to see the principal of the college; and the first thing the principal said on hearing the story was, 'I think you need to see a psychiatrist.' That seems to have become almost the routine advice given to Christians in perplexity these days. So the young man was seeking the name of a Christian psychiatrist. I said to him, 'I do not think you need to see a psychiatrist at all. The very fact that you are perplexed and confused and feel you cannot go on, shows me quite clearly that you have "come to yourself" again, and that you are in a healthy state and have a sound mind.' I added, 'The time to go to the psychiatrist was when you listened to the evangelist and went to the college. You have now come to see the position as it really is. Go back and take up your work as a baker again and use the voice, the gift that God has given you to sing. Recognise that you are not called to the ministry and go on doing what you can do.' The man literally had not got the mental equipment, and he knew it, and had seen it clearly. He was immediately relieved and left me rejoicing. He acted on my advice and resumed his valuable and happy service to the glory of God in his local church.

*   *   *

These are the ways in which the Church tests a man who says that he has received a call. My contention is that God works through the man himself and through the voice of the Church. It is the same Spirit operating in both, and when there is agreement and consensus of opinion you are right in assuming that it is a call from God. A man does not appoint himself; he is not put into the ministry merely by the pressure of the Church. The two things go together. Both sides have been neglected. I have known many men who have deceived themselves. I have also known many cases where men have been pushed into the ministry, who were never meant to be there, by false teaching on the part of the Church. The two things must go together.

*   *   *

Here, then, is the beginning of a process, here is a man called to preach the Gospel. Now comes the whole question of training and of preparation. I do not propose to go into this, or to pass judgment on theological seminaries, but there are a few things I would like to say in general in passing. My view is that the whole question of training for the ministry needs to be reviewed urgently, and that drastic and radical changes are needed. What does this man need by way of training? He needs, first and foremost, a certain amount of general knowledge and experience of life. He is a Christian. He has had an experience of conversion. But that alone does not fit him to be a preacher. That is true of many people who are not called to be preachers. This man also needs a certain amount of general knowledge and experience of life.

Why do I emphasise this? For the reason that if he has not got this, his tendency will be to be too theoretical in his preaching, too intellectual. He will probably go into the pulpit and deal with his own problems rather than the problems of the people who are sitting in the pews listening to him. But he is there to preach to them, and to help them, and not to try to solve his own individual problems and perplexities. The way to safeguard against that is that this man should have a modicum of general knowledge and experience of life, and the more the better. There are those who say, and I tend to agree with them, that it would be good for all men who enter the ministry to have some preliminary experience of living life in the world, in a business or profession. They query the wisdom of a system whereby a young man goes from school and college directly to a seminary and then into the ministry without having any experience outside that. There is the danger, putting it at its lowest, of an over-theoretical and intellectual approach; so that the man in the pulpit is really divorced from the life of the people who are sitting in the pews and listening to him. So general knowledge and experience are of inestimable value.

Then I would greatly emphasise the importance of a general training of the mind. We all need to have our minds trained. We may have a good intellect but it needs to be disciplined. And so a good general training in any arts or science course is good because it teaches one how to think and to reason systematically and logically. I stress this because, as we have seen, in the sermon there must be this element of reason and progression of thought. To secure that end necessitates a certain amount of training. To throw out a number of thoughts at random without setting them in order does not help the congregation, so the preacher needs to have his mind trained in that general sense. The particular form of training is immaterial as long as it produces a trained mind; this trained mind can then apply itself to the particular task of the preacher.

In the same way general knowledge and information will be of great value to the preacher and his preaching. It will help him to illustrate and clothe the message which he is giving to the people and make it easier for them to follow and to assimilate it.

But leaving general training we come to the more special training. What is needed here? I shall only give abroad general outline. First and foremost there must be given a knowledge of the Bible and its message. A man who is deficient in this respect cannot be a true preacher. I have emphasised 'the whole counsel of God'; I have emphasised the whole scheme and plan of salvation and the importance of 'systematic theology'. You cannot have that without having a thorough knowledge of the Bible, a knowledge of the whole Bible and its message. This is therefore a vital part of the training.

What is the place of a knowledge of the original languages? They are of great value for the sake of accuracy; no more, that is all. They cannot guarantee accuracy but they promote it. This is a part of the mechanics of preaching, not the big thing, not the vital thing; but it is important. The preacher should be accurate, he should never say things that some learned member of his congregation can show to be wrong and based upon a misinterpretation. Knowledge of the original languages is important in that way. But let us never forget that the ultimate object of this man's training is to enable him to preach, to convey the Bible message to the people—the vast majority of whom will not be experts on languages or on philosophy. His business is to convey the message to them, to be 'understanded of the people'. The object of the training is not to make the student a great expert in linguistics so much as to make him an accurate man.

I put it like this because so much training in these days spends time in dealing with negative criticism, the dry bones, and men have become more concerned about this than about the message. They 'miss the wood because of the trees', and they forget that they are meant to be preachers conveying a message to the people who are in front of them, as they are. Therefore if they get lost in, and spend all their time in dealing with, matters of criticism—higher criticism and so on, and the defence and the answers—and think that that is all, they do not know what preaching is, and 'the hungry sheep look up and are not fed'. All that is but part of the scaffolding, as I shall call it later on. You do not stop at putting up the scaffolding; that is but preliminary to the building. Or look at it in terms of a skeleton. A skeleton is essential, but a skeleton alone is a monstrosity, it needs to be clothed with flesh.

We then go on to a study of theology. This again is obvious from what we have already been saying. It is not enough merely that a man should know the Scriptures, he must know the Scriptures in the sense that he has got out of them the essence of biblical theology and can grasp it in a systematic manner. He must be so well versed in this that all his preaching is controlled by it.

Next to that I would put the study of the history of the Church. Here I would emphasise in particular the importance of learning the danger of heresies. A man may be a good Christian, he may have had a great experience, and he may therefore think that nothing more is necessary. He has the Scriptures, he has the Spirit of God in him, he is out to do good and so on, and so he tends to think that he is quite safe and that all is well. But he may find, perhaps, at some later time that he is accused of heresy; and he is astonished and amazed at this. The way to safeguard yourself against that is to learn something about heresies—how they arose in the past generally through very good and conscientious men. History shows how subtle it all is, and how many a man lacking balance, or by failing to maintain the proportion of faith, and the interrelationship of the various parts of the whole message, has been pressed by the devil to put too much emphasis on one particular aspect, and eventually pressed so far as to be in a position in which he is really contradicting the Truth and has become a heretic. So Church history is invaluable to the preacher. It is not the preserve of the academics. I would say that Church history is one of the most essential studies for the preacher were it merely to show him this terrible danger of slipping into heresy, or into error, without realising that anything has happened to him.

At the same time Church history will tell him about the great Revivals in the history of the Church. I know of nothing, in my own experience, that has been more exhilarating and helpful, and that has acted more frequently as a tonic to me, than the history of Revivals. Take the time we are living in. What discouraging days they are, so discouraging that even a man with an open Bible which he believes, and with the Spirit in him, may at times be discouraged and cast down almost to the depths of despair. There is no better tonic in such a condition than to familiarise yourselves with previous eras in the history of the Church which have been similar, and how God has dealt with them. The preacher is a man—I hope to deal with this in a subsequent lecture—who is attacked on many sides, and perhaps his greatest danger is the danger of becoming discouraged and depressed, and of feeling that he cannot go on any longer. Church history, and especially the history of Revivals is one of the best antidotes to that.

I remember reading somewhere about the French novelist Anatole France that he used to say, whenever he felt tired and jaded with a tendency to be depressed and downcast, 'I never go into the country for a change of air and a holiday, I always go instead into the eighteenth century.' I have often said exactly the same thing, but not in the same sense in which he meant it, of course. When I get discouraged and over-tired and weary I also invariably go to the eighteenth century. I have never found George Whitefield to fail me. Go to the eighteenth century! In other words read the stories of the great tides and movements of the Spirit experienced in that century. It is the most exhilarating experience, the finest tonic you will ever know. For a preacher it is absolutely invaluable; there is nothing to compare with it. The more he learns in this way about the history of the Church the better preacher he will be.

At the same time let him, of course, during this training become familiar with the stories of the great men of the past, the great saints and preachers. It will not only act as a wonderful tonic to him in times of depression, it will keep him humble when tempted to pride and a spirit of elation. That is equally necessary. When a man starts preaching, and has just one or two sermons, he really thinks he is a preacher! The best treatment for that is to make him read about Whitefield or Jonathan Edwards, or Spurgeon, or some such mighty man of God. That will soon bring him to earth.

Lastly, and only lastly, Homiletics. This to me is almost an abomination. There are books bearing such titles as *The Craft of Sermon*

Construction, and *The Craft of Sermon Illustration.* That is, to me, prostitution. Homiletics just comes in, but no more.

What about preaching as such, the act of preaching of which I have spoken? There is only one thing to say about this; it cannot be taught. That is impossible. Preachers are born, not made. This is an absolute. You will never teach a man to be a preacher if he is not already one. All your books such as *The A.B.C. of Preaching,* or *Preaching Made Easy* should be thrown in to the fire as soon as possible. But if a man is a born preacher you can help him a little—but not much. He can perhaps be improved a little here and there.

How can that be done? Here I am probably going to be somewhat controversial. I would say: Not in a sermon class, not by having a student to preach a sermon to other students who then proceed to criticise matter and manner. I would prohibit that. Why? Because the sermon in such circumstances is being preached with a wrong object in view; and the people who are listening to it are listening in a wrong way. The message of the Bible should never be listened to in that way. It is always the Word of God, and no one should ever listen to it except in a spirit of reverence and godly expectation of receiving a message.

When you come to further modern refinements of that such as television video-tapes so that a man may subsequently see his own gestures and so on—this to me is reprehensible in the extreme. The same applies to instruction in 'pulpit deportment' as it is called, or 'television deportment'. There is only one word for all this; it is sheer prostitution, it is instruction in the art of the prostitute. The preacher must always be natural and un-selfconscious; and if in your training you tend to make him become conscious of his hands, or what he does with his head, or anything else, you are doing him great harm. It should not be done, it should be prohibited! You cannot teach a preacher in these ways; and I feel that to attempt to do so is an injustice to the Word of God.

What then is the young preacher to do? Let him listen to other preachers, the best and most experienced. He will learn a lot from them, negatively and positively. He will learn what not to do, and learn a great deal of what he should do. Listen to preachers! Also read sermons. But make sure that they were published before 1900! Read the sermons of Spurgeon and Whitefield and Edwards and all the giants. Those men themselves read the Puritans and were greatly helped by them. They seem to have lived on the Puritans. Well, let the young preacher in turn live on them, or perhaps be led by them to the Puritans. Just here—perhaps I shall elaborate this later—I draw a great distinction between the preaching of the Puritans and the preaching of the eighteenth-century men. I myself am an eighteenth-century man, not seventeenth-century; but I believe in using the seventeenth-century men as the eighteenth-century men used them.

What then is the chief thing? I say, none of these mechanics except a bare minimum. What matters? The chief thing is the love of God, the love of souls, a knowledge of the Truth, and the Holy Spirit within you. These are the things that make the preacher. If he has the love of God in his heart, and if he has a love for God; if he has a love for the souls of men, and a concern about them; if he knows the truth of the Scriptures; and has the Spirit of God within him, that man will preach. That is the big thing. The other things can be helpful; but keep them in their right place, and never allow them to usurp any other position.

As we go on to consider the people to whom this man is preaching we shall discover further matters in connection with the training of the preacher.

CHAPTER SEVEN

The Congregation

WE ARE STILL looking in general at this picture of a man standing in a pulpit and preaching to a number of people. We have already looked at the preacher and his calling and what he has to do, in a general manner. Now, it seems to me to be equally essential that we should look at the people who are listening to him, the people who are sitting in the pews. After all he is preaching to them; he is not just standing there to voice certain of his own ideas and opinions, nor to give any kind of theoretical or academic disquisition on the teaching of the Scripture. He is there, primarily, to address people who have come together in order to listen to him and to what he has to say. So this raises the question of the relationship between the pew and the pulpit, between the people who listen and the man who is preaching. This has become quite an acute problem at this present time, and in a new way. The old traditional idea of this relationship seems to be disappearing. It is at any rate being questioned and queried very seriously, and clearly this has reference to the last subject with which we dealt, namely the training of the preacher. Obviously the relationship between the pew and the pulpit must affect the training of the preacher, and that this is so is becoming increasingly evident at the present time.

It is quite clear that the new factor in this respect is the great emphasis that is being placed today upon the pew. In the past, let us admit, there may have been too much of a tendency for the pulpit to be almost independent of the pew; and for the people in the pew to revere the preacher sometimes almost to the point of idolatry. You may remember the story of the poor woman leaving a service in a famous church in Edinburgh where a great and learned professor had been preaching. Somebody asked her on the way out whether she had enjoyed the sermon, and on her saying that she had, asked her further, 'Were you able to follow him?' To which she replied, 'Far be it from me to presume to understand such a great man as that!' That was the old attitude far too frequently; but that has gone, that is no longer the case. We are now in a new position in which the pew is asserting itself and more or less trying to dictate to the pulpit.

This is something which expresses itself in many different ways. Here are some statements of it from different angles. One writer, for instance, says, 'The world is dying for want, not of good preaching but of good hearing.' That is a criticism of the listener in the pew. So he feels that the great problem today is good hearing and not good preaching. However, whatever particular form the criticism takes the great emphasis is upon modern man, and the modern situation confronting us. Here are statements by the Dutch theologian Kuitert, of the Free University, Amsterdam, who is becoming increasingly popular in Europe. He says, 'Moreover it is of no genuine help to a Christian trying to find his way through God's world of this day and this place.' That is his criticism of the traditional theology and the traditional type of preaching. Or again: 'A great many Christians, convinced that faith and works are inseparable, are none the less unable to discover for themselves how to focus this unity on the issues of our own time.' That is the emphasis. Or again: 'We have to know the issues, what is at stake in our time and place. It is here and nowhere else that the truth must be done.' Note the constant emphasis on, 'here and now', 'the situation today', 'the man of today'. The same emphasis is found in Bultmann whose basic argument for demythologising the Gospel is that you cannot expect the modern man, with his scientific background and outlook to believe the Gospel —the message which he says he is anxious to convey—as long as it is tied up with the miraculous element which such a man cannot possibly accept. In other words, you see, it is what the modern man can 'accept' that becomes the determining factor. It is the same as all the talk about 'man come of age', and other characteristic modern clichés.

We must look at some of the ways in which this attitude tends to express itslf. It does so in its approach to what we may call 'the ordinary people'. We are told that today they cannot think and follow reasoned statements, that they are so accustomed to the kind of outlook and mentality produced by newspapers, television and the films, that they are incapable of following a reasoned, argued statement. We must therefore give them films and filmstrips, and get filmstars to speak to them, and pop-singers to sing to them and give 'brief addresses' and testimonies, with just a word of Gospel thrown in. 'Create your atmosphere' is the great thing, and then just get a very brief word of Gospel in at the end.

Another form which it takes is to say that these people cannot understand the biblical terminology, that to talk about Justification and Sanctification and Glorification is meaningless to them. We must realise that we are living in a 'post-Christian' era and that this is the greatest obstacle to preaching today, that people do not understand our terms. They sound archaic to them, they are not modern, they are not up to date. The result is this great modern craze for new translations of the Scriptures in familiar, ordinary everyday language, and the fashion of no longer addressing God as 'Thee' and 'Thou', but 'You'. This, we are told, is all-important, that when the modern man hears Thee and Thou it is almost impossible for him to listen to the gospel, leave alone to believe it. So we have to change our language, and we do this in our new translations of the Scriptures, and in our prayers, and in general in our style of preaching and all our religious activities. That is how this modern attitude, which regards the pew as controlling the pulpit, expresses itself with respect to the ordinary person.

Then, when you come to the intellectuals, we are told that they are now scientific in their outlook, that they accept the theory of evolution and the entire scientific outlook which makes a three-dimensional world impossible, etc, and that therefore we must make it plain to them that the Bible only deals with matters of salvation and religious experience and living. If we fail to show that the Bible and Nature (as expounded by scientists) are complementary and equally authoritative forms of revelation we shall offend this modern intellectualist and he will not even listen to the Gospel. So we must stop talking, as we have done in the past, about the origin of the world and of man, about the Fall, and about miracles and supernatural interventions in history, and we must concentrate only on this religious message. Of course there is nothing new about this; Ritschl said it all a hundred years ago. But it has now returned in a new form.

Another point which is being increasingly stressed is that we have to realise that the modern man, this intellectual type, is sophisticated, that he thinks in terms of modern literature and modern art and modern dress, novels and so on, and that unless we can address him in this idiom, with which he is so familiar, we are not likely to make any impact at all on him. We must understand that this is what controls his thinking. We had an extraordinary illustration of this attitude not many months ago in a review of a book in a religious periodical in Britain. The writer ended his review by saying that he believed that if all preachers were to read this book there would be a new hope for preaching, because this book would induce preachers to realise that their Saturday nights would be most profitably spent in watching what is called 'Saturday Night Theatre' on the television. By watching 'Saturday Night Theatre' they would come to know and understand the mentality and the outlook and the jargon of the modern man; and therefore they would be more qualified to preach to him on the Sunday! So this is the way in which the preacher is to prepare himself for Sunday—no longer prayer and meditation, but 'Saturday Night Theatre' and understanding 'the modern mentality'.

Another form which this thinking takes is to emphasise that modern sophisticated man has a particular dislike of dogmatic assertions, and that he will not tolerate the old dogmatic pulpit pronouncements. He is a learned man and is not to be 'talked down to'; he is the equal of the man in the pulpit, possibly his superior. He believes in examining things carefully and rationally and scientifically and putting up the different possible points of view. Indeed I read in a magazine belonging to an evangelical students' organisation recently a plea to the effect that what the pulpit should be doing now is to read out portions of Scripture, particularly the newer translations, make a few comments, and then invite questions and have a discussion. So you would have an 'intelligent service' instead of one man standing up and laying down the law' as it were, and telling other people 'all about it'. Participation by the people in the pew is essential. So the man in the pulpit is really just there to read the Scriptures in an intelligent slow manner, according to these different translations, and then the discussion takes place. Exchange of views, confrontation, dialogue, are the order of the day!

Then on the practical level with regard to the training of ministers, this new attitude comes out like this. There are those who say that a man is not really fit to preach to an industrial community unless he has had a certain amount of factory experience himself. There has been a serious proposal that all preachers, having finished their academic training, should then go and work in a factory, say for six months, in order that they may get to understand the outlook and the mentality of the factory worker. They must get to understand his language and how he expresses himself; for it is well-nigh impossible for him to preach to them unless he has had this experience.

* * *

There I have stated the position in general and as it most commonly expresses itself. What are we to say to this? To what extent is the pew to control the pulpit? I maintain that this new kind of thinking about these matters is entirely wrong, and for the following reasons. Let me divide my answers into general and more particular categories. It is wrong in general, first of all, because it is wrong in fact, and it is wrong in experience. It is wrong in its whole psychological understanding of the situation.

Let me elaborate that. I shall never forget—and I recount it here because I think it helps to make the point clear—I shall never forget preaching some twenty-seven years ago at a college chapel in the University of Oxford on a Sunday morning. I had preached in exactly the same way as I would have preached anywhere else. The moment the service had finished, and before I had scarcely had time to get down from the pulpit, the wife of the Principal came rushing up to me and said, 'Do you know, this is the most remarkable thing I have known in this chapel.' I said, 'What do you mean?' 'Well,' she said, 'do you know that you are literally the first man I have ever heard in this chapel who has preached to us as if we were sinners.' She added, 'All the preachers who come here, because it is a college chapel in Oxford, have obviously been taking exceptional pains to prepare learned, intellectual sermons, thinking we are all great intellects. To start with, the poor fellows often show that they do not have too much intellect themselves, but they have obviously been straining in an attempt to produce the last ounce of learning and culture, and the result is that we go away absolutely unfed and unmoved. We have listened to these essays and our souls are left dry. They do not seem to understand that though we live in Oxford we are nevertheless sinners.' Now that was a statement of fact by a highly intelligent lady, the wife of the Principal of a college.

I remember a preacher, a good man who had done good work in a church in a working-class area. He then got a call to a church in the suburb of another town. I remember noticing after a while—he came into the presbytery to which I belonged—that the man was beginning to look tired and strained; and I talked to him about this. We were talking together one day and he admitted that he felt very strained and tired. I said, 'Well, what is the matter? You have had experience, you have had a number of years in the other church and were very successful.' 'Ah well, you see,' he said, 'I have a different type of congregation now. I have to preach to people who are living in the suburbs.' Some of them were professional people, others were business people who had done well and had moved from living over their shops into the suburbs. And here he was, poor man, trying to produce great intellectual sermons for those people whom he assessed in that way. The actual fact was, I knew, that his people were complaining about the dryness of his preaching. It was not what they wanted. Indeed, I have very little hesitation in saying that that poor man ultimately killed himself because of his wrong attitude to preaching. His health broke down and he died at a comparatively early age. It was not what the people wanted at all, not what they needed and expected.

Then take this talk about the inability of people in general today to listen to sermons and especially long sermons. I was ill a year ago and at that time received a number of letters. The letter that I shall always treasure more than any other is this. I should say that according to modern standards my ideas on preaching are all wrong; I tend to be long—forty-five minutes or so—and I certainly do not spend my time in telling stories! However, the letter that I prize was from a little girl aged twelve who wrote on behalf of herself and her brother, unbeknown to their parents, saying that they were praying for my recovery and hoping that I would soon be back in the pulpit. She then gave the reason for this, and that is what pleased me so much. She said, 'because you are the only preacher we can understand.' According to the modern ideas and theories I am not an easy preacher, I am too much of a teacher, and there is too much reason and argumentation in my sermons. I have heard that certain people never take their newly converted friends to listen to me, or advise anyone who seems to be under conviction to listen to me. They say it would be too much for them, that they would not be able to follow, and so on. Later on, yes, but not at this stage. But here is a young child who says, 'You are the only preacher that we can understand.' I am sure she is right!

But to enforce this still further, I have often had the experience of people who have been converted, and have then gone on and grown in the Church, coming to me some time later and telling me about what happened to them. What they have so often said is, 'When we first came to the Church we really did not understand much of what you were talking about.' I have then asked what made them continue coming, and have been told again and again that, 'There was something about the whole atmosphere that attracted us, and made us feel that it was right. This made us come, and we gradually began to find that we were absorbing truth unconsciously. It began to have meaning for us more and more.' They did not get as much as some others out of a sermon, but they got something, and that something was of great value. And they had continued to grow in their understanding until now they were able to enjoy the full service, the full message. This is a very common experience; people at different levels seem to be able to extract, under the influence of the Spirit, what they need, what is helpful to them. That is why you can preach to a mixed congregation of varying intellects and understanding and knowledge and culture, and all can derive benefit from it.

But further, this modern idea is entirely refuted by the tradition of the centuries. We are not the first or the only people who have lived in this world. We tend to talk as if we were, or as if we are some peculiar special race. But that is not so, for in this world you have always had these different types. This is what Luther has to say about this matter, 'A preacher,' says Luther, 'should have the skill to teach the unlearned simply, roundly and plainly; for teaching is of more importance than exhorting.' Then he adds, 'When I preach I regard neither doctors nor magistrates, of whom I have above forty in the congregation. I have all my eyes on the servant maids and the children. And if the learned men are not well pleased with what they hear, well, the door is open.' That, surely, is the right attitude. Some 'doctors and magistrates' perhaps may feel like that, that not sufficient attention is being paid to them by the preacher in the pulpit. But the wise preacher keeps his eye on the servant maids and the children. If this great and learned man feels that he does not get anything he is condemning himself. He is condemning himself in the sense that he is not spiritually minded, that he is not able to receive spiritual truth. He is so 'puffed up' and blown up with his head knowledge that he has forgotten that he has a heart and a soul. He condemns himself, and if he walks out, well, he is the loser. I am assuming, of course, that the preacher is really preaching the Word of God!

Let me enforce this point by reporting an incident which happened in my experience, strangely enough, once more in that University of Oxford. I was invited to preach in a University mission there in 1941. It fell to my lot to preach on the Sunday night, the first service of the mission, in the famous pulpit of John Henry Newman—afterwards Cardinal Newman—in St. Mary's Church, where he preached while he was still in the Church of England. It was of course, chiefly a congregation of students. I preached to them as I would have preached anywhere else. It had been arranged, and announced, that if people had any questions to put to me that an opportunity would be given to them if they retired to another building at the back of the church after the service had ended. So the vicar and I went along expecting just a few people. But we found the place packed out. The vicar took the chair and asked if there were any questions. Immediately a bright young man sitting in the front row got up. I discovered afterwards that he was studying Law and was one of the chief officials at the famous Oxford University Union Debating Society where future statesmen, judges, barristers and bishops often learn the art of public speaking and debating. His very dress and stance betrayed what he was. He got up and said that he had a question to put; and he proceeded to put it with all the grace and polish characteristic of a union debater. He paid the preacher some compliments and said that he had much enjoyed the sermon; but there was one great difficulty and perplexity left in his mind as the result of the sermon. He really could not see but that that sermon, which he had listened to with pleasure, and which he admitted was well constructed and well presented, might not equally well have been delivered to a congregation of farm labourers or anyone else. He then immediately sat down. The entire company roared with laughter. The chairman turned to me for my reply. I rose and gave what must always be the reply to such an attitude. I said that I was most interested in the question, but really could not see the questioner's difficulty; because, I confessed freely, that though I might be a heretic, I had to admit that until that moment I had regarded undergraduates and indeed graduates of Oxford University as being just ordinary common human clay and miserable sinners like everybody else, and held the view that their needs were precisely the same as those of the agricultural labourer or anyone else. I had preached as I had done quite deliberately! This again provoked a good deal of laughter and even cheering; but the point was that they appreciated what I was saying, and gave me a most attentive hearing from there on. Indeed it was as the result of that that I was invited to have the debate, to which I referred in a previous lecture, with the famous Dr. Joad, in the Oxford Union. There is no greater fallacy than to think that you need a gospel for special types of people. It is entirely contrary to plain biblical teaching; it is also contradicted completely by what we read in the biographies of all the great preachers such as Whitefield, Spurgeon and also in the stories of evangelists such as D. L. Moody. They never recognised these false distinctions, and their ministries were blessed to all types—intellectual, social, etc.—of people.

In the third place, this modern idea is really based on false thinking. This, to me, is most important. It assumes that the difficulty and the trouble with the modern man, the thing that prevents his believing the Gospel, is almost entirely a problem of language and of terminology, what is described grandiloquently today as 'the problem of communication!' That is the reason behind so much of this thinking.

Let me say at once that I agree entirely that we should always seek the best translations possible. We must not be obscurantist in these matters. Let us have the best that the translators can give us. But that is not the real point behind the idea that you must now address God as 'You' rather than 'Thee' or 'Thou' if you are to 'communicate' the Gospel to the modern man. The basic assumption behind that thinking is that the reason these people do not believe in God, and do not pray to Him and accept the Gospel, is the archaic language of the A.V., and if only that is put right the whole situation will be changed, and the modern man will be able to believe these things. The simple answer to all that is that people have always found this language to be strange. The answer to the argument that people in this post-Christian age do not understand terms like Justification, Sanctification and Glorification is simply to ask another question. When did people understand them? When did the unbeliever understand this language? The answer is: Never! These terms are peculiar and special to the Gospel. It is our business as preachers to show that our gospel is essentially different and that we are not talking about ordinary matters. We must emphasise the fact that we are talking about something unique and special. We must lead people to expect this; and so we are to assert it. Our business is to teach people the meaning of these terms. They do not decide and determine what is to be preached and how: it is we that have the Revelation, the Message, and we have to make this understood. That was the great principle on which the Protestant Reformers worked. That is why they produced their new translations; they wanted the message as they put it, 'to be understanded of the people'. There is all the difference in the world between the failure of a man to understand Latin and his failure to understand the terms connected with salvation, such as Justification. It is always right that the Bible and preaching should be in the native language of any people, but that still leaves untouched the problem of understanding the special terminology of salvation. This is the special business of preaching. We should not expect people to understand these terms; the whole point of preaching is to give them this understanding. 'The natural man receiveth not the things of the Spirit of God: for they are foolishness unto him: neither can he know them, because they are spiritually discerned' (1 Cor. 2:14). We do well to heed the words of Professor J. H. S. Burleigh in his Croall Lectures on St. Augustine's Philosophy and especially on Augustine's *City of God*. Quoting Augustine he says:

'If Moses were alive, I would lay hold of him and ask him and entreat him to unfold these things to me. I would offer my bodily ears to the sounds breaking forth from his mouth. But if he should speak in the Hebrew tongue in vain would his words impinge upon my organs of hearing. They would never reach my mind at all. Even if he spoke Latin would his words be the cause of my understanding?'

Professor Burleigh goes on to say:

In the *De Magistro* St. Augustine analysed the complex process of the communication of truth from one mind to another. Besides the physical process of speech and hearing, there must also be a spiritual process at work. Words, whether spoken or written, are indispensable mechanical helps to understanding, but are not the cause of understanding. They are signs indicating truth, which is only grasped because the mind has its own interior teacher identified with Christ Who is Truth itself, speaking to the inward ear.

Many who would claim to agree with this in theory seem to be forgetting it completely in their practice.

Then take that other false argument, that we have got to know the exact condition of people before we can truly preach to them, and that therefore the preacher should go and work in a factory for six months in order that he may preach effectively to factory workers. This is to me the most monstrous and fatuous argument of all, because, if this is true, and is pressed to its logical conclusion, your training will never be finished, because, if you are to preach to drunkards you will have to spend six months in the drinking saloons and bar-parlours and so on, you will have to go round all the various trades and professions and departments and spend six months in each. Then, and only then, will you be ready to preach to them. The whole idea, I say, is utterly ridiculous because on that argument and supposition one could never preach to a mixed general congregation. You would have to have one service for, and one congregation of, the non-intellectuals; then you would have a special service for the intellectuals, and then you would have one, probably, for those who are somewhere in between. Then you might have services for the different ages, then one for the factory workers and one for professional people and so on endlessly. The result would be that you would be dividing up and atomising your congregation; you would never have a common public act of worship, and a sermon preached, at all. You would have to be dividing yourself up in this way and your work would be endless. In any case it would be entirely destructive of this great fundamental principle of the New Testament, that we are all one: 'There is neither Jew nor Gentile, Barbarian, Scythian, bond nor free, male or female.' I add, there is neither intellectual nor non-intellectual, factory worker, professional man or anything else. We are all one in sin, one in failure, one in hopelessness, one in need of the Lord Jesus Christ and His great salvation.

Let me put it in this way. Having spent the first part of my adult life as a physician in medicine I have often been interested in the difference between the work of the physician and the work of the preacher. Of course there are many similarities, but there is one essential difference which comes out in this way. How does the physician deal with his patient? Well, the first thing he does is to ask the patient to give an account of his symptoms and his troubles—his aches and pains, where it is, how long he has had it, how it began, has it varied, etc. All this has to be gone into in great detail. The doctor takes a careful history of the case and then enquires as to the patient's previous history from childhood onwards. Having done that he takes the family history, for that may throw considerable light upon this particular ailment. There are hereditary and familial diseases, and familial predispositions to disease, so the family history is most important. Having ascertained these facts he then proceeds to make his physical examination of the patient.

Now without this detailed, specific, special personal knowledge of the patient the physician cannot do his work; and it is at this point, I say, that there is such a striking contrast between the work of the physician and that of the preacher. The preacher does not need to know these personal facts concerning his congregation. This is a point, incidentally, that arises in another connection, namely in the giving of testimonies in evangelistic campaigns. Some attach great importance to this and argue that if a man hears the story of someone else who once had his particular weakness and sin and of how he was delivered from that by 'accepting Christ' he will be helped. The same argument applies to that. The difference is this: the preacher does not need to know these details. Why not? Because he knows that all the people in front of him are suffering from the same disease, which is sin—every one of them. The symptoms may vary tremendously from case to case, but the business of the preacher is not to medicate symptoms, it is to treat the disease. The preacher therefore should not be over-interested in the particular form the sin takes.

The same point arises, and is equally important also, when the preacher interviews people in his vestry at the end of the service. Some of these people will come in to talk to you, and you will find that, almost invariably, they want to talk about their particular sin. They seem to have the feeling, some of them, that if they could but get rid of this one problem all would be well. But it is just here that the preacher has to take charge and to correct them. We have to show them that though they get rid of that particular sin they are still in as great need as they were before, and that the business of salvation is not merely to get rid of particular problems but to put the 'whole man' right in his relationship to God.

So the preacher does not need to know these particular detailed facts about the people because he knows that there is this general, common need. It is a vital part of preaching to reduce all listeners to that common denominator. The preacher has to show the self-satisfied Pharisee that his need is terribly great, that it is as great as that of the Publican, if not greater. He has to show the great intellectualist, who boasts of his knowledge and of his understanding, that he is guilty of intellectual pride, which is one of the greatest of all sins, much worse than many sins of the flesh. He has to expose this pride of man trusting to himself and to his learning and his knowledge. He has to humble through his message this man who comes to listen more as an inspector and a judge rather than as a sinner. He has to be convicted, he has to be made to realise his terrible need. So the preacher is in the position that he does not need to go into these different sections and grades and divisions of society. He knows the problem of the factory worker, he knows the problem of the professional man; because it is ultimately precisely the same. One may get drunk on beer and the other on wine, as it were, but the point is that they both get drunk; one may sin in rags and the other in evening dress but they both sin. 'All have sinned and come short of the glory of God.' 'There is none righteous, no, not one.' 'The whole world lieth guilty before God.'

This modern approach is based on entirely false thinking. Indeed, it is ultimately due to bad theology. It is based on a failure to realise the true nature of sin, and that sin is the problem, not sins, and that specialisation on the particular forms and manifestations of sin is irrelevant and very largely a waste of time. The history of the Church and her preaching throughout the centuries substantiates this argument. The general preaching of the Gospel is applied in particular by the Holy Spirit to the particular cases. Men and women are brought to see their same common fundamental need, and they are converted and regenerated in the same way by, the same Spirit. So they mix together in the same Church; and if they feel that they cannot, and do not, well then they are not regenerated. It just comes to that. If some of them feel that they are being neglected because of their great intellects it shows that there is a fundamental lack of humility in them; they have not been humbled as they should have been. The glory of the Church is that she consists of all these types and kinds and all the possible varieties and variations of humanity; and yet because they all share this common life they are able to participate together and to enjoy the same preaching.

* * *

There is the case in general. But I can imagine a question being raised at this point. 'What about 1 Corinthians 9, verses 19–23?' Paul describing his own ministry says:

135

For though I be free from all men, yet have I made myself servant unto all, that I might gain the more. And unto the Jews I became as a Jew, that I might gain the Jews; to them that are under the law, as under the law, that I might gain them that are under the law; To them that are without law, as without law, (being not without law to God, but under the law to Christ,) that I might gain them that are without law. To the weak became I as weak, that I might gain the weak: I am made all things to all men, that I might by all means save some. And this I do for the gospel's sake, that I might be partaker thereof with you.

This is a highly relevant passage. Looked at superficially it might seem to be the justification of much of this present-day argumentation which suggests that the pew should really control the pulpit. The Apostle on the surface seems to be saying that what he does is determined by the people to whom he is speaking.

How do we deal with this? There can be no doubt that in the main the Apostle was dealing here with his general conduct and behaviour rather than his actual preaching; but I believe that at the same time he was also dealing with the method or way in which he presented the Truth. We can surely come to certain conclusions. This Apostle, of all Apostles—but it was true of all the others also—obviously does not mean that the content of his message varied with the people. He is only concerned here with the form of presentation. But when we come to this matter of presentation—which is our concern at the moment—what is the teaching? It is obvious that there is clear teaching here to this effect, that as preachers we must be flexible: we must not be traditionalists, we must not be legalists in this matter. There is grave and real danger for many of us to become traditionalists and legalists. There are some people who seem to delight in using archaic phrases; and if you do not use them they doubt whether you are really preaching the Gospel at all. They are slaves to phrases. I have observed that certain young men who have developed a new interest, for instance, in the Puritans, start speaking and writing as if they lived in the seventeenth century. That is quite ludicrous. They use phrases that were current and common then, they even try to affect the kind of stance and appearance which I imagine was characteristic of the Puritans, but which is no longer characteristic of Christian people today; and they affect certain mannerisms. All this is entirely wrong.

We should not be interested in the incidentals, in the temporary or the passing aspects of religion; we should be interested in the principles and the things that are permanent. And surely that is what the Apostle is saying. He had to fight a great fight over this whole matter. He has been dealing in that First Epistle to the Corinthians, with the question of meats offered to idols, in the previous chapter. He deals with it also in the Epistle to the Romans in chapter 14. People were tied by traditions belonging to their unconverted state, and they were in genuine trouble about these matters. The Jewish Christians were in trouble, as were also some of the Gentile Christians, over meats that had been offered to idols and various other matters. What the Apostle says repeatedly is that while we must hold on to the essentials we must be elastic with regard to things that are not essential. He qualifies this because he is concerned about 'the weaker brother'. You must not trample on the tender conscience of such a brother, you must try to help him, and you must even cease to do things which are legitimate in and of themselves if they are an offence to your brother. 'Wherefore,' he says, 'if meat make my brother to offend, I will eat no flesh while the world standeth, lest I make my brother to offend.' 'Conscience, not thine own but of the other also,' and so on. But what he says, and that very plainly and clearly is that you must not allow prejudice to stand between people and your message; you must not allow your own personal foibles to control you. You must do your utmost to help these people to whom you are preaching to come to a knowledge of the Truth. So you do not, when you are preaching to the Gentiles, insist upon things which certain Jewish Christians are still insisting upon; for they are insisting upon them wrongly. You remember also how Paul had to 'withstand Peter to the face' at Antioch over this very matter. Peter had become confused over all this, and Paul had to correct him in public. He tells us about that in Galatians 2. It is the same essential principle with which he is dealing here.

Let me sum it up in modern terms by asserting that it is always our business to be contemporary; our object is to deal with the living people who are in front of us and listening to us. I must not go into the pulpit with some ideal picture of the preacher in my mind, say that of the Puritan preacher of three hundred years ago, or that of one hundred years ago, and act as if that were still the position. To do so will be to do harm. It will be an offence to a modern congregation; it will make it more difficult for them to listen; in any case it is not an essential part of the message at all. I can learn from the preachers of the past, and should; but I must not be a slavish imitator of them. I am helped by their knowledge of the Truth and their expositions, but as for the things that were merely incidental to their preaching—the things that were passing and temporary and mere customs and fashions of their day—I must not hold on to them and make them almost as essential as the Truth itself. That is not 'holding on to the Truth'; that is traditionalism. This applies of course not only to the manner of preaching but also to forms of service, dress, and many other matters.

The Apostle's argument, surely, is that there must be elasticity in our actual mode of presentation. But let us be clear that there are certain limits even to this principle. We must not be archaic and legalistic, but there are limits, and one limit, obviously, is that 'the end does not justify the means'. This is a very common argument today. The argument put so frequently is, 'But people are converted as the result of this.' We must not accept that Jesuitical argument, and we have good reasons for not doing so.

Secondly, our methods must always be consistent and compatible with our message, and not contradict it. This again is a most important point at this present time. There are men who are quite sincere and genuine and honest, and whose motive is undoubtedly good, and whose concern is to bring people to salvation. But this so runs away with them that in their desire to make contact with the people and to make it easy for them to believe the message, they do things which I suggest often contradict that very message. The moment the method contradicts the message it has become bad. Let us have elasticity, but never to the point of contradicting your message.

This is not only true in terms of biblical principles but it is even proved to be right in practice. What always amazes me about these people who are so concerned with modern methods is their pathetic psychological ignorance; they do not seem to know human nature. The fact is that the world expects us to be different; and this idea that you can win the world by showing that after all you are very similar to it, with scarcely any difference at all, or but a very slight one, is basically wrong not only theologically but even psychologically.

Let me illustrate what I mean by a well-known example. At the end of the First World War there was in England a famous clergyman who was known as 'Woodbine Willie'. Why was he called 'Woodbine Willie'? The explanation is that he had been a chaplain in the army and had been a very great success in that capacity. His success he attributed to the fact—and many agreed with him in this—that he mixed with the men in the trenches in a familiar manner. He smoked with them, and in particular he smoked their cheap brand of cigarette known as 'Wild Woodbine' commonly called 'Woodbines'. In pre-1914 days you could buy five such cigarettes for a penny. Now this cheap type of cigarette was not the brand of cigarette that an officer generally smoked, but the ordinary soldier did. So this man, whose name was Studdert-Kennedy, in order to put the men at ease, and in order to facilitate his work as chaplain smoked 'Woodbines', hence the name 'Woodbine Willie'. Not only that, he noticed also that most of the men could not speak without swearing, so he did the same. It was not that he wanted to swear, but he held the view that if you want to win men you have to use their language and you have to be like them in every respect. All this certainly made him a popular figure—there is no doubt about that. After the end of the Second World War he used to go round the country teaching this and urging that preachers must do this; and many tried to do so and began to do so. But the verdict of history on this was that it was a complete failure, a temporary 'stunt' or 'gimmick' that achieved notoriety for a while but soon entirely disappeared from the thinking of the Church. But it had a great temporary vogue.

From the standpoint of the New Testament it was based on a complete fallacy. Our Lord attracted sinners because He was different. They drew near to Him because they felt that there was something different about Him. That poor sinful woman of whom we read in Luke 7 did not draw near to the Pharisees and wash their feet with her tears, and wipe them with the hair of her head. No, but she sensed something in our Lord—His purity, His holiness, His love—and so she drew near to Him. It was His essential difference that attracted her. And the world always expects us to be different. This idea that you are going to win people to the Christian faith by showing them that after all you are remarkably like them, is theologically and psychologically a profound blunder.

This same principle has a further application at the present time. There are foolish Protestants who seem to think that the way to win Roman Catholics is to show them there is practically no difference between us, whereas the converted Roman Catholic will always tell you that what appealed to him was the contrast. 'Action and reaction are equal and opposite.' The modern idea is wrong psychologically as well as theologically.

What makes this to be inevitably the case is that the subject matter with which we are dealing is so different. In this realm we are dealing with God, and our knowledge of God, and our relationship to God. So everything here must be 'under God' and must be done 'with reverence and godly fear'. We do not decide this; we are not in charge and in control. It is God. It is His service, and He has to be approached 'with reverence and with godly fear, because our God is a consuming fire'.

Furthermore, light entertainment, easy familiarity and jocularity are not compatible with a realisation of the seriousness of the condition of the souls of all men by nature, the fact that they are lost and in danger of eternal perdition, and their consequent need of salvation. Not only that, such methods cannot bring out the Truth; and our business is to preach the Truth. These methods may affect people psychologically and in other respects, and they may lead to 'decisions'; but our object is not merely to get decisions, it is to bring people to a knowledge of the Truth. And beyond this, we must never give the impression that all that is needed is for people to make a little adjustment in their thinking and ideas and behaviour; that is to militate against our message. Our message is that every man 'must be born again', and that whatever may happen to him short of that is of no value whatsoever from the standpoint of his relationship to God. The New Testament teaching is that the unbeliever is all wrong. It is not merely his ideas of art or drama that are wrong; everything about him is wrong. His particular views are wrong because his whole view is wrong, because he himself is wrong. The rule is, 'Seek ye first the kingdom of God and His righteousness, and all these (other) things shall be added unto you'. If you put your emphasis on these 'other things' instead of on 'seeking first the kingdom of God' you are doomed to failure, and you are doing despite to the message that has been committed to you.

No one has ever been 'reasoned' into the Kingdom of God; it is impossible. It has never happened, it never will happen. We are all one in sin—'The whole world lieth guilty before God.' We are all in the same spiritual condition. So I argue that all that is taught in that passage in 1 Corinthians 9:15–27 is that we are to do our utmost to make ourselves clear and plain and understood. We are never to allow our own prejudices, or foibles, or things that are merely incidental to the message to be a hindrance to the message. We are to be 'all things to all men' in that sense, and in that sense only.

* * *

My final comment is that the real trouble with this modern outlook is that it forgets the Holy Spirit and His power. We have become such experts, as we think, in psychological understanding, and at dividing people up into groups—psychological, cultural, national, etc.—that we conclude as a result that what is all right for one is not right for another, and so eventually become guilty of denying the Gospel. 'There is neither Jew nor Gentile, Barbarian, Scythian, bond nor free.' This is the ONE Gospel—the ONLY Gospel. It is for the whole world, and the whole of humanity. Mankind is one. We have fallen into the grievous error of adopting modern psychological theories to such an extent that we evade the truth, sometimes to protect ourselves from the message, and certainly often to justify methods that are not consistent and consonant with the message which we are privileged to deliver.

CHAPTER EIGHT

The Character of the Message

THIS MATTER OF the relationship of the pew to the pulpit, or the listener to the preacher, is of the greatest possible importance. Having looked at the teaching of the Apostle in 1 Corinthians 9 in its bearing on this, let me draw certain conclusions.

I would lay it down as being axiomatic that the pew is never to dictate to, or control, the pulpit. This needs to be emphasised at the present time.

But having said that I would emphasise equally that the preacher nevertheless has to assess the condition of those in the pew and to bear that in mind in the preparation and delivery of his message. Notice how I put it. It is not that the listener is to control, but that the preacher is to assess the condition and the position of the listener. Let me give my scriptural warrant for making this assertion. There are several, so I pick out some of the more obvious ones. Take for instance what the Apostle Paul says in 1 Corinthians 3 at the beginning: 'And I, brethren, could not speak unto you as unto spiritual, but as unto carnal, even as unto babes in Christ. I have fed you with milk, and not with meat: for hitherto ye were not able to bear it, neither yet now are ye able. For ye are yet carnal . . .' Obviously he is saying there that what he did was influenced by the condition of the people in Corinth. It was not that they were dictating to him; it was that he was making an assessment of them, and that this partly determined how he preached to them.

But take a second example. It is in the Epistle to the Hebrews in chapter 5 beginning at verse 11. The author has been referring to our Lord as 'an high priest after the order of Melchisedec'. He goes on to say:

> Of whom we have many things to say, and hard to be uttered, seeing ye are dull of hearing. For when for the time ye ought to be teachers, ye have need that one teach you again which be the first principles of the oracles of God; and are become such as have need of milk, and not of strong meat. For every one that useth milk is unskilful in the word of righteousness: for he is a babe. But strong meat belongeth to them that are of full age, even those who by reason of use have their senses exercised to discern both good and evil.

There again you have exactly the same thing. He wants to tell them about this doctrine concerning our Lord as the great High Priest, but he feels that he cannot do so because he estimates that they are not yet capable of receiving it.

This is, of course, an elementary point in connection with teaching. The first thing a teacher in any realm has to do is to assess the capacity of his hearers, his pupils, his students, whatever they are. This fundamental rule should be constantly in the mind of the preacher, and we need to be reminded of it constantly, and particularly when we are young. The chief fault of the young preacher is to preach to the people as we would like them to be, instead of as they are. This is more or less inevitable. He has been reading biographies of great preachers, or perhaps he has been reading the Puritans, and as a result has a picture in his mind, a kind of ideal picture of what preaching should be. He then proceeds to try to do that himself, forgetting that the people who listened to the Puritans—who sometimes preached for three hours at a time—had been trained to do that in various ways more or less for a century. I must not digress on this, but it seems to me that people often forget that the works of the major Puritans, which are most accessible to us, were written about the middle of the seventeenth century when Puritanism had been established for about a hundred years. The people listening to those sermons were a prepared people, trained and instructed and therefore capable of following the close reasoning and argumentation of these long sermons. If a young preacher today does not understand this point, and tries to preach as the Puritans preached, and preaches for a couple of hours, he will soon find that he will have no congregation to preach to. It is vitally important that the preacher should make an assessment of the people to whom he is preaching.

Let me give you an example which sounds ridiculous but which actually happened recently. A women's meeting was held each week in connection with a certain church in London. It was not for the women members of the church but for the poorer women in the district. It had served a useful purpose for years, and it was primarily evangelistic in nature. Different speakers were invited to address the meeting each week. The majority of the listeners were poor old women; the average age was tending to go up higher and higher because the younger women were busy in their homes and going out to work in various ways. But there they were, about forty to fifty came to the meeting each week. The problem of finding speakers became greater and greater but many were ready to help. One week a young professional man who was a member of the church was present to address them. He gave an address on 'The Trinity' to those old ladies! I tell this story in order to ridicule such a procedure. Here was a man, an intelligent trained professional man whom you would have thought would have some idea of addressing people; but he clearly had not given even a thought to that and probably had been reading an article or a book on the Trinity recently. But, of course, what he did was utterly useless. You do not give 'strong meat to babes', you give them milk. That is the principle which is taught both by the Apostle Paul and in the Epistle to the Hebrews.

But I must add something to that. While it is the duty and the business of the preacher to make an assessment of his congregation, he must be careful that this is a true assessment and an accurate one. This surely needs no emphasis. The danger arises both from the standpoint of the pulpit and of the pew. The pulpit may make a wrong assessment of the pew; and the pew may make a wrong assessment of itself. I have a feeling that both errors are much in evidence, and that this is one of the chief causes and explanations of our present position.

The main danger confronting the pulpit in this matter is to assume that all who claim to be Christians, and who think they are Christians, and who are members of the Church, are therefore of necessity Christians. This, to me, is the most fatal blunder of all; and certainly the commonest. It is assumed that because people are members of the Church that they are Christian. This is dangerous and wrong for this reason, that if you assume that, you will tend therefore, in all your services, to preach in a manner suited to Christian believers. Your messages will always be instructional, and the evangelistic element and note will be neglected, perhaps, almost entirely.

This is a very great and grievous fallacy. Let me give you reasons for saying that. I would start with my own personal experience. For many years I thought I was a Christian when in fact I was not. It was only later that I came to see that I had never been a Christian and became one. But I was a member of a church and attended my church and its services regularly. So anybody assuming, as most preachers did, that I was a Christian was making a false assumption. It was not a true assessment of my condition. What I needed was preaching that would convict me of sin and make me see my need, and bring me to true repentance and tell me something about regeneration. But I never heard that. The preaching we had was always based on the assumption that we were all Christians, that we would not have been there in the congregation unless we were Christians. This, I think, has been one of the cardinal errors of the Church especially in this present century.

But this has been reinforced many times in my experience as a preacher and as a pastor. I think I can say quite accurately that my most common experience in conversation with people who have come to me in my vestry to discuss the question of becoming members of the church, has been this. I have questioned them as to why they want to become members, and what their experience is and so on. The commonest answer I have had, particularly in London for over thirty years, has been something like this. These people—and quite frequently they were either undergraduates or young graduates—would tell me that they came up to London to the University from their home churches fully believing that they were Christians. They had no doubt about that, and either they had asked their home church, before coming up to London, where they should go on Sundays, or else they had been referred to us by their home church. They went on to tell me that having come in that way, and having listened to the preaching, and especially on Sunday nights, when, as I have already said my preaching was invariably evangelistic, the first thing they discovered was that they had never been Christians at all and that they were living on a false assumption. At first, some of them were honest enough to confess, they had been rather annoyed at this. They did not like it, and they had resented it; but that was the fact. Then, realising that though they did not like it, that this was the truth, they continued to come. This might go on perhaps for months, and they would pass through a period of repentance in great trouble about their souls. They were afraid to trust almost anything because, having previously assumed wrongly that they were Christians, they were now afraid of repeating the same error. Then eventually they had come to see the truth clearly and had experienced its power and become truly Christian. That has been my commonest experience in the ministry. It shows the complete and dangerous fallacy of assuming that anybody who comes to a service regularly must be a Christian.

Let me tell another story, a still more striking one. I am doing this simply to bring out this vital point. It was my pleasure and privilege to preach for nine Sundays in Canada, in Toronto, in 1932. I well remember being welcomed on the first Sunday morning by the minister of the church who, though on vacation, was still not out of town. He introduced me, and in responding to the welcome I thought it would be wise for me to indicate to the congregation my method as a preacher. I told the congregation that my method was to assume generally on Sunday morning that I was speaking to believers, to the saints, and that I would try to edify them; but that at night I would be preaching on the assumption that I was speaking to non-Christians as undoubtedly there would be many such there. In a sense I just said that in passing.

We went through that morning service, and at the close the minister asked if I would stand at the door with him to shake hands with people as they went out. I did so. We had shaken hands with a number of people when he suddenly whispered to me saying, 'You see that old lady who is coming along slowly. She is the most important member of this church. She is a very wealthy woman and the greatest supporter of the work.' He was, in other words, telling me to exercise what little charm I might possess to the maximum. I need not explain any further! Well, the old lady came along and we spoke to her, and I shall never forget what happened. It taught me a great lesson which I have never forgotten. The old lady said, 'Did I understand you to say that in the evening you would preach on the assumption that the people listening are not Christians and in the morning on the assumption that they are Christians?' 'Yes,' I said. 'Well,' she said, 'having heard you this morning I have decided to come tonight.' She had never been known to attend the evening service; never. She only attended in the morning. She said, 'I am coming tonight.' I cannot describe the embarrassment of the situation. I sensed that the minister standing by my side felt that I was ruining his ministry and bitterly regretted inviting me to occupy his pulpit! But the fact was that the old lady did come that Sunday night, and every Sunday night while I was there. I met her in her house in private conversation and found that she was most unhappy about her spiritual condition, that she did not know where she stood. She was a fine and most generous character, living an exemplary life. Everybody assumed—not only the minister but everybody else—that she was an exceptionally fine Christian; but she was not a Christian. This idea that because people are members of the church and attend regularly that they must be Christian is one of the most fatal assumptions, and I suggest that it mainly accounts for the state of the Church today. So we must be very careful at this point.

The same thing applies to, and the same wrong assumption tends to be made by, the listeners. Because such people assume that they are Christians they tend to resent preaching which assumes that they are not Christian, though it is what they need most of all. This again can be illustrated by a story. I knew a lady who left a certain chapel after listening to the preaching of a new minister for about a year. She gave her reason for doing so. She said, 'This man preaches to us as if we were sinners.' That was terrible! She was made to feel uncomfortable and forced to examine herself and to see herself truly; and she did not like it. She had been attending that church for nearly thirty years; but she showed that she was antagonistic to the Truth when really faced with it in a direct, personal way. She liked general expositions of Scripture, and sermons based on the Scriptures for believers; they did not hurt her, they did not trouble her, they did not examine her, they did not convict her. She revelled in that but she did not like preaching when it became personal and direct.

This is a very common attitude, and this is where we must be careful in this whole matter of assessment. I remember receiving a letter once from one of the more prominent leaders of a well-known body of evangelical Christians in London. I knew his name well but I had never met him. On opening the letter I recognised the name. He told me that he had been in the congregation at our church on the previous Sunday night, and that he had made a strange discovery. It was that it was possible for a believer of his age and standing to derive benefit from what was clearly and obviously an evangelistic service. He had assumed, he told me, all his life, that this was impossible, that when a believer like himself went on a Sunday evening all he had to do was to pray for the unconverted, that he must not expect to derive any benefit from it because he had already passed through that stage. In spite of that he had discovered to his great astonishment that the service had moved him and gripped him, had done something to him, and had given him something. Hitherto he had thought that that was not possible. He had made this discovery for the first time in his life and felt that he must write to let me know.

This, obviously, is a very serious matter, because it has such an influence on the preacher and what he does. How can we explain this false assumption? It seems to me that it arises from the fact that many people who think they are Christian, and who have accepted the teaching of the Scriptures intellectually, have never come under the power of the Word. They have never experienced its power, they have accepted a purely intellectual teaching. And because they have never really come under its power they have never truly repented. They may have known some kind of sorrow for sin, but that can be different from repentance. This is often the explanation of their position. The true believer always feels the power of the Word and can always be convicted by it. Belief in a sense is once and for ever, but in another sense it is not. There is something essentially wrong with a man who calls himself a Christian and who can listen to a truly evangelistic sermon without coming under conviction again, without feeling something of his own unworthiness, and rejoicing when he hears the Gospel remedy being presented. That is what had happened to that man who wrote to me. His heart was much sounder than his head and the teaching he had accepted.

If a man can listen to such a sermon without being touched or moved I take leave to query whether he is a Christian at all. It is inconceivable to me that a man who is a true believer can listen to a presentation of the exceeding sinfulness of sin and the glory of the Gospel, without being moved in two ways. One is to feel for a while, in view of what he knows about the plague of his own heart, that perhaps he is not a Christian at all; and, then, to rejoice in the glorious Gospel remedy which gives him deliverance. Many and many a time have I been told, at the close of such a service, something like this. A man, or a woman, would come in to see me and say, 'You know, if I had not been converted before I would certainly have been converted tonight.' I always like to hear that. That means that they have felt the power of the Gospel again, they have seen the whole thing again, and they have, as it were, almost gone through the experience of conversion again. What I am asserting is that there must of necessity be something wrong, radically wrong, with one who claims to be a Christian who does not come under the power of this glorious Gospel every time it is presented, and in whatever form.

In other words we must be very careful as preachers not to be guilty of a too-rigid classification of people saying, 'These are Christians, therefore . . .' You have to be very sure that they are Christians, for the tendency of many is to say, 'Yes, we became Christians as the result of a decision we took at an evangelistic meeting, and now, seeing that we are Christians, all we need is teaching and edification.' I contest that very strongly and urge that there should always be one evangelistic service in connection with each church every week. I would make this an absolute rule without any hesitation whatsoever. I do so, as I say, because I believe that this confusion is the main trouble today in the churches in every land.

I always remember something said to me by an old man many years ago. We were discussing together the sad decline in spiritual tone and spirituality of the Churches in Wales in particular. We were concerned most of all with the Presbyterian Church which had started in the eighteenth century as the result of the Evangelical Awakening—the Calvinistic Methodist Church. I had read the history of that great and glorious period, so I said to him, 'When did the transition take place from what one reads about in the early history and the first hundred years of this denomination, and what you and I know to be the situation now—when did this transition take place?' He replied, 'I have no hesitation in telling you that the answer is that it took place just after the Revival of 1859.' 'But how?' I asked. 'Well, in this way,' he said. 'That Revival was so powerful that it more or less swept everybody into the Church. Before that there had been a distinction between "the Church" and "the world". The tests of admission to membership had been very strict, with the result that prior to 1859 there were always a number of people attending public worship and preaching who were listeners and adherents only and had not become members of the Church.'

This is a most interesting and important point. How rarely does one find this in the Church today. But until about the middle of last century there were always listeners and adherents as well as members in most non-episcopal Churches. The change took place partly as the result of the great movement of the Spirit in revival, and the increasing tendency to regard the baptised children of church members as Christians. The result was that the preachers regarded all the listeners as Christians and stopped preaching evangelistically, and there was often no evangelistic service at all. It was assumed that everyone was a Christian, and the ministry was devoted entirely to edification, with the result that a generation grew up that had never known the power of the Gospel, and never really heard preaching which was likely to convict of sin. As I have said I personally belong to that generation. It was the second generation after the revival of 1859, and I discovered later that I had never really heard a truly convicting evangelistic sermon. I was received into the Church because I could give the right answers to various set questions; but I was never questioned or examined in an experimental sense. I cannot reprobate too strongly this tendency to assume that because people come to church that they therefore must be Christian, or that the children of Christians are of necessity Christians. Looking at it from another aspect I would say that one of the most exhilarating experiences in the life of a preacher is what happens when people whom everybody had assumed to be Christians are suddenly converted and truly become Christians. Nothing has a more powerful effect upon the life of a church than when that happens to a number of people.

I am urging that all the people who attend a church need to be brought under the power of the Gospel. The Gospel is not merely and only for the intellect; and if our preaching is always expository and for edification and teaching it will produce church members who are hard and cold, and often harsh and self-satisfied. I do not know of anything that is more likely to produce a congregation of Pharisees than just that. A further result of this wrong attitude is that such people only attend one service each Sunday; once is enough for them, they do not need any more! They generally attend on Sunday morning only; they have become 'once-ers' as they are called.

This is truly deplorable; and my first point is that it is to be traced to this wrong assessment of people on the part of the pulpit and the pew. Both agree in their diagnosis that these people are Christians, and so they never hear preaching of the type that will make sure that they really are. The way to correct this, as I have said, is to ensure that one service each week should be definitely evangelistic in a biblical sense.

That, of course, means that all this has to be explained clearly to the listeners. This is a part of our preaching, because, acting on this wrong assumption, many of these listeners will not come to the evangelistic service because they feel that they have no need of it, that it has nothing to give them.

This to me is of the very essence of the whole problem of the Church today. What do we say to such people? We must convince them of the importance of being present at every service of the church. Every service! Why? The first answer—and I have often used this argument and people have come to see it—is that if they are not present at every service they may well find one day that they were not present when something really remarkable took place.

This raises again the whole question of, What is preaching? I am referring once more to what I have called its essence, the power of the Spirit. I shall develop this further later. This is the all-important element that we must recapture in connection with our church services, the idea that you never know what is going to happen. If the preacher always knows exactly what is going to happen, in my view he should not be in a pulpit at all. The whole glory of the ministry is that you do not know what may happen. In a lecture you know what is happening, you are in control; but that is not the case when you are preaching. Suddenly, unexpectedly, this other element may break into a service—the touch of the power of the Spirit of God. It is the most glorious thing that can ever happen to any individual or company of people. So I say to these 'once-ers', if you do not come to every service you may live to find a day when people will tell you of an amazing occurrence in a service on a Sunday night or on a Sunday morning—and you were not there, you missed it. In other words we should create this spirit of expectation in the people and show them the danger of missing some wonderful 'times of refreshing . . . from the presence of the Lord' (Acts 3:19).

That should be followed by a question: Why is it that any Christian should not long for as much of this as he can possibly get? Surely this is quite unnatural. It is certainly un-scriptural. Take the way in which the Psalmist in Psalm 84 expresses his misery and sorrow because he could not go up with the others to the House of the Lord. 'How amiable are Thy tabernacles, O Lord of Hosts!' 'My soul longeth, even fainteth for the courts of the Lord: my heart and my flesh crieth out for the living God.' He thinks then of those who are having the privilege: 'Blessed are they that dwell in thy house; they will be still praising thee.' He thinks of them with envy because he cannot be with them. Nothing is comparable to being in the House of God. 'A day in thy courts is better than a thousand . . .' Surely this ought to be instinctive in the true Christian. There is something seriously wrong spiritually with anyone who claims to be a Christian who does not desire to have all that can be obtained from the ministry of the Church.

Or take another aspect of the same subject. I hear from many sources in many countries that there is an increasing tendency among congregations to dictate to the preacher as to the length of his sermon. I have been told by many young preachers that when they have arrived at a church to preach, they have been handed an Order of Service paper on which everything has been put down in detail and timed: 'Eleven o'clock, Call to worship—Twelve noon, Benediction'.

And as they demand one or two Scripture readings, several prayers, three or four hymns, a children's address, an anthem or solo, and time for the announcements and the receiving of an offering the sermon of necessity must be very brief.

Now why is this? Is there not something seriously wrong with such people? This is not their attitude to a play or some other programme on the television. The trouble there is that it ends too soon It is the same with a football match or a baseball match, or whatever else interests them—the pity is that these things come to an end so soon. But why the difference here? This is a most serious question. In those other realms they do not object to the length because they enjoy it, they like it, and they want more and more of it. Why then is it not the same with the Christian? I am again raising the question of assuming that these people are Christians simply because they come to the service at all. I am suggesting that if they put these time limits on sermons they are more or less confessing that they are not Christians, that they are lacking in spiritual life. Why is it also that so often they are listless in their listening? They often give the preacher the impression that he is allowed to preach by their leave, and only on condition that it will be brief. There are even some people who in a literal physical sense settle down to endure the sermon.

I recall that one of my predecessors at Westminster Chapel, John A. Hutton, to whom I have already referred, used to tell a very amusing story in this connection. He held this view that I am putting forward, that it is the pulpit that really determines the character of the pew and the listener. Good listeners are produced by good preaching. He used to tell this story. He was preaching in a church on one occasion, and as he was just announcing his text he saw that a man who was sitting far back in a corner of the church was settling down into the corner and actually putting his feet up on the seat—obviously settling down to sleep. Now John Hutton could not pass a thing like that, so he addressed this man directly. He said, 'Sir, I do not know you, but whoever you are, I do not think you are being quite fair.' He went on, 'If at the end of my sermon you are asleep, well then the blame will be mine, but, you know, you are not even giving me a chance; you are settling down to sleep even as I am giving out my text. You are not fair.'

It is undoubtedly true that many members of congregations come in such a frame of mind and with such an attitude. Indeed I have come to the conclusion during this last year, during my convalescence, and while sitting at the back of many congregations, that a number of people seem to go to a place of worship and to a service in order to go home! Their main idea seems to be to get out and to get home. Why do they go at all? That is the question, I think, that needs to be asked. Why this great anxiety for the service, and especially the sermon, to finish? There is only one conclusion to be drawn; these people need to be humbled. These people are lacking in spirituality, in a spiritual mind and outlook, and in spiritual understanding.

This is not simply a matter of opinion. I say this on the basis of comparing them with what we are told about the early Christians in Acts 2, which is surely the norm of what we should all be. This is what we are told: 'And they continued stedfastly in the apostles' doctrine and fellowship, and in breaking of bread, and in prayers.' 'And they, continuing daily'—daily!—'with one accord in the temple, and breaking bread from house to house, did eat their meat with gladness and singleness of heart, Praising God, and having favour with all the people. And the Lord added to the church daily such as should be saved.'

Here were Christians who met every day for preaching and teaching and instruction. Not only on Sunday, or once on Sunday, and anxious to get home as soon as they could, hoping it would be short, and annoyed with the preacher if it is not short. 'Daily!' 'Continued stedfastly, daily.' That was what they wanted and enjoyed above everything else. And of course that is inevitable in the true Christian. The Apostle Peter puts it thus: 'As newborn babes, desire the sincere milk of the word, that ye may grow thereby' (1 Peter 2: 2). The new-born babe in Christ does desire the sincere milk of the word. If he does not he is ill, he is marasmic, he is in a bad state, and you had better take him to see a doctor. Nature cries out for the nutriment that is appropriate to it; and if you know people whom you think are Christians, and who themselves think they are Christians, but who do not want the preaching of the Word, and do not revel in it, and rejoice in it, and want as much as they can possibly get of it, I suggest that the right question to ask about them is, 'Are these people Christians?' This behaviour is contrary to nature. They do not conform to what we are told about Christians in the New Testament. They revelled in it, they gloried in it; and they were a praising people. They did not attend their meetings mechanically, they did not do so as a matter of duty, they did not do it merely because it was the expected thing, saying to themselves, 'Well, I have been to the service, I have done my duty, and now I can write my family letters and spend the rest of the day reading and doing various other things which I enjoy.' Not at all. They could not get enough of it.

The New Testament preachers, the Apostles, did not have to go round the houses and urge people to come to the services. The difficulty confronting the Apostles was to send them home! They wanted to spend the whole of their time in this atmosphere; and the more they received the more they wanted. Daily! Steadfastly! You could not keep them away. And this has been the characteristic of the Church always in every period of Reformation and of Revival. John Calvin used to preach every day in Geneva. Every day! And people were thirsting to hear him, and the others. This was true also of Martin Luther. This has always been true in every period in the life of the Church when she has been truly functioning as the Church. My contention is that the people do not attend places of worship today because of this wrong assessment which leads to the wrong type of preaching. Either the preaching is wrong, or the listening is wrong, or, most likely, both are wrong.

I would put my exhortation to these listeners at its very lowest by telling them that if they have no other reason for being present at every service of the Church, that they should at any rate realise that there is great value in numbers. Look at it like this. Think of a man who is not a Christian, a man of the world who suddenly finds himself in great trouble. He has a terrible problem and no one seems able to help him, Walking along the streets aimlessly he happens to pass a church, a place of worship, and he decides to go in wondering whether he will find help there. Now if he finds just a little handful of people there, people who look miserable and, as the preacher begins to preach, keep looking at their watches repeatedly, he will come to the conclusion that there is nothing in it. He will conclude that this handful of people do this sort of thing probably because they were brought up to do so, and have not thought sufficiently about it even to stop doing it. It obviously does not mean much to them; they are doing it clearly as a matter of routine or tradition, or out of a sense of duty. The poor man will be entirely put off; it will not help him at all. But if he goes into a church which is packed with people and becomes conscious of a spirit of anticipation, and sees a people who are eagerly looking forward to something, he will say, 'There is something in this. What is it that brings these people here, this great crowd of people?' So he is interested immediately and begins to pay close attention to everything. The very fact of a crowd of people doing this has often been used by the Spirit of God to lead people to conviction and conversion. I have known this happen many times.

The trouble is that so many do not stop to think about these matters. They just go to the service as a matter of duty, and having done so feel better because they have done their duty. That attitude to a service obviously expresses itself and visitors sense this and draw the conclusion that there is not much value in it if this is the attitude of the regular attenders. But, conversely, when they enter a place of worship where people attend because they feel that God meets them there, this also will transmit itself to them in some strange way that one does not quite understand. So they will feel that something real is happening, and it may well be used of God to bring them to a knowledge of the truth.

What all this amounts to is that what is needed in the pulpit is authority, great authority. The pew is not in a position to determine the message or method or dictate to the pulpit. I would lay that down as an absolute. The pulpit is to make its assessment, and it is to do so with authority. The greatest need in the Church today is to restore this authority to the pulpit.

How is this to be done? How can this authority be restored? We have to be very careful here for this has often been the problem before and has often been faced in the wrong way. That was the case with the Tractarian Movement of the last century connected with the names of Keble, Cardinal Newman, E. B. Pusey, Cardinal Manning and others. They were concerned about this question of authority. They were conscious of the fact that the pulpit, the Church, had lost her authority and they began to search for a way of regaining and restoring that. But they, from the Protestant standpoint, took an entirely wrong step. They said that the way to restore authority was to remove the preacher or minister farther away from the people. The way to do this was to put vestments of various descriptions upon him to emphasise the priestly and the mysterious element in his functioning. In other words they tried to build up his authority in this outward spectacular manner, they called him a priest and claimed that he had special authority through the sacraments and so on. Let us grant that the motive was good, but they took a false step which led in the end to a depreciation of preaching and to a false emphasis upon sacraments and in many cases upon the mere aesthetic aspect of worship.

As for the non-episcopal churches in the last century it seems to me that they also made a false move; they believed that the key to authority in the pulpit was scholarship. Now scholarship is obviously of great value and importance; but scholarship alone will not give authority to the preacher. It will give him standing among other scholars and make him attractive to 'the wise'; but that is not what is needed primarily in the pulpit. The prime and greatest need in the pulpit is spiritual authority. I have already said that the abler a man is the better preacher he should be. Knowledge and culture are invaluable but only on condition that they are used as servants and handmaidens; in and of themselves they do not give authority. There is but one thing that gives a preacher authority, and that is that he be 'filled with the Holy Spirit'. The history of the Church throughout the centuries, and especially during the last hundred years proves and substantiates what I am saying.

At this point I would add a word which may come as a surprise to some, and indeed sound almost ridiculous in view of what I have been saying. I believe it is good and right for a preacher to wear a gown in the pulpit. How do I reconcile that with what I have just been saying about spiritual authority? The gown to me is a sign of the call, a sign of the fact that a man has been 'set apart' to do this work. It is no more than that, but it is that. Of course, I must hastily add that while I believe in wearing a gown in the pulpit I do not believe in wearing a hood on the gown! The wearing of a hood calls attention to the man and his ability, not to his call. It is not a sign of office but a sign of the man's scholastic achievements; so one has a B.D. gown, another a D.D. gown, another an M.A. and so on. That is but confusion; but above all it distracts attention from the spiritual authority of the preacher. Wear a gown but never a hood!

In these varied ways I am therefore asserting what many modern intellectuals, who rather object to authority in the pulpit, and who just want the simple reading of the Scriptures with a few comments and discussions, need to be told—that that man in the pulpit is there not because he is abler than others, but because God has given him certain special gifts which He has not given to others. He is there because he has had this 'call', which has been confirmed by the Church. They should not feel that they are in competition with him, and query his right to address them in an authoritative manner because they have as much knowledge as he has, and can read the same books as he does. All that may be quite true, they may well be even abler, and have more knowledge; but still this man has been set apart. Why? Not because of his natural gifts alone, but specifically because of what God has done to him. That is what gives him this authority that is not given to all; and if a Christian man, however able and learned and knowledgeable he may be, is not ready to sit down and listen to this man whom God has called, and appointed, and sent to perform this task, with joy and with keen anticipation, I take leave to query whether that man is a Christian at all. It is a matter of spiritual authority, not intellectual or cultural authority; and all should recognise this and therefore be ready to listen to the preacher.

*   *   *

This brings us to the end of this general consideration of what preaching is, this 'act' of preaching. In order to make it complete I must add another word which may sound most un-spiritual after what I have been saying. But it is really important; and that is, the building. After all the congregation is in a building, sitting and listening to the man who is preaching to them. The building is therefore of importance. It can help or hinder the carrying out of the purpose of their coming. The building has its importance, but it must not be overdone. The Roman Catholics and their various successors and imitators have overdone this. One can recognise that at their best they were animated by excellent motives. The great and imposing and ornate buildings that they erected—the cathedrals and so on—were an attempt to give expression to their sense of the glory and greatness of God Whom they desired to worship 'in the beauty of holiness'. But they so over-did that as to make such places almost impossible from the standpoint of preaching, and so they became guilty of neglecting the most important thing of all. A church building tells us a great deal about the people who built it.

A most interesting change took place about the middle of the last century, not only in Britain but also in the U.S.A. Until then the churches, the chapels, were generally very simple buildings. They were called 'meeting-houses' because they were built in order that people might meet together to worship God and to listen to the preaching of the Gospel. What was needed was a place that was appropriate and suitable for that end. But towards the middle of the last century a change came in and they began to erect these great and ornate buildings in the mock-Gothic style. Vast sums of money were spent in order to produce these high vaulted buildings with transepts. The emphasis was on beauty and magnificence. How sadly did these people betray themselves. They began to say, 'We Nonconformists and Free-Churchmen are now becoming respectable. We are becoming more educated and cultured and taking our place in society with the learned and the ruling classes.' So they began to imitate the Anglican and the Catholic church buildings, and to introduce great domes and pillars and other ornamentations which render most buildings acoustically impossible. The idea was to show how they had advanced from illiteracy and the coarseness of evangelicalism, but what it actually proclaimed was a tragic decline in spirituality. As the building becomes more ornate the spirituality invariably declines Buildings tell us a great deal about the people who meet in them and delight in them, still more about the people who built them.

What, then, should we desiderate in a building? Surely the first absolute essential is good acoustics. This cannot be over-emphasised. I speak out of considerable experience over many years of preaching in church buildings in various countries. It sounds almost incredible but it is the simple truth to say that I cannot think of a single instance of a new building put up in Great Britain since the last war—many had to be rebuilt because of bombing—I cannot think of a single one where they have not already had to put in a public address system. Why? Not because they are big buildings—some of them are quite small buildings—but because the acoustics are hopeless. Why should this be so? Because the architects, generally speaking, know nothing about acoustics. They are interested in beauty, in the appearance, they are interested in lines and curves and so on; they know nothing about acoustics, they know nothing about preaching. The first essential in a church building is that it should have good acoustic properties. How do you ensure that? The one great rule, the essential rule in that respect is a flat ceiling. Any variation from that, however slight, always produces trouble. Curves and angles are an abomination. Flat ceilings should be compulsory. Our forefathers knew this. They built square buildings with flat ceilings, and the result was, and is, that however big they might be, they are acoustically almost perfect. It is not the size of the building that matters; the acoustics are mainly determined by the ceiling. Alcoves are ruinous, and it is a mistake also to have too high a building. That is where the tendency to imitate the Catholics and the Anglicans has done such harm to preaching. The presence of sounding boards above so many of their pulpits bears eloquent testimony to what I am saying. Eloquent? Perhaps I should have said 'reverberating'! The preacher must be free. To have to concentrate on voice production will detract from the efficacy of his preaching. He should be free, and the character of the building plays an important part in this.

What about the pulpit? Put it in the centre; do not push it to the side somewhere. Preaching is the greatest act in connection with the Church and her function; it is what is needed above everything else. So put the pulpit in the centre. What about the height of the pulpit? It is important that it should be in the right relative height in relation to the listeners. The tendency now is to have low pulpits; that is because the designers do not know what preaching is! Do not misunderstand this, but, architecturally, mechanically, the preacher should preach down to his congregation always. The pulpit should therefore always be at an appropriate height. If there is a gallery in the church the test is that when the preacher stands in the pulpit his eyes should be more or less level with the people sitting in the front row of the gallery facing him. If they are higher he will have to bend his head backwards when looking at them and that is bad for his throat which should always be relaxed. Then, the actual height of the reading desk in the pulpit is again important. I found it extremely difficult to preach in a certain church recently because the reading desk was about level with the upper part of my chest. I felt as if I was struggling constantly to do the breast stroke in swimming. From the standpoint of preaching the situation was utterly ridiculous. I need scarcely say that it was a new building. You cannot preach when you are confined in a kind of box. The preacher is not a prisoner in a dock. He must have freedom; and he must insist upon having it.

Let me end this lecture with a story to illustrate this point. I remember going to preach in a very big chapel in North Wales almost forty years ago. The minister of that church was well known as what was called a 'popular preacher'. I shall never forget what he did in his vestry before the service. He received me in a very gentlemanly, indeed lordly manner, for which he was famous, and then he proceeded to eye and to examine me up and down. I wondered whether I was not sufficiently well dressed to please him, or whether there was something seriously wrong that I was not aware of. He then came right on to me and touched me in the region of my epigastrium. By now I began to wonder what was happening. He then said partly to me and also to a number of deacons who were there with us, 'I think two platforms will be sufficient.' The explanation of this strange procedure I subsequently discovered was this. His chapel was a large building that seated up to 1400 people. He knew it was likely to be full and he was anxious that the little preacher should be assisted in every way to command such a congregation. He said, 'You know, no man can preach if the desk in front of him is higher than roughly the pit of his stomach.' So, in the interests of visiting preachers, he had got his people to fix three platforms into the front of the pulpit. A very tall man would not need an extra platform at all, the other man might need one platform, another would need two, some indeed even three. He thus made sure that each preacher should be in the same relative position with respect to the congregation. This may appear to be ridiculous, but as one who has suffered in many pulpits I can assure you that it has real importance. It is the Oliver Cromwell principle, is it not—'Trust in God, and keep your powder dry'.

CHAPTER NINE

The Preparation of the Preacher

WE COME NOW to a new aspect of our study of preaching or the preacher and preaching. We have been looking at what takes place when a man stands in a pulpit and preaches in a service in a church. We had to start with that. There is the fact, that is what is taking place; and we have therefore considered what preaching is, in general, and the preparation of the man who is preaching.

We now turn to a different aspect of the matter. So far our approach has been general. We now come to the specific matter of how this man actually prepares for this week by week. I trust that my broad division of the subject is clear. As I view this all-important matter we must be clear and right in our understanding of the whole before we come down to any particulars. We have now reached that point and so can look at this man, who is conscious of his call, preparing himself for the exercising of this ministry of preaching.

How does he do so? What is the process of preparation? I would lay it down as a first postulate that he is always preparing. I mean that literally. That does not mean to say that he is always sitting at a desk; but he is always preparing. As it is true to say that there is no such thing as a holiday in the spiritual realm, I always feel that in the same sense the preacher never has a holiday. He has times of absence from his normal work, he has vacations, but because of the nature and character of his calling he is never free from his work. Everything he does, or that happens to him, he finds to be relevant to this great work, and is therefore a part of his preparation.

But turning to certain specific matters, the preacher's first, and the most important task is to prepare himself, not his sermon. Any man who has been any length of time in the ministry will agree whole-heartedly with me concerning this. It is something that one has to learn by experience. At first one tends to think that the great thing is to prepare the sermon—and the sermon, as I have been saying, does need most careful preparation. But altogether more important is the preparation of the preacher himself.

In a sense the preacher is a man of one thing. There are those who have said in the past, like John Wesley, that they had become 'a man of one Book'. While that is true, speaking generally, it is even more true that the preacher is a man of one thing. This is the thing to which he is called, and it is the great passion of his life.

So what does he do about this? The first great rule is that he must be very careful to maintain a general discipline in his life. There are many dangers in the life of a minister. Unlike men in professions and in business he is not tied of necessity by office hours and other conventions, or with conditions determined outside himself; he is, as compared with them, his own master. I mean in reference to men. He is not his own master, of course, with reference to God. But there is this obvious distinction between the life of a minister and the life of most other men, and because things are in his own hands he must realise that there are certain serious dangers and temptations which confront him in a very special manner. One of these is the danger of just frittering away your time, particularly in the morning. You start with the newspaper, and it is very easy to spend a great deal of time on this, quite unconsciously. Then there are weekly magazines and journals, and interruptions on the telephone and so on. You may well find that your morning has gone whether you are working in your home or in an office in your church. So I have felt always, and increasingly with the years, that one of the great rules for a preacher is to safeguard the mornings. Make an absolute rule of this. Try to develop a system whereby you are not available on the telephone in the morning; let your wife or anyone else take messages for you, and inform the people who are telephoning that you are not available. One literally has to fight for one's life in this sense!

How often has a morning's work in the study been interrupted by a phone call about some matter of no urgency, sometimes about a preaching engagement in two years' time! That is the kind of thing that happens. You can deal with that situation in one of two ways. One is to ask the good man to write to you so that you may consider the matter carefully. But the second, and the more effective way, is not to answer the telephone yourself at all in the morning, and to give instructions to someone to say on your behalf, 'Would you mind telephoning again at such-and-such a time' —lunch time or some other time when you have finished your morning's work. Such interruptions are really bad; the only possible good they can do is to help in the matter of one's sanctification! Do not allow even the affairs of the Church to interfere with this. Safeguard your mornings! They must be given up to this great task of preparing for your work in the pulpit.

I want to add a word here which to me is important, but which may not be acceptable to all. I am an opponent of universal set rules for all. Nothing is more important than that a man should get to know himself. I include in that that he should get to know himself physically as well as temperamentally and in other respects. I say this because there are those who would prescribe a programme for a preacher and minister; they tell him when to get up in the morning, what to do before breakfast, and what to do later and so on. They do not hesitate to draw up systems and programmes and to advocate these, and indeed almost to suggest that if a man does not follow such a programme that he is a sinner and a failure. I have always been an opponent of such ideas for this reason, that we are all different, and that you cannot lay down a programme of this nature for everybody.

Let me illustrate what I mean. We live in the body, and our bodies differ from case to case. We also have different temperaments and natures, so you cannot lay down universal rules. Let me use an illustration from the realm of dietetics. This has always been the subject of much discussion. What should one eat? What diet should one follow? There are always those ready to come forward who have worked out and advocate a kind of universal diet. Everybody should be on this diet, and if you go on to this diet you will never have any more trouble. There is one final answer to all that. I hold that the first rule of dietetics is simply that 'Jack Spratt could eat no fat, his wife could eat no lean'. That is just sheer fact. Jack Spratt was so constituted that he could not digest fat. He had not decided that; he was born like that. This is a matter of the metabolic processes of the body which one does not determine. His wife was entirely different; she could not digest lean meat, but thrived on fat. Well now, to prescribe a common diet for Jack Spratt and his wife is obviously just sheer nonsense.

The same principle, I maintain, applies on a higher level also. Some of us are slow starters in the morning; others wake up fresh and brimful of energy in the morning, like a dog at the leash, waiting to go to work. We do not determine this; it is something constitutional. It depends on many factors, partly, if not chiefly, on blood pressure and such matters as your nervous constitution, the balance of your ductless glands, etc. All these factors come in. I argue therefore that our first business is to get to know ourselves, get to know how you, with your particular constitution, work. Get to know when you are at your best and how to handle yourself. Having done so, do not allow anyone to impose mechanical rules upon you or to dictate to you how you should work and divide up your day. Work out your own programme; you know when you can do your best work. If you do not do so you will soon find that it is possible for you to sit at a desk—according to the rules and regulations—for a couple of hours with a book open in front of you, and turn its pages, but actually absorb practically nothing. Perhaps later on in the day you could do much more in half an hour than you have tried to do in the two hours in the morning. That is the kind of thing I mean.

This means that this question of discipline is thrown right back on to the man himself. Nobody can tell him what to do. What controls everything is his realisation that if he is to be what he should be, if he is to be a true preacher, a spiritually minded man who is concerned about ministering to the glory of God and the edification and salvation of souls, he must do this. That should compel him to exercise this discipline. If he has the right motive and the right objective, if he is truly called, he will be so anxious to do all he has to do in the most effective manner that he will take the trouble to find out how best to order and organise himself and his day. I have known many men who have got into difficulties because they have had a system imposed upon them which was not suited to them.

*   *   *

I approach the next matter with great diffidence, much hesitation, and a sense of utter unworthiness. I suppose we all fail at this next point more than anywhere else; that is in the matter of prayer. Prayer is vital to the life of the preacher. Read the biographies, and the auto-biographies of the greatest preachers throughout the centuries and you will find that this has always been the great characteristic of their lives. They were always great men of prayer, and they spent considerable time in prayer. I could quote many examples but I must refrain as there are so many, and they are well known. These men found that this was absolutely essential, and that it became increasingly so as they went on.

I have always hesitated to deal with this subject. I have preached on prayer when it has come in a passage through which I have been working; but I have never presumed to produce a book on prayer, or even a booklet. Certain people have done this in a very mechanical manner, taking us through the different aspects, and classifying it all. It all seems so simple. But prayer is not simple. There is an element of discipline in prayer, of course, but it surely cannot be dealt with in that way because of its very nature. All I would say is this—and again I am speaking here from personal experience—that once more it is very important for one to know one's self in this matter. Whether this is a sign of a lack of deep spirituality or not I do not know—I do not think it is—but I confess freely that I have often found it difficult to start praying in the morning.

I have come to learn certain things about private prayer. You cannot pray to order. You can get on your knees to order; but how to pray? I have found nothing more important than to learn how to get oneself into that frame and condition in which one can pray. You have to learn how to start yourself off, and it is just here that this knowledge of yourself is so important. What I have generally found is that to read something which can be characterised in general as devotional is of great value. By devotional I do not mean something sentimental, I mean something with a true element of worship in it. Notice that I do not say that you should start yourself in prayer by always reading the Scriptures; because you can have precisely the same difficulty there. Start by reading something that will warm your spirit. Get rid of a coldness that may have developed in your spirit. You have to learn how to kindle a flame in your spirit, to warm yourself up, to give yourself a start. It is comparable, if you like, to starting a car when it is cold. You have to learn how to use a spiritual choke. I have found it most rewarding to do that, and not to struggle vainly. When one finds oneself in this condition, and that it is difficult to pray, do not struggle in prayer for the time being, but read something that will warm and stimulate you, and you will find that it will put you into a condition in which you will be able to pray more freely.

But I am not suggesting for a moment—quite the reverse—that your praying should be confined only to the morning when you start your work in your study. Prayer should be going on throughout the day. Prayer need not of necessity be long; it can be brief, just an ejaculation at times is a true prayer. That is, surely, what the Apostle Paul means in his exhortation in 1 Thessalonians 5:17, 'Pray without ceasing'. That does not mean that you should be perpetually on your knees, but that you are always in a prayerful condition. As you are walking along a road, or while you are working in your study, you turn frequently to God in prayer.

Above all—and this I regard as most important of all—always respond to every impulse to pray. The impulse to pray may come when you are reading or when you are battling with a text. I would make an absolute law of this—always obey such an impulse. Where does it come from? It is the work of the Holy Spirit; it is a part of the meaning of, 'Work out your own salvation with fear and trembling. For it is God which worketh in you both to will and to do of his good pleasure' (Phil. 2:12-13). This often leads to some of the most remarkable experiences in the life of the minister. So never resist, never postpone it, never push it aside because you are busy. Give yourself to it, yield to it; and you will find not only that you have not been wasting time with respect to the matter with which you are dealing, but that actually it has helped you greatly in that respect. You will experience an ease and a facility in understanding what you were reading, in thinking, in ordering matter for a sermon, in writing, in everything, which is quite astonishing. Such a call to prayer must never be regarded as a distraction; always respond to it immediately, and thank God if it happens to you frequently.

From every standpoint the minister, the preacher, must be a man of prayer. This is constantly emphasised in the Pastoral Epistles and elsewhere, and, as I say, it is confirmed abundantly in the long history of the Church, and especially in the lives of the outstanding preachers. John Wesley used to say that he thought very little of a man who did not pray four hours every day. Nothing stands out so clearly likewise in the lives of people like David Brainerd and Jonathan Edwards, Robert Murray McCheyne and a host of other saints. That is why one is so humbled as one reads the stories of such men.

* * *

That brings us to the next essential in the preacher's life—the reading of the Bible. This is obviously something that he does every day regularly. My main advice here is: Read your Bible systematically. The danger is to read at random, and that means that one tends to be reading only one's favourite passages. In other words one fails to read the whole Bible. I cannot emphasise too strongly the vital importance of reading the whole Bible. I would say that all preachers should read through the whole Bible in its entirety at least once every year. You can devise your own method for doing this, or you can use one of the methods devised by others. I remember how after I had worked out a scheme for myself and the members of my church in my early years in the ministry, I then came across the scheme that Robert Murray McCheyne worked out for the members of his church in Dundee. It is in his biography by Andrew Bonar. By following that scheme of Robert Murray McCheyne you read four chapters of the Bible every day, and by so doing you read the Old Testament once, but the Psalms and the New Testament twice, each year. Unlike many modern schemes he did not just pick out little sections, or a few verses or small paragraphs here and there, and thus take many years to go through the whole Bible, and in some cases omit certain passages altogether. The whole object of his scheme is to get people to go right through the Scriptures every year omitting nothing. That should be the very minimum of the preacher's Bible reading.

I have found this to be one of the most important things of all. Then, having done that, you can decide to work your way through one particular book, with commentaries or any aids that you may choose to employ. The reading I have been describing so far has been general reading; but now you proceed to study one particular portion, one of the chapters you have been reading, if you like, in detail and carefully with all the aids that you can find, and with your knowledge of the original languages and all else.

I would emphasise this yet more strongly. One of the most fatal habits a preacher can ever fall into is to read his Bible simply in order to find texts for sermons. This is a real danger; it must be recognised and fought and resisted with all your might. Do not read the Bible to find texts for sermons, read it because it is the food that God has provided for your soul, because it is the Word of God, because it is the means whereby you can get to know God. Read it because it is the bread of life, the manna provided for your soul's nourishment and well-being.

The Preparation of the Preacher

The preacher, I say, does not read his Bible in order to find texts; but as he reads his Bible in this way—as indeed all Christians should—he will suddenly find as he is reading that a particular statement stands out, and as it were hits him, and speaks to him, and immediately suggests a sermon to him.

Here, I want to say something that I regard as in many ways the most important discovery I have made in my life as a preacher. I had to discover it for myself, and all to whom I have introduced it have always been most grateful for it. When you are reading your Scriptures in this way—it matters not whether you have read little or much—if a verse stands out and hits you and arrests you, do not go on reading. Stop immediately, and listen to it. It is speaking to you, so listen to it and speak to it. Stop reading at once, and work on this statement that has struck you in this way. Go on doing so to the point of making a skeleton of a sermon. This verse or statement has spoken to you, it has suggested a message to you. The danger at that point I had to discover is to say to oneself, 'Ah yes, that is good, I will remember that', and then to go on with the reading. Then you find yourself towards the end of the week without a sermon for the Sunday, without even a text, and you say to yourself, 'Now what was that that I was reading the other day? Oh yes, it was this verse in that chapter.' You then turn back to it and find to your dismay that it says nothing at all to you; you cannot recapture the message. That is why I say that whenever anything strikes you you must stop immediately and work out a skeleton of a sermon in your mind. But do not stop even at that: Put it down on paper.

For many many years I have never read my Bible without having a scribbling-pad either on my table or in my pocket; and the moment anything strikes me or arrests me I immediately pull out my pad. A preacher has to be like a squirrel and has to learn how to collect and store matter for the future days of winter. So you not only work out your skeleton, you put it down on paper, because otherwise you will not remember it. You think you will, but you will soon discover that it is not so. The principle involved here is precisely the one that operates with regard to examinations. We all know what it is to sit and listen to a lecture and to hear the lecturer saying certain things. As you listen you say, 'Yes, all right, I know that.' Then later you go to the examination hall and you have to answer a question on that very matter, and you suddenly find that you do not know much about it. You thought you did, but you do not. So the rule is, whenever anything strikes you put it down on paper. The result is that you will soon find that you have accumulated a little pile of skeletons—skeletons of sermons—in this way. Then you will be truly rich.

I have known ministers to be frantic on a Saturday with no texts or sermons for the Sunday, and trying desperately to get hold of something. That is simply because they have not practised what I am advocating. This is, I would say, if I had to single out one thing as being more important than anything else in the life of a preacher, this is beyond all question on the practical level the most important of all. I remember once that, looking through my pile of skeletons just before leaving for my summer vacation, I happened to notice that there were ten skeletons bearing on the same theme. I there and then arranged them in order and so knew that I had a series of ten consecutive sermons ready for my return. In a sense I no longer needed the holiday!

Next in order I would say is—and I cannot think of a better term though I do not like it in some ways because it has been so abused— 'devotional reading'. I do not mean by that what are called devotional commentaries. I abominate 'devotional' commentaries. I do not want other people to do my devotions for me; yet I cannot think of a better term here. I am thinking of a type of reading which will help you in general to understand and enjoy the Scriptures, and to prepare you for the pulpit. This type of reading comes next to the Scriptures. What is it? I would not hesitate to put into this category the reading of the Puritans. That is precisely what they do for us. Those men were preachers, they were practical, experimental preachers, who had a great pastoral interest and care for the people. So as you read them you find that they not only give knowledge and information, they at the same time do something to you. Again I would emphasise that it is most important that the preacher should know not only himself in general but also his particular moods and states and conditions. The preacher should never be moody; but he will have varying moods. No man can tell what he will feel like tomorrow morning; you do not control that. Our business is to do something about these changing moods and not to allow ourselves to become victims of them. You are not exactly the same two days running, and you have to treat yourself according to your varying conditions. So you will have to discover what is the most appropriate reading for yourself in these varying states.

You will find, I think, in general, that the Puritans are almost invariably helpful. I must not go into this overmuch, but there are Puritans and Puritans! John Owen on the whole is difficult to read; he was a highly intellectual man. But there were Puritan writers who were warmer and more direct and more experimental. I shall never cease to be grateful to one of them called Richard Sibbes who was balm to my soul at a period in my life when I was overworked and badly overtired, and therefore subject in an unusual manner to the onslaughts of the devil. In that state and condition to read theology does not help, indeed it may be well-nigh impossible; what you need is some gentle tender treatment for your soul. I found at that time that Richard Sibbes, who was known in London in the early seventeenth century as 'The Heavenly Doctor Sibbes' was an unfailing remedy. His books *The Bruised Reed* and *The Soul's Conflict* quietened, soothed, comforted, encouraged and healed me. I pity the preacher who does not know the appropriate remedy to apply to himself in these various phases through which his spiritual life must inevitably pass.

This may sound strange to some, even wrong. You may have a theoretical outlook; you have not been in the ministry and you know nothing of its problems and cares and trials. The Apostle Paul knew what it was to experience 'without were fightings, within were fears'. He knew what it was to be 'cast down' and 'in great conflict' and to be in the midst of a great fight; and any minister worth his salt is bound to know this. 'The care of all the churches', says the Apostle elsewhere. All these various factors—problems with people, problems with yourself, physical states and conditions—lead to this kind of variation in the level of one's spiritual experience. This has also been the testimony of the saints throughout the centuries. I am always very distrustful of any Christian who tells me that he or she knows nothing about such variations. There is a chorus which says, 'And now I am happy all the day.' I do not believe that; it is not true. There will be times when you will be unhappy. There are these states and conditions of the soul, and the sooner you learn how to deal with them, and how to handle them, the better it will be for you and for the people to whom you preach.

Under this same heading I would put the reading of sermons. I must be careful about this. I have already indicated that there are sermons and sermons, and that the date at which they were published is somewhat important. I can simply testify that in my experience the help that I derived in my early years in the ministry from reading the sermons of Jonathan Edwards was immeasurable. And, of course not only his sermons, but also his account of that Great Awakening, that great religious Revival that took place in America in the eighteenth century, and his great *The Religious Affections*. All that was invaluable because Edwards was an expert in dealing with the states and conditions of the soul. He dealt in a very practical manner with problems arising in a pastoral ministry among people who were passing through the various phases of spiritual experience. This is invaluable to the preacher. The preacher has thus to choose his reading judiciously, not only for the sake of his own soul but also that he may be able to help others, not only directly but also in their reading. Much harm is often done by advising people to read the wrong type of book—you can make them worse instead of better. If a man is already slightly melancholic, and tends to morbidity and introspection, and you give him a book to read that is mainly designed to produce conviction of sin and to awaken and alarm, you may well drive him mad. He does not need that, he needs encouragement and positive instruction at that point; and vice versa. So you have to know what to read for yourself, and also for others. I leave it at that. There is ample material; indeed the preacher's great difficulty is to find sufficient time for reading; it is a constant battle.

Time must be found for reading, and we turn now to the more purely intellectual type of reading. The first is theology. There is no greater mistake than to think that you finish with theology when you leave a seminary. The preacher should continue to read theology as long as he is alive. The more he reads the better, and there are many authors and different systems to be studied. I have known men in the ministry, and men in various other walks of life who stop reading when they finish their training. They think they have acquired all they need; they have their lecture notes, and nothing further is necessary. The result is that they vegetate and become quite useless. Keep on reading; and read the big works. I have many reasons for saying that. We shall return to it later.

Then I come back again to what I emphasised when considering the training of the preacher—the importance of reading Church history. That must never be regarded as just a subject to be studied for examination purposes; it is of much greater value to the preacher than to the student. And he needs to be reminded constantly of the great facts. In exactly the same way one should continue to read biographies and the journals of men of God, especially these men who have been greatly used as preachers—Whitefield, the Wesleys and so on. Keep on with this; it is never ending. The more you read along those lines the better equipped you will be. All this, remember, comes under the heading of the preparation of yourself.

Next in order I would put apologetic reading. I mean by that that there are fashions in theology and philosophy; they come and go. It is the business of the preacher to be acquainted with all this, so he will have to read some of these books. He cannot read them all because there are too many of them, far too many; but he will have to read some of them. Then there are questions connected with science, where science seems to come into conflict with faith and with the teaching of the Scriptures. All these matters have to be considered. Then, of course, there is psychology and its particularly subtle attacks on the Faith.

Now no one man can be expert on everything; but he has to try to keep up to date and abreast of all this as best he can. So he must read about these matters so that he may know what is happening. So far I have been thinking mainly in terms of books. But in addition there are the journals and periodicals, not only those that belong to one's own denomination, but others that are relevant to the work, and especially in these ecumenical days. All this is necessary to help the preacher to make an assessment of the people who are going to listen to him. He must know something about their background and their outlook, and what they are thinking, and what they are reading, and the influences that are being brought to bear upon them. People in their innocence and ignorance are still ready to listen to plausible speakers and to believe anything they read in a newspaper or popular journal, and it is our business to help them and to protect them. We are shepherds, we are pastors, and we are to look after and care for these people who have been committed to our charge. It is our business therefore to equip ourselves for that great task.

Before I go on to other types of reading I would emphasise strongly the all-importance of maintaining a balance in your reading. I cannot stress this too much. Because of our natural differences we all have our prejudices and preferences, so there is the type of man who spends the whole of his time reading theology, another reading philosophy, another psychology; they tend to read practically nothing else. This is really dangerous, and the way to counteract it is to prescribe balanced reading for yourself. What I mean is this. Read theology, as I say, but always balance it, not only with Church history but with biographies and the more devotional type of reading. Let me explain why this is so important. You are preparing yourself, remember, and the danger for the intellectual type of man, if he is only reading theology or philosophy, is to become puffed up. He persuades himself that he has a perfect system; there is no problem, there is no difficulty. But he will soon discover that there are problems and difficulties; and if he wants to avoid shipwreck, the best thing he can do when he feels that he knows all, and is elated and tempted to intellectual pride, is to pick up say the Journals of George Whitefield. There he will read of how that man was used of God in England, Wales, Scotland and America, and also of his experiences of the love of Christ; and if he does not soon feel that he is but a worm, well then I suggest that he has never been regenerated. We continually need to be humbled. That is why balanced reading is an absolute essential. If your heart is not as much engaged as your head in these matters, your theology is defective—apart from anything else. There is this real danger of becoming over-theoretical, over-academic, over-objective, over-intellectual. That will mean not only that you are in a dangerous spiritual state yourself, but also that to that extent you will be a poor preacher and a poor pastor. You will not help your people and you will be failing at the task to which you are called.

The way to counteract, and to safeguard yourself against that, is to balance your reading. Never fail to do so. I maintain that one should always be reading along these differing lines daily. I have developed a sort of routine which I think is sound and profitable almost from the physical standpoint as well as the other. If I am reading the stiffer and the more difficult books, or the more directly theological books in the morning, I read the other types at night. It is good that the mind should not be too much exercised or stimulated before you go to bed, if you want to avoid the problem of insomnia. It does not matter so much when you are young—at that stage you can do almost anything you like and still sleep—but as you get older you will find that it is not quite so easy. I have often had to say that to men who have been in trouble nervously, and on the verge of a breakdown. It has been obvious to me from listening to their stories that they were in the habit of reading really difficult matter which called out all their reserves of mental ability right up until they retired to bed; and then they were surprised when their minds refused to stop working, and they could not relax and sleep. This is sheer common sense; but it is very important. So balance your reading for all these reasons.

What is the purpose of all this reading? I reiterate that the object of all this reading is not primarily to get ideas for preaching. That is another terrible danger. As men tend to read their Bibles in order to get texts for sermons, so they tend to read books in order to get preaching material. I would almost describe this as the occupational disease of the ministry. I remember a minister telling me in 1930 that he had been to a conference, or house-party designed to deepen people's spiritual experiences. He told me of the great benefit he had derived from the conference. I was expecting him to tell me something about what he had experienced, or of what it had meant to him spiritually; but that is not what he told me. He said, 'I got wonderful preaching stuff there.' Preaching stuff! Preaching material! He did not go to the conference to derive spiritual benefit, but simply to get material—illustrations, stories of other people's experiences, etc—for his sermons. He had virtually immured himself from any spiritual influence because he approached everything in this way. He had become a professional. He would read his Bible to get texts, he would read books to get ideas and so on.

In fact this can become quite ludicrous; and I am glad that this is so for this reason, that preachers who have to go to books to get sermons are generally caught out! This was brought home to me when I lived in South Wales. There was a famous religious bookshop in a certain town, and preachers from the outlying district used to go into the market and to visit the bookstall once a week or oftener. They all went to this bookshop and bought the various books. The tendency was, naturally, for all to buy the same books, and the result was that many of them were preaching the same sermon! But, unfortunately for them, their people, their church members, knew one another and when they met they would talk about their respective churches and ministers. One would talk about a wonderful sermon he had heard the previous Sunday. 'What was the text?' the other would ask. On being told the questioner would begin to smile, because he had also been listening to much the same thing. There were slight variations of course, but essentially it was the same sermon! These poor men had become dependent upon books for their ideas.

I remember another minister, who was a good preacher, telling me on one occasion when I happened to be travelling in the same compartment in a train and found him reading Robert Bridges' *Testament of Beauty* that he 'got' much more from 'these fellows' than he did from anybody else. What he meant was that he got more ideas and preaching material there. There are men who get their ideas from books and journals, indeed from all sorts of strange places.

I maintain that this is not the primary object of reading. What then is its main purpose and function? It is to provide information; but still more important, it is because it is the best general stimulus. What the preacher always needs is a stimulus.

In a sense one should not go to books for ideas; the business of books is to make one think. We are not gramophone records, we are to think originally. What we preach is to be the result of our own thought. We do not merely transmit ideas. The preacher is not meant to be a mere channel through which water flows; he is to be more like a well. So the function of reading is to stimulate us in general, to stimulate us to think, to think for ourselves. Take all you read and masticate it thoroughly. Do not just repeat it as you have received it; deliver it in your own way, let it emerge as a part of yourself, with your stamp upon it. That is why I emphasise the general principle that that is the chief function of learning. It is tragic when men become mere gramophone records, or tape-recording machines with the same thing being churned out and repeated endlessly. Such a man will soon become barren; he will soon be in difficulties; and his people will have recognised it long before he does.

* * *

One further remark about reading. General reading is also important. Why? Well, if there were no other reason—merely for the sake of relief for the mind. The mind needs rest. The man who is too tense and who over-taxes his mind will soon get into trouble. The mind must be given relief and rested. But to relieve your mind does not just mean that you stop reading; read something different. Read something quite different, and as you do so the mind can relax. A change in this respect is as good as a rest. And at the same time you will be adding to your stock of good general information, which is excellent as a background to preaching. So I advocate the reading of history. I mean now secular history, biographies, the history of statesmen, even the history of war, if you like. You may have some special interest in some such subject, a hobby; well, make use of it, develop it. But once more, a solemn warning! Do not give too much of your time to it. That is the danger. You will always be fighting in this respect. There will always be the tendency to go to extremes. But if you have a special interest, cultivate it in moderation. It will be good for your mind; it will preserve resilience and freshness. I have therefore always tried to do this, and to take certain journals which deal with general affairs and literary matters, and where there are good well-written articles and good book reviews which will suggest other books for reading. I am not a believer in digests and encyclopaedias which encourage a 'ready-reckoner' mentality rather than thought.

The minister should always be reading in this balanced way which he maps out for himself. It was always my practice many years ago when on my summer vacation to take one big book with me. At that time it was generally the latest Bampton Lectures. These were generally by men who were not evangelical, but they were men who could take a broad survey of a particular aspect of Truth. The Bampton Lectures or the Hibbert Lectures I found to be of great value. A busy preacher rarely has the time for the consecutive reading that that type of book demands, so I took advantage of a vacation to read such works. My wife was very ready to agree with my scheme, and the children equally so later. They gave me the mornings to myself that I might do this; then, having done that, I was prepared to do anything they proposed. Looking back I am glad that I had the sense and the wisdom to do that.

*   *   *

I must say a word about music. Music does not help everyone, but it greatly helps some people; and I am fortunately one of them. Someone recently said to me that he was astonished when reading the obituary notices at the time of the death of Karl Barth to find that Barth used to start the morning by listening to a record of music by Mozart. He said that he could not understand this. I said, 'What is your difficulty?' 'Well,' he replied, 'I am surprised that a thinker like Karl Barth went to Mozart; I would have expected him to go to Beethoven or Wagner or perhaps Bach.' He was astonished. My feeling about this man was that he evidently did not know the real value of music, or how to use it. 'I can tell you why Karl Barth went to Mozart' I said, 'He did not go to him for thoughts or ideas, he went to Mozart because Mozart did something to him in a general sense. Mozart put him into a good mood, and made him feel happy in his spirit. He released him, and set him free to do his own thinking.' A general stimulus in that way is often more helpful than a more particular intellectual one. The man himself is bigger than his intellect. Is not that the reason why the prophets of old had music played to them on the harp or some other instrument? I shall refer to this again later. Anything that does you good, puts you into a good mood or condition, anything that pleases you or releases tensions and relaxes you is of inestimable value. Music does this to some in a wonderful way. Remember that we are still dealing with the ways in which the preacher treats and handles himself and prepares himself. So put on your gramophone record, or whatever it is—anything you know that will help you.

I end as I began, by saying—Know yourself. You will find that there will be variations in your life; you will pass through phases and experience various states. Get to know yourself. You will find that there will be periods, perhaps of days, even weeks, when for some amazing reason your mind is working at its very best, and you are in a fecund condition finding ideas for sermons everywhere—'Tongues in trees, books in the running brooks, Sermons in stones, and good in everything.' When that happens, hold out both hands, take it all in; write down on paper as much as you can, so that when the dry and barren and arid periods come you will have something to fall back upon. 'Know thyself' was the advice given by the Greek philosophers of old; and there is still no more important injunction for preachers.

CHAPTER TEN

The Preparation of the Sermon

WE HAVE TRIED, however inadequately, to deal with the preparation of the preacher himself. No man can do this adequately, but we must be deeply aware of the need of it, and go on struggling with it for the rest of our lives. Having done that we come now to the preparation of the sermon.

Let me emphasise again that we are dealing in these lectures with preaching. Someone has asked, 'What about visiting?' I am not attempting to deal with all the aspects of a minister's work but with preaching, because I believe that this comes first and is most important. Visiting, or any other activity, can never compensate for a lack of preaching. Indeed I suggest that visiting will not have much meaning unless the preaching has been what it should be, and has prepared the way. It will probably be just a social visit including perhaps a cup of tea and a pleasant talk; but that is not pastoral visiting. Preaching prepares the way for all the other activities of a minister. As I have shown, it prepares the way for personal work, and it equally prepares the way for visiting.

I am not going to deal with the subject of visiting. Indeed you may have noticed that I have not even dealt with the question of pulpit prayers, or praying in public. That, obviously, is not because I do not regard that as of the greatest importance; it is simply because time and other factors compel me to confine myself to preaching. Pulpit praying is most important; the conduct of the service as a whole is most important. But again I suggest that this will be very largely determined by preaching, and by one's approach to this. Of course, if you belong to a church which has a liturgical service this does not follow, although I would have thought that, even there, the way in which the minister reads the Liturgy will depend very largely upon what he has been doing during the preparation of his sermon. But I am not concerned to deal with all these various other matters; I desire to emphasise what I regard as the chiefest thing of all—preaching. I cannot emphasise this too much; preaching controls everything and determines the character of everything else.

As we turn to the preparation of the sermon we find ourselves confronted at once by a major decision to which I have already referred in my general introduction. What type of sermon is it to be? Is it to be evangelistic? Is it to be for the edification, the comfort and the building up of believers, the members of the Church? Or is it to be a more general type of instruction in the message of the Scriptures? This is obviously a major decision, and having referred to it before, I only repeat it now because it is an issue that arises at once at this point.

Having decided which particular type of sermon it is to be, you then come to the very practical question of the actual preparation. Some seem to think that there are absolute rules in this matter; but I suggest that that is not so. I therefore merely put forward some tentative suggestions based on my own understanding, and my own experience, of these matters.

On the whole I would say that one should not preach on subjects as such. What I mean is this. I remember a chaplain in the U.S. forces during the last war telling me of what he did on one occasion while in Britain. He was stationed in a certain part of the country and was asked to preach one Sunday in the local church which he had been attending. He had come to certain conclusions concerning the spiritual state of that church, 'So,' he said to me, 'in view of what I had observed I decided to give them my sermon on "Justification by faith".' I then put some questions to him and discovered that, after he had finished his training in the well-known seminary he had attended, this man had immediately prepared a series of sermons on various theological and doctrinal subjects. He had a sermon on justification, another on sanctification, another on providence, another on eschatology and so on. In other words he started with a subject, and then looked for a text through which he could deal with it. But what he was actually doing was to give lectures on 'justification by faith' and so on. That is what I mean by not preaching on subjects.

I venture to go a step further, and to expose myself to some criticism, by saying that on the whole I do not believe in preaching through a catechism. There are those for whom I have great respect who do this regularly; but I suggest that this is not a wise procedure, chiefly for the reason that it tends to produce a theoretical attitude to the Truth, an over-intellectual attitude to the Truth. It is not that I do not believe in teaching people the Catechism. I do. But my view is that this should be done at another time and in a different way. I would place this under the heading of instruction and deal with it in a series of lectures. But, still better, it seems to me, is to tell the people to read and study the Catechism for themselves and then consider it together in discussion groups.

I say all this because I believe, as I have been indicating, that in preaching the message should always arise out of the Scriptures directly and not out of the formulations of men, even the best men. After all, these catechisms were produced by men and men who were concerned to emphasise certain things in their peculiar historical situation, over against certain other teachings and attitudes. At their best, therefore, they tend to be incomplete, they tend to have a particular emphasis; and therefore they tend to leave out certain things. But my final argument against preaching through the Catechism is that the same object can be achieved by preaching from the Scriptures in the way that I have indicated; for after all, the catechisms derive from the Scriptures. The function of a catechism, I would have thought, ultimately, is not to provide material for preaching; it is to safeguard the correctness of the preaching, and to safeguard the interpretations of the people as they read their Bibles. As that is the main function of creeds and catechisms, it is surely wrong therefore to just preach constantly year after year on the Catechism, instead of preaching the Word directly from the Scripture itself, with the Scriptures always open before you, and the minds of the people directed to that rather than to men's understanding of it. Though what you are preaching is your understanding of the meaning and the teaching of the Scriptures this method preserves, and emphasises in a clearer manner, the idea that you are giving the message of the Bible rather than the dogma of a particular church.

Assuming that that is true on the whole with regard to subjects and catechisms you then come to the great question—'What exactly am I going to do? Shall I preach on odd texts?' What I mean by odd texts is that they do not belong to a series, but that you take a particular verse or paragraph here and another there, so that there is no sequence or connection between the sermons from Sunday to Sunday. Should it be preaching from odd texts, therefore, or should it be a series of sermons?

Preachers have often held strong views on this, and it is a very interesting and, of course, a very important question. One of the greatest preachers of the last century, if not the greatest of all, Charles Haddon Spurgeon, took a very strong line on this. He did not believe in preaching a series of sermons; indeed he opposed doing so very strongly. He said that there was a sense in which it was impertinent for a man to decide to preach a series of sermons. He held that the texts should be given to the preacher, that he should seek the Lord in this matter and ask for guidance. He held that the preacher should not decide but pray for the guidance and the leading of the Holy Spirit, and then submit himself to this. He will thus be led to particular texts and statements which he will then expound in sermonic form. That was the view held by Spurgeon and by many others. I myself was brought up in a tradition which adhered to that view. We never heard a series of sermons based on a book, or part of a book, of the Bible or on a theme.

But over and against that you have the position of the Puritans who were clearly great believers in preaching series of sermons. It is interesting to note, in passing, that though Spurgeon was such a great reader of the Puritans, and such a great admirer of them, at this point he disagreed with them entirely.

What, then, does one say about this? All I can say is that it seems to me to be quite wrong to be rigid in this matter, and to lay down any hard and fast rule. I cannot see why the Spirit should not guide a man to preach a series of sermons on a passage or a book of the Bible as well as lead him to one text only. Why not? What is important—and here I am with Spurgeon whole-heartedly—is that we must preserve and safeguard 'the freedom of the Spirit.' We must not be in control in this matter; we must not decide in cold blood, as it were, what we are going to do, and map out a programme, and so on. I am sure that that is wrong. I have known men who have done that. I have known men who, at the beginning of a season after a vacation, would actually hand out a list of their texts for many months ahead and would indicate what was going to be preached every particular Sunday during that period of time. I reprobate that entirely and completely. I am not saying, I dare not presume to say, that this is impossible: under the freedom of the Spirit it is not impossible, because 'the wind bloweth where it listeth'. We must not say that the Spirit will always, and must always, work in one particular way. But, speaking generally, I feel that to plan and publish such a programme is surely to put certain limits upon the sovereignty and the leading of the Spirit in this matter. So, having asserted that we are subject to the Spirit, and that we must be careful to make sure that we really are subject to Him, I argue that He may lead us at one time to preach on odd texts and at another time to preach a series of sermons. I would humbly claim that I have known this many times in my experience.

There is a volume of sermons preached by me published under the title *Spiritual Depression*. The story of how I came to preach that series may help to illustrate this matter. I had actually determined— it seemed to me that I was being led in that way, but undoubtedly it was my own determination—to start a series of sermons on the Epistle to the Ephesians. However, one morning while dressing, quite suddenly and in an overwhelming manner, it seemed to me that the Spirit of God was urging me to preach a series of sermons on 'spiritual depression'. Quite literally while I was dressing the series took order in my mind, and all I had to do was to rush as quickly as possible to put down on paper the various texts, and the order in which they had come to me, in that way. I had never thought about preaching a series of sermons on spiritual depression; it had never occurred to me to do so; but it came just like that. I always pay great attention to such happenings. It is a very wonderful and glorious experience apart from anything else; and I would not dare to disobey what I regard as a very definite injunction coming in that manner. I am quite confident that the preaching of that series of sermons was dictated to me by the Spirit Himself.

I would add a further word to justify my attitude that we should avoid an over-rigidity in this matter. I am suggesting that it is right both to preach on odd texts and a series; and, in any case, a series can always be broken into. Indeed a series should always be broken into if you feel a particular pressure on your spirit urging you to do so. That is why I would never print a programme of what I proposed to preach even for the next three months. You cannot tell what you should do— at least I could never tell. Circumstances may arise which demand attention and provide a wonderful opportunity for preaching. Indeed I could never give a guarantee that I would finish the sermon I had prepared on any one occasion. Many and many a time I have found myself in the position that the usual amount of time for the sermon had gone and I had only preached half my sermon! How can you tell what may happen? You are not in control, at least you should not be. The Spirit is using you, and dealing with you, as you are preaching, quite as much as He was at the time of preparation. Do not misunderstand this; I am not advocating or excusing slovenliness. I have gone out of my way to emphasise the opposite. But, still, with all your preparation and forethought you have to maintain 'the freedom of the

Spirit', and try to keep yourself open and sensitive to His every movement. So, to me, a printed programme would have been ridiculous because of the constant possibility of interruptions and variations, and the development of certain themes in an entirely unforeseen manner either during preparation or actually while preaching. Whatever your decision with regard to this matter, keep yourself free.

Or let me put it like this. I would lay it down as a rule that there are special occasions which should always be observed. At this point I have the temerity to express a criticism of the Puritans. I believe in preaching special sermons on Christmas Day and during the Advent season; I also believe in preaching special sermons on Good Friday, Easter Sunday and Whit Sunday.

How do I justify this? Well, why did the Puritans object to it? The answer is, of course, that they objected to these special occasions because of their violent reaction to Roman Catholicism. The Roman Catholics had turned the celebration of the birth of our Lord into a Mass; and so the Puritans, being creatures of reactions, as we all are, tended to react too violently, with the result that their desire to get rid of everything savouring in any way of the Mass, and everything else associated with Roman Catholic thinking, went to the other extreme and opposed any observance of these days.

While I fully understand their attitude and entirely sympathise with it in general, I nevertheless think they were mistaken. I say that because I believe that the danger confronting most of us is to become so interested in the implications and the outworking of the Christian faith that we tend to forget the essence and the very foundations of the faith. We assume them but perhaps never preach them. And if that is true of the preaching, the same will obviously be true of the people who listen to us. But when we turn to the New Testament Epistles we find that the Apostles cannot deal with any subject without constantly referring back to these basic facts of the Christian faith. In any case there are the four Gospels reminding us of the facts and the historicity.

Surely the great danger today, and especially in certain circles, is over-intellectualisation. I have often striven to persuade people to become more intellectual and to be less sentimental in their approach to the Christian faith, but at the present time I am equally certain that some people need to be warned of the danger of being over-intellectual and of losing contact with the great historic facts on which our faith is based. Any Christian who does not respond to a sermon on the Nativity had better re-examine his whole position in Christ. If you yourself as preacher cannot still be moved by a sermon which just deals with the facts and details of the death of our blessed Lord on the Cross on Calvary's hill, if you do not feel as if you had never preached it before, and if you are not as moved by it as you have ever been, I say again that you had better examine your foundations. And the same is true of the people. So these special occasions have great value in this respect, that they, in a sense, compel us to go back, and to remind ourselves of these things which after all are the fundamentals on which our whole position rests.

I go even further; I believe in using almost any special occasion as an opportunity for preaching the Gospel. So in addition to what I have mentioned I have always taken advantage of the first Sunday of a New Year in this way. You may ask, 'What is the difference between the first of January and the thirty-first of December?' And of course in a sense you are right. That is the purely intellectual attitude. To it all days are the same. But to the average person there is a difference. New Year! the time for making resolutions. Of course we know that it is nonsense and that it will lead to nothing. People do it every year and probably do not remember their resolutions even for a week. Nevertheless they do this. 'But,' you say, 'what then is the point of paying any attention to that?' Once more that is the theoretical view-point. But we must not take these theoretical views, as I have been trying to show; we have to assess our congregations and our people, and we must deal with them as human beings. Remembering that 'he who winneth souls is wise' we must take advantage of anything and everything that will bring home the truth of the Gospel to people. So when you start a New Year there is an obvious opportunity of reminding people of the fleeting nature of life. We all tend to forget this; you can be so interested in great theological and intellectual and philosophical problems that you tend to forget that you are going to die. And the people, immersed in business and pleasure and the family, and 'the affairs of this life' are equally forgetful.

Here, then, is an opportunity made for you, presented to you, to bring home to all the fleeting character of life in this world, and to remind them that none can afford to sit back as spectators or as critics of preachers and preaching. You can remind them that they are involved in all this, and that you are not addressing them on some theoretical subject, but dealing with the most vital matter of all, and that, whether they like it or not, they are moving on to an inevitable and unavoidable end, and that the Final Judgment is coming. A preacher who does not take advantage of these things is a fool, and is not fit to be in a pulpit.

I shall never forget my sense of disappointment a few years back when I had the following experience. Being somewhat over-tired I took a rest at the change of the year and went to a service conducted by a young minister on the first Sunday morning of a New Year. To my utter astonishment he began his sermon by saying, 'Well, you remember that last Sunday we were dealing with such and such a verse; this Sunday we go on to the next verse.' He made no reference whatsoever to the New Year or to any of these matters at all. I felt sorry for him, sorry that he was capable of missing such an opportunity. Apart from anything else these special occasions help to make our work easier—they are opportunities made for the preacher.

Anything that happens in the world, anything striking, any phenomenon, is something we should always take advantage of. I remember reading of an incident in the life of John Fletcher of Madeley, that great and saintly man who lived two hundred years ago. He was a vicar in Madeley in Staffordshire, in England. Suddenly there was a terrible disaster on the River Severn. The Severn Bore that year was bigger than usual with the result that large numbers of people were drowned as the result of the flood. This catastrophe led John Fletcher

to preach a remarkable sermon in which he made frequent references
to that tragic happening and which led to tremendous consequences.
I also remember reading how at just about the same time, incidentally,
a number of those great preachers of that eighteenth century made use
of the earthquake that took place in Lisbon, in Portugal, in 1751. They
all took advantage of such events. They did not preach on the earthquake as such but they used it to bring home to the people the fleeting
nature of life, and to enforce their call to repentance. An earthquake
makes people think, as does a tornado, or hurricane; and so they give
the preacher an opportunity. 'Because thine heart was tender' is the
favourable comment on King Josiah in the Old Testament; and we
remember the lines of the hymn, 'Saviour while my heart is tender, I
would yield my heart to Thee'. There are times when our hearts are
tender, and we are more likely to respond. It is the essence of wisdom,
it is indeed but common sense, that we should take advantage of all
these things. Though you may have planned out the greatest series of
sermons the world has ever known, break into it if there is an earthquake! If you cannot be shaken out of a mechanical routine by an
earthquake you are beyond hope!

*   *   *

Those are my sentiments concerning the question of whether to
preach on odd texts or to take a series. With regard to preaching on
odd texts I have already referred to this when dealing with the preparation of the preacher. I warned against the bad habit of reading the
Scriptures 'for' texts, and emphasised that we should always read
them for our own good and edification. I pointed out how in doing so
you would find that certain statements would hit you and strike you;
and I told you what to do about that. Anyone who follows that practice will find that he will never be short of texts; he will have accumulated a pile of skeletons which he has prepared while reading the
Scriptures for his own edification.

But in addition to that you will find that sermons are as it were
given to you. They come to you directly, and you have very little to do

about them. I do not know whether all would agree with me in this, but my own experience certainly was that this happened to me more frequently in the early years of my ministry than has been the case since. I think that that is entirely due to the kindness of God. He known us, 'He knoweth our frame'; and He knows that we need this kind of help much more at the beginning. As you give extra encouragement to children, and do things for them which you do not do later because you want them to grow up, so God, I think, deals with the preacher. You will find that He will be kind and very gracious to you at the beginning, and will give you texts and sermons; sometimes perhaps a complete sermon will come to you. But then at other times you will find that you will have to work it out and labour and sweat in the way I have indicated. I leave the question of preaching on odd texts at that.

Turning to the preparation of a sermon there are several possibilities. One is that you work through a book of the Bible and just go systematically through the book. Another is that you work systematically through a section of a book, the Sermon on the Mount or something like that; or perhaps even a portion of a chapter. There are many possibilities in this respect. Or, as I have indicated previously, you can have a series of sermons dealing with a particular aspect of the Christian life and living.

I have given the example of 'spiritual depression'. Let me say a little more about that. What determined my preaching of that series was really a combination of some of these things I have been mentioning. I have explained how you can accumulate a large number of skeletons. I had been doing this for a number of years and so I had a pile of skeletons. What happened on that occasion, while I was dressing that morning, was that I was shown that in my pile of skeletons there was a ready-made series on spiritual depression. It was not that the whole pile dealt with this, but that in the pile there were odd sermons that could be put in order to form a series. This was to me such a remarkable experience that I have never forgotten it, and never shall. I was more or less able there and then, if I remember rightly, to put down on paper some twenty-one outlines of sermons. I had got the skeletons there, and all that seemed to happen at that moment was that the Spirit put them into order for me. So all I had to do was to go to the bundle of skeletons and pull out the particular ones indicated and look at them. It seemed to me immediately that this suggested arrangement was a perfect one, and I dared not vary it in any way. I added one or two at the end—but even the skeletons of those were also in the pile.

This method, I say once more, is not only right in and of itself, it greatly eases the burden and the labour of the minister. It avoids that terrible position which I have known men to be in so often, of having frantically to look for texts on Saturday for the coming Sunday. I have even known men to go to bed on Saturday night without being prepared for their task. But if you do what I am suggesting you will find that it will work out in a most interesting, and even in an exciting manner.

I would emphasise again that while doing all this you must always be expository. Always expository. If you follow the method I have been advocating you will be expository, because as these texts have hit you, you will have paused and looked at them, and have examined them, and then have worked out your skeletons. In other words your skeletons are the headings of an exposition. I do not approve of the method whereby you take a subject like 'spiritual depression' and then think and work it out for yourself, and then look for texts which will be convenient pegs on which to hang these thoughts of yours on the subject. That is what I am opposing. The matter should always be derived from the Scriptures, it should always be expository. And if you are true to the teaching of the Scriptures you will find that you will cover all the different aspects of truth, and do so in a very much better way than by trying to work these things out for yourself in a more or less philosophical manner.

A series of sermons may be long or short. How does one decide? I remember years ago being in a theological students' conference in which we had a great discussion on this question regarding the length of a series of sermons. I remember that on that occasion I took up the cudgels for short series. How one lives to un-say what one has said previously! However, that was my position at that time, and I want to justify it. You cannot lay down rules and regulations in these matters; and this is where I think we have to be judicious in our use of preachers like the Puritans. The danger is that we read them and say, 'This is marvellous, this is the way to do it.' But if you try to emulate them you may find that it is not the way for you to do it. Why not? One reason is that it depends so much upon the preacher. What one man can do another cannot, and it is dangerous for him to attempt to do so. It not only depends upon the particular person of the preacher, it also depends upon his stage of development. A preacher should be always growing and advancing and developing, so that what he cannot do in his younger days he should be able to do in middle age and old age. So any rigidity in these matters must be avoided.

I remember hearing of a very able man—belonging to the nineteenth century—a fine theologian who, before he became principal of a theological college, had been pastor of a church in London. He had started preaching to his people, who were chiefly tradesmen and their wives, on Sunday nights, a series of sermons on the Epistle to the Ephesians. The result was that he more or less lost his congregation. They all had the greatest possible respect and admiration for him, and liked him as a man; but the fact was that they just could not take it. He was preaching over their heads and so was not feeding them. His intention was good but his sermons were, as they put it, too deep for them, and the series was too long. They could not take this, and cried out for some relief.

So you have to be careful about this. In other words I come back to something I have said already but which I must emphasise again, namely that you have to be constantly reassessing yourself and your people. And you must always be ready to make readjustments. Do not go on with a rigid set plan from which you will not vary. I remember hearing of a foolish preacher who had undergone a change in his thinking and outlook and who as a result was preaching constantly on one line and on one theme. Someone told him that he had heard complaints about this from some of his people. His reply was, 'They have got to take it whether they like it or not.' There is a sense in which I would justify him for saying that, but as he said it it was surely quite wrong. The business of the preacher is to persuade people to 'take it', to teach them to 'take it', to wean them out of the false, not to throw the truth at them. So he must be constantly readjusting as he becomes aware of changing conditions.

This may sound difficult, and there is a sense in which it is; yet, to me, it is one of the most glorious aspects of the ministry. It is a part of the romance of preaching that it is always living and alive; it is never set, it is never formal. There is this constant interplay and reaction between the preacher and his people. You grow and develop together, and you have to make these adjustments. After all, what is the purpose of preaching? What are you doing; what are you trying to do; what is your object? It is, is it not, to help these people, and to bring them to God, and to a knowledge of God, and to build them up in our 'most holy faith'. Be ready always therefore to readjust.

I emphasise at the end of this section, as I have been doing all along, that you must make certain that each particular sermon is complete in itself, and is an entity in and of itself. This applies even when you are preaching a series. The way to do this is to take a few minutes at the beginning of the sermon in which to give a brief resumé of what you have been saying previously. I emphasise the word 'brief'. There was a popular preacher—not popular in the usual acceptation of that term, but a man who achieved a certain amount of notoriety—in England a number of years ago. His popularity seemed to be due very largely to the depth of his voice which led to his speaking frequently on the radio, and that in turn filled his church. I remember speaking to a lady who used to go to listen to this man, but who told me that she had stopped doing so. I asked her why she had stopped. 'Well,' she said, 'he spends so much time in telling us what he said last time, and then so much time in telling us what he hopes to say next time, that he tells us very little each time.' This had so upset her that she had actually stopped listening to him. This is a very real snare and temptation to the preacher. Though that tendency to be too long in giving a synopsis of the previous sermon must be firmly resisted, a summary is nevertheless essential for the people. It will help all of them, even those who attend regularly; and for strangers who may attend, it is essential. So you must show the context of this particular sermon in the series, and its relationship to the whole, and perhaps throw out a hint of what is going to follow. But it must be an entity in itself—that is most important.

We have been dealing with a major decision. Having arrived at this major decision you now have to come down to the actual work of preparing the sermon, the particular sermon. How do you approach this? Well, obviously, the first thing you have to do is to deal with the meaning of your text. At this point there is one golden rule, one absolute demand—honesty. You have got to be honest with your text. I mean by that, that you do not go to a text just to pick out an idea which interests you and then deal with that idea yourself. That is to be dishonest with a text. Perhaps a few illustrations will help to make this point clear.

I well remember the first time I heard a certain famous preacher on the radio. He told us that he was going to preach on 'Turning the place of your crucifixion into a garden'. One wondered immediately as to the possible source of that theme. He soon told us that his text was to be found at the beginning of the eighteenth chapter of John's Gospel where we read, 'In the place where He was crucified there was a garden'. That was what the text said. But, you see, the sermon was on 'turning' the place of your crucifixion into a garden. But there was nothing about that in the text. There was a garden there; the garden was there before the crucifixion. It was not the crucifixion that produced the garden. However, in order to give himself the opportunity of preaching a very sentimental sermon about how people suffering from illnesses could and should react to their trial, he did violence to his text. He told us that good people who took it in a beautiful spirit, and never grumbled and never complained, turned their place of crucifixion into a garden. We were then treated to a series of affecting sentimental stories of such people for about twenty-five minutes to half an hour. Now there is only one thing to say about that—that is just utter dishonesty; there is nothing else to say about it.

Or take another example, that of a man preaching on Naaman the Syrian. You remember the point in the story about his strong objection to the command to go to dip himself in the river Jordan—a miserably small river as contrasted with the rivers Abana and Pharpar. But the theme of the sermon was 'The importance of the unimportant in life'. That, again, is nothing but a sheer misuse of a text. The meaning of that text and its context is not to show 'the importance of the unimportant in life' but to show that Naaman could not be healed by God without being humbled, and that all of us have to submit to God's way of salvation. But that was literally not mentioned at all in the sermon. The idea behind this affront to a text is that you just extract an idea, anything that pleases you, such as the fact that the river Jordan was actually smaller than the other rivers, and ignore the real meaning of the text and its context. It is not only superficial, it is actually dishonest and an abuse of scriptural statements.

Or take another and still more striking example. I am deliberately giving illustrations from popular preachers. This man announced his theme as 'My Gospel'. His text was Paul's statement in 2 Timothy 2:8: 'Remember that Jesus Christ of the seed of David was raised from the dead according to my gospel.' He started with the question, 'Can you say "my" gospel?' 'Of course,' he added immediately, 'it may not be my gospel, but is it yours?' This was the real point, 'Can you say "my" gospel?' Then there was a tirade against traditionalism, orthodoxy, systematic theology, indeed any kind of theology. The one thing that mattered was personal experience—'my gospel'. What was truly amazing and almost incredible was that the man could possibly say that, because what Paul is obviously saying there is that it was not his own gospel, not something that arose from his experience, but 'that Jesus Christ of the seed of David was raised from the dead.' The Apostle indeed was writing specifically to counter the kind of thing that this preacher was saying, and emphasising that there is only one Gospel—the one he preached—the Gospel which is based upon the vital historical fact that Jesus the Christ is the incarnate Son of God, born of the seed of David according to the flesh, and that He literally rose in the body from the grave. All that was completely ignored, indeed denied. The great thing was, Have you had some personal experience; has your life changed? He just extracted 'My gospel' and completely ignored even the rest of the verse, leave alone the context. It was really a tirade against a theological understanding of the Gospel or of being 'able to give a reason for the hope that is in you'. It was an exaltation of personal experience, irrespective of the cause of the experience. There is, again, only one thing to say—this is utterly dishonest, it is an abuse, a travesty of what the text says.

We must be honest with our texts; and we must take them always in their context. That is an absolute rule. These other men do not observe that; they are not interested in that, they are always looking for 'ideas'. They want a theme, an idea; and then they philosophise on that, giving expression to their own thoughts and moralisings. That is utterly to abuse the Word of God. You must take your text in its context, and you must be honest with it. You must discover the meaning of the words and of the whole statement. We have gone into this before, but what I want to emphasise at this stage is the spiritual meaning of the verse or passage. Accuracy first, but then, and more important, the spiritual meaning. What determines the accuracy of your understanding of particular words ultimately is not scholarship but the spiritual meaning of the passage. You will find that the learned authorities often, if not generally, disagree with one another completely, and the meaning ultimately has to be determined not by some exact science but by spiritual perception, spiritual understanding; that 'unction' that John talks about in 1 John 2:20 and 27.

This procedure leads you to the thrust of the message of this particular statement. In order to arrive at this you will have to learn how to ask questions of your text. Nothing is more important than this. Ask questions such as, Why did he say that? Why did he say it in this particular way? What is he getting at? What was his object and purpose? One of the first things a preacher has to learn is to talk to his texts. They talk to you, and you must talk to them. Put questions to them. This is a most profitable and stimulating procedure. But at the same time never force your text. An idea may occur to you and it may excite you and thrill you; but if you find that you have to do some manipulating or forcing in order to make that fit into this particular text, don't do it. You must sacrifice a good sermon rather than force a text. After this, or while doing this, you must check this understanding you have arrived at by consulting your lexicons and commentaries.

What I am leading to, the thing I am concerned about, is that you make certain that you really are getting the main message, the main thrust and import of this particular text or statement. It is quite astonishing to note how good men can avoid doing this. I have reached a stage in which I am not quite sure whether one learns more about preaching by preaching oneself, or by listening to others! I suppose it is a combination of both. But during a recent illness, and while recuperating from an operation, I was a listener for nearly six months, and I learned a great deal. One Sunday morning I heard a man preaching on Galatians 3:1: 'O foolish Galatians, who hath bewitched you that ye should not obey the truth, before whose eyes Jesus Christ hath been evidently set forth, crucified among you?' The theme of the sermon was 'the danger of being side-tracked'. The introduction, I felt, was good and legitimate apart from over-elaboration of the theme of the 'witching eye', and a little disquisition of mesmerism. All right —I was quite prepared even for that. But then the rest of the sermon was devoted to the things that tend to distract us, and particularly theology and orthodoxy.

Now to me, this good man was missing the main message. Surely what the Apostle is saying is this: 'O foolish Galatians who hath bewitched you, that ye should not obey the truth, before whose eyes Jesus Christ hath been evidently set forth, crucified among you?' The Apostle is amazed at these Galatians. In what respect? Well, what Paul was amazed at was that anything could distract the attention of these foolish Galatians from the great and glorious truth which he had placarded before them, the amazing fact of the death of 'the Son of God' on the Cross on Calvary's hill, which he had 'evidently set forth', 'placarded' before them. Paul was amazed that anything could distract them from 'the glory of the Cross'. But the Cross, and its meaning and message was literally not mentioned in that sermon. The time was taken in telling us about 'the side-shows', the things that tend to distract us. But we were told nothing about the object from which they distracted us. Surely Paul is expressing his utter amazement and astonishment that a man who has ever had a glimpse of this should ever forget it in his preoccupation with matters like circumcision. But that did not come out at all. In a sense that preacher was saying nothing wrong apart from his passing attack on orthodoxy, but what interested me was that he completely failed to bring out the main thrust of his own text, the very text on which he was preaching. He had obviously been bewitched by 'the witching eye'!

Nothing is more important than that we should be sure that we have got at the main thrust of the text, and let that come out. We must not be like another man whom I heard preaching on Romans 1 : 1-4: 'Declared to be the Son of God with power, according to the spirit of holiness, by the resurrection from the dead,' on Easter Sunday. What astonished me on that occasion was that there was very little about the Resurrection. The good man explained the meaning of the words in an excellent manner and certainly emphasised that Jesus is the Son of God, but I went away without a sense of astonishment at this amazing event of the Resurrection, the thing which according to the Apostle finally 'declared' Him to be 'the Son of God'. That was not at all the thrust of the sermon on that Easter morning; but surely it is the thrust of what the Apostle himself is saying.

I remember a well-known preacher preaching on a Good Friday morning on the text, Romans 8 : 2: 'The law of the Spirit of life in Christ Jesus hath made me free from the law of sin and death.' His theme turned out to be his particular brand of holiness teaching—he was a believer in 'entire sanctification'. On that Good Friday morning, when the very day, and the very occasion which had brought us together, was making people think of the actual death of our Lord, the historical Fact, our minds were directed away from that to a particular theory of holiness. And, once more, that happened not only because of a misunderstanding of the particular verse but because of a complete ignoring of the previous and the following verses. I cannot over-emphasise the importance of our arriving at the main thrust, the main message of our text. Let it lead you, let it teach you. Listen to it and then question it as to its meaning, and let that be the burden of your sermon.

CHAPTER ELEVEN

The Shape of the Sermon

HAVING DISCOVERED THE main message and thrust of your text you must proceed to state this in its actual context and application. For instance, it might be in its application to the particular church to whom the Apostle was writing. You must show its original context and application.

Then you go on to show that this is also the statement of a general principle that is always valid. It was true then in those special circumstances, but it is a spiritual principle that applies always. So you demonstrate the truth that it had not merely a temporary local application but a more general one as well.

At this point I always feel that it is wise to enforce this by calling attention to parallels in other places in the Scriptures. This, I believe, is a very valuable and important principle, that you buttress what you find in a text by similar statements in other portions of Scripture, so showing that it is not something isolated. This is a wise procedure for many reasons. Heretics are generally people who have got hold of an idea from a particular statement which they have misinterpreted, and have then allowed it to run away with them, instead of checking it with other portions of Scripture. It is always helpful to the listener to see that what is being preached is sound and solid biblical teaching. So you must look for these parallels elsewhere, and show how this same thing is stated in somewhat different circumstances perhaps, but is essentially the same point. Having done that you can show its relevance for today and for the immediate people to whom you are preaching.

That is the introduction to the sermon; that is how you lead up to your handling of the theme, the subject matter or the principle which you have discovered in this way.

Now while I believe that this is the procedure which one should adopt in general, I hasten to say that surely there is nothing wrong in varying it at times. In other words, sometimes you may start with the situation today, and outline and delineate that, and then ask, 'Well, now, what have the Scriptures to say about this?' It is not that you have actually arrived at it like that in your own preparation but it is sometimes a good way of putting it. If there is some acute problem or situation that has arisen in your local church, or in a more general way, that is not a bad way of dealing with it. It will arrest interest, it will focus attention, it will certainly enable the people to see clearly that what you are doing is not something theoretical and academic. At times, therefore, it is good to start with a statement of the position and then show that the passage you are expounding deals with this very thing. That shows that the Scriptures are always contemporary, that they are never out of date, and that they never fail to deal with any situation whatsoever. At the same time it emphasises again that your preaching always comes out of the Scriptures. So while I advocate what I have suggested as a general habit and practice, I also say that we must not become slaves to any method; we must always be free and prepared to vary our method for the sake of the proclamation of the Truth.

*   *   *

We have now arrived at the principle or teaching that you want to put to the people. The next step is to divide this up into propositions or heads, headings—call it what you like. There are a number of things to say about this. Perhaps I had better deal first with the numerical question. There are some preachers who are absolute slaves in this respect. You must have three 'heads', and three only. If you have fewer than three heads you are a bad preacher; if you have more than three you are an equally bad preacher. This is quite ridiculous, of course, but it is amazing to notice how easily one falls into habits and becomes the slave of a tradition. I was certainly brought up in this tradition of 'always an introduction and three heads'. People looked for them; that was the almost invariable custom of the preachers.

That it had become the tradition in that particular Church—the Welsh Presbyterian—was unusually ridiculous because one of the greatest preachers of that denomination, indeed its greatest preacher, and one of its founders, Daniel Rowlands, often had as many as ten headings to a sermon. A contemporary writer said that listening to Rowlands was like watching an apothecary with a number of bottles containing wonderful perfumes. He would take the first bottle and pull out the stopper or the cork and release the wonderful aroma which was then wafted over the entire congregation. Then he would put that bottle down and take up the second one and do the same with that. And there were often as many as ten bottles. I tell that story in order to enforce the point that we must not become slaves in this matter.

However, let us turn to something more important. The important thing about these 'heads' is that they must be there in your text, and that they must arise naturally out of it. This is vital. The actual division into heads, as I am going to show you, is not as easy as it may sound. Some people seem to be gifted with an unusual facility in this respect. It used to be said of Alexander Maclaren—a Baptist preacher in England at the end of the last century and the beginning of this century, and whose volumes of sermons are still being reprinted—that he seemed to have a kind of golden hammer in his hand with which he just tapped a text, and immediately it divided itself up into inevitable heads. However it is not given to many of us to have this golden hammer; but we must always make sure that these divisions arise naturally out of the text. Let me first put this negatively; because it is so important. Never force a division. And do not add to the number of divisions for the sake of some kind of completeness that you have in your mind or in order to make it conform to your usual practice. The headings should be natural and appear to be inevitable.

Let me tell you a story in order to ridicule this notion that you must have three heads, and also at the same time to warn against false additions. There was a quaint old preacher whom I just remember—I cannot remember hearing him but I certainly remember seeing him and remember many stories concerning him. He was a true eccentric. There have been such men in the ministry at various times in the past; there may still be an occasional one. This man was preaching on one occasion on the text, 'And Balaam arose early and saddled his ass'. After introducing the subject and reminding his hearers of the story, he came to the headings, the divisions. 'First,' he said, 'we find a good trait in a bad character—"Balaam arose" early. Early rising is a good thing; so that is the first head. Secondly, The antiquity of saddlery— "he saddled his ass". Saddlery is not something modern and new, it was an ancient craft.' And then the inspiration seemed to have vanished and he could not think of another heading. Yet he felt that he must have three heads to the sermon, otherwise he would not be a great preacher. So the divisions of the sermon were eventually announced as—'A good trait in a bad character.' 'The antiquity of sadlery.' 'Thirdly and lastly, a few remarks concerning the Woman of Samaria!' Now that literally happened. From that let us learn not to force the text and not to add to it. Do not become a slave to these mechanical notions.

I hasten to add something equally important: Do not be too clever in your divisions, do not be too smart. This has been a real snare to many preachers. It may not be quite as true today, but certainly in the earlier part of this century there was probably nothing that did greater harm to preaching than this very thing. Clever headings. Slick and smart divisions in which the preacher displayed his cleverness. One of the great dangers always facing the preacher (I hope to deal with this later) is the terrible danger of professionalism. I have often found that ministers when they meet with one another, instead of 'swapping jokes' as the men of the world do, say to each other 'What do you think of this? What do you think of the following divisions of this verse?' They would exchange these and almost have a competition in that respect. Now that is professionalism—and we are all subject to it. But it is thoroughly bad from every standpoint. We should never handle the Word of God in that way. So avoid cleverness and smartness. The people will detect this, and they will get the impression that you are more interested in yourself and your cleverness than in the truth of God and their souls.

Then there is, of course, what has been described as, 'Apt alliteration's artful aid'. There are those who believe that it is helpful that their headings should all start with the same letter of the Alphabet—three Bs or three Ms, etc. They must introduce this alliterative element. I hesitate to say that this is actually wrong, but I am sure that it is a snare to many men. In order to get the third heading to start with the same letter as the other two they sometimes have to manipulate their matter just a little. But that is precisely what I say we must not do. I have always been puzzled as to why those who regard themselves as 'devotional' or holiness preachers should have been most addicted to this practice. For myself, I am acutely allergic to the practice and generally find it to be a hindrance to the truth, and an annoyance. Avoiding every suspicion of artificiality or cleverness, our headings should appear to be the inevitable way of dividing up the matter.

There are a number of further points about this question of headings or divisions in a sermon. Take time over this because the whole purpose of dividing up the subject in this way is to make it easier for the people to take in the Truth and to assimilate it. That is the sole reason for having divisions. We should not be believers in 'Art for Art's sake'. As we do this in order to help the people it should be done well.

The question of the form of the sermon, to which I have referred previously, also comes in at this point; that is why you should take time over this. But sometimes you will find that it is extremely difficult to get exactly the right form. You have got your message, and you are beginning to see the 'form' in which you are going to present it, but you cannot quite work out the divisions to your own satisfaction. I advocate taking great care over this; we must not rush it or force it. It is here, especially, that one's knowledge of oneself is most helpful and rewarding. I was making the point in a previous lecture that a man has to know himself and his own temperament, and his own differing mental and physical and spiritual conditions and states, and that he has to treat himself accordingly. Very often I have found that in struggling to get the matter of a sermon into the right divisions, and into the form that seems to be appropriate to it, one can get into a kind of mental tangle. You find that you can no longer think clearly and you become tense. It is possible to spend hours in this way trying in vain to get the sermon into shape. The ways in which release comes are many and various. What happens to us at this point can happen equally well to a man who is not a Christian at all. One of the best treatments of this subject is a book by Arthur Koestler, published a few years ago under the title *The Act of Creation*. He is not interested of course in what we are discussing, but he is interested in the way in which great scientific discoveries in particular are made, and also in poetry. One of the big points he makes is that it is generally the case that the most notable scientific discoveries have not been the result of a pure logical process of thinking. That has played a part in the process, but the big things, he says, have generally come suddenly and unexpectedly; they have been 'given'. The story is not that the scientist has gone on from step to step and then eventually arrived at the ultimate step—the vital thing has often come in a kind of flash of revelation.

To illustrate his thesis he tells a story of Poincaré, one-time President of the French Republic and also Prime Minister more than once. He was also a great mathematician, and at one time he was working on some mathematical problem. He had been engaged on it for months but could not get the solution. He could get so far each time, but he could not get any further. He knew that there was a solution but he could not arrive at it. After months spent in this way, he began to feel a bit stale and so he went off to stay at a small seaside village, partly to have a change of air and for the good of his health. He had taken his work with him, thinking that he might be able to do a bit now and again; and this had been going on for some time. He eventually reached a point when he felt he must pay a visit to Paris to consult some of his colleagues in order to get some further help concerning this problem. Now this is what happened. He had to take a little bus from the village to a kind of county town where he would get a larger bus that would take him to a large town, and then the final bus to Paris.

He set out on the journey little knowing what was to happen. The local bus had been delayed on its journey so that when Poincaré arrived at the county town he saw that the bus he had to take for the second stage of his journey was on the verge of starting, and that it was very doubtful whether he would catch it. So he hurriedly picked up his bag, got off his little bus, and running as fast as he could just managed to get hold of the rail at the back of the second bus and succeeded in hauling himself on to the platform. As his two feet landed on the platform, suddenly the solution to his mathematical problem appeared before him plainly and clearly! That is sheer fact; that is the sort of thing that happens. It is a most astonishing phenomenon, and I find it to be a very fascinating study. I have had this kind of experience on several occasions.

We are all different, I know, and one can only speak for oneself, but as far as I am concerned if my sermon is not clear and ordered in my mind I cannot preach it to others. I suppose I could stand up and talk, but that would probably muddle people rather than help them. That is why I regard this ordering and shaping of the sermon as most important, and I advocate that you should struggle with this until you get it into shape. I well remember how on one occasion I was struggling with a text and had spent a whole morning on it, but simply could not get it in shape. My wife then called me to lunch. At that time— this was many years ago—there was a man named Christopher Stone who had a weekly radio programme of new gramophone records. We used to enjoy listening to that programme while having our lunch. We began to do so on this occasion. He had put on two or three records which had not interested me at all. Then he announced that he was going to put on a record of two very famous singers singing a very well-known duet. I believe one of them was Beniamino Gigli. Listening to this record with these two superb voices perfectly blended, and singing most thrilling music, I was not merely pleased but deeply moved emotionally, and, immediately, the problem I had been struggling with for hours throughout the morning was entirely resolved, everything fell into place at once—order, divisions, shape, everything. The moment the record finished I rushed to my study and put it down on paper as quickly as I could, trusting that I had not forgotten or missed anything. That singing and that music provided the release I needed from my mental tangle and stalemate.

I am ready to confess that I regard this question of form, and true division, as being so important that when I have failed to find the desired division to my satisfaction with a given text, rather than preach on it in this unsatisfactory state I have put it aside and taken another text, and more or less 'made' a sermon on the other text. Rather than ruin a message which I feel has been given to me, and which I feel has something special about it, which God is likely to honour in the preaching, and which is likely to help the people—rather than ruin something which one feels is going to be better than usual, or mar it or deliver it imperfectly, I put it aside for the moment. I have put such a message aside for a week or a fortnight or even longer. I have then come back to it; and it is only when I have finally satisfied myself as to the shape and form that I have preached it.

It is good to make a rule of this—never to spoil something which you feel within yourself is going to be good. Sermons vary tremendously; and you will have a feeling at times that what you are preparing is going to be one of the best sermons you have ever preached in your life. Whenever you have that feeling do not spoil it, do not ruin it by hasty and inadequate preparation; take time over it.

The next point is whether you should announce the headings all together. I have known people who insist upon your announcing all the headings immediately at this stage before you go on to deal with point number one. That was the old tradition. You will find that the Puritans did so, as did also Spurgeon.

I have tended to rebel against that tradition in spite of my admiration for its practitioners. The reason is that I feel that people have become mechanical over this question also, and I have felt that it is bad for the congregations. It cannot be repeated too frequently that as long as one is preaching one is always in a battle, and the battle is one between the substance and the form of the sermon. Both, of course, are important, and that is why there is this tension between them. While I have asserted as strongly as I can the importance of form, I want also to assert equally strongly the danger of allowing the form to become the master of the substance. It is because I feel that this stating of the headings all together at the beginning, before taking up the first division, has often encouraged the people to take too much interest in the form and the mechanics and the cleverness of the construction, rather than in the truth preached, that I have tended to avoid doing this.

At this point you should check what you have done by turning to your commentaries once more. You have already consulted them about the exact meaning of the words, the context, and so on, but you come back again to them to check yourself as to the message and the way in which you have divided it. You do this for the sake of accuracy once more. So now you have prepared your skeleton, and you have seen to it that the divisions lead up to a climax and to an application. That, of course, is the whole point and purpose of preparing the sermon and of preaching.

All this can be done in one of two ways. There are those who do all this in their minds without writing anything at all. I on the other hand would urge, once again, the importance of putting this skeleton, which you have thus prepared, in writing. I suggest that this is better because I have found that this helps to stimulate one's mind yet further. I know that there are those who can think 'inwardly' as it is sometimes described. There are different ways of thinking; and we are all different in this matter. Some people think best as they are speaking; some think best as they are writing; and it has been said that 'the salt of the earth' think inwardly. Well, find out the group to which you belong; but make sure that you are right in your assessment. It is probably true to say of most of us that it is good for us to put our 'skeleton' down on paper. I have known many a man to whom a good idea had come, and who, because it had thrilled him when it came to him, thought all would be well, but who found when he came to preach his sermon that he had not got as much as he thought he had. So put it down on paper!

Having arrived at this point you are face to face with a major decision. What are you going to do with this skeleton that you have prepared? There are two main possibilities open to you: Should this be written out in full, or should it not? Once more it seems to me that the only sane thing to say is that you must not lay down an absolute law about this matter; because you will find that your laws will not stand up to the test of the history of preaching. Charles Haddon Spurgeon, that great preacher, did not write out his sermons in full; he just prepared and used a skeleton. He did not approve of the writing of sermons, in general. He would write articles and did so constantly, but he did not write his sermons. On the other hand, Dr. Thomas Chalmers, the great leader of the Free Church of Scotland, and a great preacher, found that he had to write out his sermons fully. He tried many times to become an extemporary preacher but felt each time it was a complete failure; he just could not do it. So he had to write his sermons out in full. The result was that that became and has continued to be a tradition in Scotland until today. Chalmers was the man who started it. There had been great preachers in Scotland before him who did not write their sermons, and were good extemporary preachers. But Chalmers was a great man, and the great leader in the Disruption of 1843; so he started a whole tradition. That is the sort of thing that happens.

Jonathan Edwards is most interesting in this respect. Until recently I was always under the impression that Edwards always wrote out all his sermons in full. It is quite certain that in his early days he did so, and that furthermore he actually read them in the pulpit to the people. There is the well-known story of how he stood in his pulpit with a candle in one hand and his manuscript in the other; that was his way of preaching. But I was interested to find in 1967—when I had the privilege of meeting the two scholars who are responsible for the re-publishing of his Works in the Library at Yale University, and who have all his MSS. there—I was very interested to see that as Edwards went on he did not write his sermons in full, but contented himself with writing some notes. He obviously varied his method as he went on and developed. How wise he was in this respect, as in many others also.

It is always wrong to lay down absolute laws in these matters. Once more, every man has got to know himself, and he has to decide for himself. What I regard as being always important is that you should preserve freedom. This element can never be exaggerated. Yet, at the same time you must have order and coherence. As is so often true in this matter of preaching you are always in the position of being be-tween two extremes, you are always on a kind of knife-edge.

But I would ask a question: What is wrong with combining both these methods—the written and the extempore? In many ways it seems to me to be the ideal; certainly it was what I did myself during my first ten years in the ministry. I tried to write one sermon a week; I never tried to write two. But I did try to write one for the first ten years. I felt that writing was good discipline, good for producing ordered thought and arrangement and sequence and development of the argument and so on. So my particular practice was to use both the written and the extempore methods; and I would be prepared to defend this.

If I am asked which sermons I wrote, I have already said that I used to divide my ministry, as I still do, into edification of the saints in the morning and a more evangelistic sermon in the evening. Well, my practice was to write my evangelistic sermon. I did so because I felt that in speaking to the saints, to the believers, one could feel more relaxed. There, one was speaking in the realm of the family. In other words, I believe that one should be unusually careful in evangelistic sermons. That is why the idea that a fellow who is merely gifted with a certain amount of glibness of speech and self-confidence, not to say cheek, can make an evangelist is all wrong. The greatest men should always be the evangelists, and generally have been; and the idea that Tom, Dick and Harry can be put up to speak on a street corner, but you must have a great preacher in a pulpit in a church is, to me, the reversing of the right order. It is when addressing the unbelieving world that we need to be most careful; and therefore I used to write my evangelistic sermon and not the other. However, I am simply suggesting that we must not be over-dogmatic or rigid about this. Then as time went on, and as with many others, I wrote less and less, and by now I cannot remember when I last wrote a sermon. However, the important point is that you have just got to know yourself, and to be honest with yourself, and do what you regard as being most effective.

However, whether you write your sermon in full, or partly, or whether you preach in a more extemporary manner, you must never just preach your skeletons. These skeletons are to be clothed; they need to have flesh upon them. We come back again to this question of the form of the sermon. A sermon is not just a collection of statements; it has this further quality about it, this form, this wholeness. The sole reason for this is that it is helpful to the people. It is not a matter of 'Art for Art's sake', it is because it greatly aids people as they listen. You can put it like this. A scaffolding is essential in putting up a building, but when you look at the completed building you do not see the scaffolding; you see the building. There is a structure there; but the structure is covered, it is only there as something to help you to put up the desired building.

The same thing precisely is true of the human body. There is the frame, the skeleton; but it must be clothed with flesh before you have a body. This is equally true of a sermon. I remember a youngish preacher, a very able man who had taken first class honours in Theology in Oxford, telling me how he was preaching on one occasion with an old preacher, a great old preacher. The older man having heard the younger man three or four times said to him, 'You know, you bring very good pedigree cattle to the market, but it is a great pity that their bones and skeletons are so obvious. They have not got enough flesh on them. A man who goes to the market to buy an animal does not want to buy a skeleton, he likes to buy a well-fed and well-covered animal—Flesh! You do not buy bones from the butcher; you want meat.' In exactly the same way we must never just throw facts at people, we must not throw thoughts or skeletons at them; we must take time to clothe the skeletons with flesh.

While that is the chief danger with regard to extempore preaching, we turn now to some of the dangers connected with the writing of sermons. The reason for writing is that you desire to clothe the skeleton, but immediately certain dangers and snares arise. The first is to affect a too-ornate style, to pay too much attention to the literary quality or the literary element. This is most interesting from the standpoint of the history of preaching. Christian preachers seem to have gone through phases with regard to this. Take, for instance, what happened in the seventeenth century, a great century in many respects. At the beginning of that century there were certain so-called classical preachers in the Church of England—Bishop Andrewes, the famous Jeremy Taylor, and John Donne, up to a point. These men were regarded and acclaimed as great preachers, and in many senses they were; and yet it seems to me, as it did definitely to the Puritans at that time, that they had gone too far in a certain direction. Their sermons had become works of art. They were literary masterpieces, perfectly constructed, freely interspersed with classical and literary allusions and quotations. The result, however, was that the people in general were more or less ignorant of saving truth, of the real truths of the Scriptures, and went merely to enjoy these perfect ornate sermons. To listen to them was a literary and aesthetic treat.

The Puritans introduced a tremendous reaction against this; and they did so quite deliberately. They felt that these perfect sermons were actually 'concealing' the Truth, whereas the whole point of a sermon is to 'declare' the Truth. Once more the form had triumphed over the substance. The best way, perhaps, to bring this point home is to tell the story concerning Thomas Goodwin, one of the greatest of the Puritans. Thomas Goodwin was a naturally eloquent man, and when he was a student at Cambridge University he used to listen to a famous orator and eloquent preacher in the University. Thomas Goodwin admired this man tremendously; he was his ideal of a preacher, and so he modelled himself on this man and his method. But Thomas Goodwin underwent a very great and profound religious experience that changed his whole outlook and affected him in a radical manner, as true conversion always does (2 Cor. 5:17). He had a great struggle with himself with respect to his preaching as the result of this. Not long after his conversion he was asked to preach the University sermon, and, of course, instinctively, he began preparing and writing in the classical manner which he had so admired. He produced a great sermon with wonderful purple patches and literary embellishments which thrilled him and moved him as he thought of them and wrote them. But then the Spirit of God, and his own conscience, began to work within him, and he went through a terrible struggle. What should he do? He knew that in his congregation there would be not only the learned people of the University, but also some ordinary people, perhaps even some uneducated servant-maids who often attended on these occasions. Thomas Goodwin now realised that he had to preach to those servant-maids as well as to the others, and he knew that these purple patches would not only mean nothing to these ordinary people but might even be a hindrance. What should he do? At last, with his heart almost bleeding and breaking, he excised the purple patches from the sermon and never delivered them. In the interests of the Truth, in the interests of the communication of the Gospel, in the interest of the souls of the people, surely he was undoubtedly right. A concern for literary form unless carefully disciplined can easily lead to an ornate and artificial style which can ruin true preaching.

There is much evidence of this tendency surely today. I remember reading in 1943 or '44 an account of the Disruption of 1843 in the Church of Scotland. In dealing with the great Thomas Chalmers this man ventured to criticise his preaching. The criticism was that there was a most regrettable absence of literary and historical allusions in Chalmers' preaching. Thus a little pygmy whose preaching efforts have never been heard of, and who had never achieved anything, ventured to criticise a giant. But what grounds of criticism! What ignorance of the true function of preaching!

Let me put it in another way. In the earlier part of this century there was a bishop of the Church of England called Hensley Henson. He wrote his autobiography in two volumes under the title *A Diary of an Unimportant Life!* I remember reading his description in one of the volumes of how on one occasion he spent three weeks writing a sermon which he had to deliver on some special occasion. He tells us how he laboured with this, re-writing certain portions, and changing others and making various additions—three weeks producing and polishing this perfect sermon!

Surely this is something which it is very difficult to reconcile with the preaching of the Gospel as one sees it in the Scriptures themselves, or as one sees it in the preaching that has characterised the great periods in the history of the Church. What has this polishing of phrases, this writing and re-writing to do with Truth? There must be form, but we must never give inordinate attention to it. Can you conceive of the Apostle Paul spending three weeks in the preparation of one sermon, polishing phrases, changing a word here and there, putting in another adjective or adding another *bon mot*? The whole thing is utterly inconceivable. 'Not with wisdom of words,' says the Apostle. 'Not with enticing words of man's wisdom.' How easily we go from one extreme to the other! So I put it in general by saying that we must always be careful to avoid this over-ornate style. Perhaps it is not as great a danger today as it once was, because people are not as interested in preaching as they used to be; but I am quite certain that it was this over-attention to the literary style and perfect form of the service towards the end of the last century, and the beginning of this century, that did such grievous harm to preaching and the whole cause of preaching.

This brings us to the question of the use of quotations. This again can be quite an involved and difficult matter. It is certainly a more acute problem today than the previous one. This is because we all think we are more learned, and that our congregations are more learned and better educated and have more knowledge. And the temptation is to think that the proof of learning is the number of quotations used. This is particularly true, as you know, with regard to books. How do you decide whether a man is a scholar or not? The simple answer is—by the number of footnotes. If he has no footnotes and copious references to other writers and quotations from them, he is not a scholar, he is not a thinker, and vice versa. This of course is just ridiculous. What we should be interested in is a man's quality of mind, his capacity for thinking, and his originality; not the number of footnotes. But this is the whole tendency at the present time. But when it comes into preaching it becomes a deadly menace. Nothing can militate more against true preaching than this.

Why do I say this? One answer is that the real object in using quotations should not be to show your learning or to call attention to yourself. If it is, you had better not use a single quotation because your motive is entirely wrong. I remember the Principal of a theological college who had a considerable vogue as a popular preacher for some few years in Britain. One day he was asked to preach a sermon on the radio in about two months' time. He immediately began to read through the Oxford Book of Religious Verse and similar books. What for? To find a striking quotation with which to start the sermon. He not only did that himself, he got some of his favourite students to do the same thing; he urged them to read such poetry on his behalf. He told them what his theme was going to be, and they were to look for some striking quotation to give an arresting opening to the sermon. It was one of these students who told me the story at the time. There is only one comment to make on that kind of thing—it is sheer prostitution. But it is also an abuse of quotations. Why is that wrong? I say it is wrong for the reason that the form, once more, becomes more important than the substance. But the form is meant to be the servant of the substance.

I remember a phrase which impressed me very much in this connection. I was reading an article in which the writer was drawing the distinction, between what he called 'The Artifice of Artistry, and the Inevitability of Art'. That states it perfectly. Artistry falls back upon artifices; you can see the man striving and straining to produce an impression. What characterises the work of the artist, the true artist, on the other hand, is always the 'inevitability'—you feel it could not have been anything else. There is something artificial about the other; it is an artifice, it is always the characteristic of the prostitute out to produce an effect to serve her own ends. We must never be guilty of that. We must always make sure that there is this quality of 'inevitability'.

It is not for me to lay down rules on this matter, but I would say that on the whole it is a good thing to avoid the use of books of quotations. The only real legitimate use of a book of quotations is to check what I think is an accurate quotation or to help to supply some missing word or words. It is there to save time. In other words you should not turn up a particular heading in your book of quotations in order to find a quotation. What should happen, rather, is that as you are thinking or writing, something comes into your mind which you have read somewhere or which you learned in school. In order to make quite sure that you are right about the words, and the author, check it with your book of quotations. But to start with your book of quotations is artificial and mechanical; and, in any case, it is a lazy way of doing your work.

I would go even further and say: Do not try to think of quotations. If you do, once more the mechanics have become too obvious and prominent in your method. In other words, only use a quotation when it comes to your mind and when it seems to you to be inevitable. Or, if you like, only use a quotation when it seems to say perfectly the thing that you were trying to say. It says it better than you can say it, it says it in what seems to you to be an almost perfect manner. You may think that I am making too much of this matter, but I can assure you that I am not. Too many quotations in a sermon become very wearisome to the listener, and at times they can even be ridiculous. I remember having a conversation one day with a man who had been professor of poetry at Oxford and who was also a clergyman. We were talking about this very matter and the way in which it was becoming quite ridiculous. He told me that the previous week he had been listening to a sermon in Westminster Abbey in London. The learned preacher having produced a mass of quotations (showing his profound reading!) actually said at one point in his sermon, 'As Evelyn Underhill has been reminding us recently, God is love.'

There is no need to comment. Everything has to be stated in the form of a quotation, and so we reach this position in which the truth is being concealed and the preacher makes himself ridiculous and disgusts the people.

A sermon is meant to be a proclamation of the truth of God as mediated through the preacher. People do not want to listen to a string of quotations of what other people have thought and said. They have come to listen to you; you are the man of God, you have been called to the ministry, you have been ordained; and they want to hear this great truth as it comes through you, through the whole of your being. They expect it to have passed through your thought, to be a part of your experience; they want this authentic personal note. I can assure you that if your sermons are nothing but a string of quotations, some, probably the more ignorant people, will say, 'What a learned man that was'; the others, and especially any preacher who may be present, will know exactly what you are doing. But what is invariably true is that there will be no power in your preaching. I can guarantee that statement. There is never any power in sermons that consist simply of 'as So-and-so has said', or 'So-and-so has reminded us' and so on. Such statements come out one after another and you feel that this good man has allowed his reading to become a substitute for his thinking. We are meant to do our own thinking, and all your reading should be designed to stimulate your thought and to give you a certain amount of information.

The next warning I would give is to be careful—this especially when you are writing—of too close reasoning. I have emphasised in general, at the beginning in my original outline, the importance of reasoning and development and sequence in the sermon; but do not make the reasoning too close or refined or subtle. Because this sermon is going to be spoken, and it is not as easy to follow a very close and well-reasoned argument when you are listening as when you are reading. So if you go too far in that respect you are hindering the people from receiving the truth. This can apply also to extemporary preaching, but it is a particular danger I feel in connection with written sermons.

So I close by saying: Prepare, but beware of the danger of over-preparation. This is particularly true of written sermons. The danger is to be too perfect. You have your ideal, you know what you want to do; but the danger is to overdo it so that the sermon becomes an end in itself. How do you avoid this? What is the antidote? It is quite simple—keep on reminding yourself right through from beginning to end that what you are doing is meant for people, for all sorts and kinds of people. You are not preparing a sermon for a congregation of professors or pundits; you are preparing a sermon for a mixed congregation of people, and it is your business and mine to be of some help to everybody that is in that congregation. We have failed unless we have done that. So avoid an over-academic theoretical approach. Be practical. Remember the people: you are preaching to them.

CHAPTER TWELVE

Illustrations, Eloquence, Humour

COMING NOW TO the extemporary type of preaching, and the preparation for it, there is much less to say. The dangers here are not so many; but there is one thing which I would like to emphasise, and I do so as the result of my own experience. It is the danger that arises when a man who generally or frequently has written his sermons decides for various reasons to do so no longer and becomes an extemporary preacher. The greatest danger confronting him will be to be content with an inadequate preparation. Instinctively one tends to feel that if one is not going to write the sermon fully, all that is necessary is to prepare the barest outline or skeleton and to leave it at that. The result of doing so can be quite disastrous in the pulpit. When the thought comes to you while you are reading your Bible, and you prepare a hurried sketch or outline of a sermon, you seem to be brimful of ideas and feel that there will be no difficulty in preaching that sermon. But, alas, you will often find that when in a few days or weeks you come to preach from this skeleton in a pulpit all your ideas seem to forsake you and there is but little to say. Try as you will, you cannot re-capture what came to you, and you will even begin to wonder how you ever arrived at the various headings. They obviously had a meaning once, but it has somehow vanished.

The way to deal with this danger may appear to be quite obvious, but if you are not aware of the problem you will have to learn by painful experience, even as I did. You must work out your points, the main headings, in a number of subordinate or subsidiary headings. In other words you must make sure that you have sufficient matter and material. The main headings can be elaborated and worked out and illustrated in various ways. Be very careful to make notes of that. As I have advised with regard to the skeleton itself, here again I emphasise the importance of putting it down on paper, so that you will be reminded as you are preaching, of what you wanted to say under this particular heading. The rule is not to let your preparation be too brief; work out your message in these sub-headings as best you can, and then you will not be short of matter. Many a preacher has relied upon the inspiration that has come to him when a text has suddenly spoken to him in the way I have described, and has found that it recurred when he was in the pulpit while actually preaching. He has then fallen to the foolish temptation of imagining that that will always happen, and that careful preparation is therefore not necessary. Experience will soon disabuse him.

Another factor which operates in this connection can be best illustrated by my telling the story of a minister I knew in South Wales. It shows how there are times and seasons, or ebb and flow, in one's spiritual experience. This particular preacher had had a great experience in the religious awakening and Revival in Wales in 1904–5. He was an able man and a good student. The Revival broke out while he was a student and he and others were greatly affected by it. Quite commonly during a time of Revival people are given an unusual ease and facility in speech, in prayer, and in preaching; and the testimony of the ministers in Wales at that time was that they had to spend very little time in preparation. Everything seemed to be given to them; they were full of matter, and out of the fullness of their hearts and their Christian joy, and their love to the Lord, they spoke without any difficulty or restraint.

But a problem often arises when a period like that comes to an end and the Revival subsides. Many of these men fail to realise that that was an exceptional time, and that now having returned to more ordinary times in the life of the Church, they will have to do much more in the matter of preparation. I have known a number of men who fell into this particular trap, and for differing reasons. Some of them even felt that it was sinful to prepare sermons. They had had this great liberty and freedom so that when it ceased some of them got into real spiritual trouble and almost mental trouble, feeling that they had grieved the Spirit or had quenched the Spirit. Others felt that they must be guilty of some sin they were not aware of. Why were they no longer given that ease and facility that they had once enjoyed? I knew several such men and had to try to help them a little out of the spiritual depression which in some cases actually crossed the line from the spiritual to the psychological.

It was the failure to understand this that led the man I am thinking of in particular into trouble. In his case the problem was not so much the fear of having 'grieved the Spirit', as that he thought that he had scriptural warrant for not preparing his sermons. He did not have to prepare during the Revival, and when the Revival ended he felt that he had spiritual warrant for continuing in the same way. It was the verse in Psalm 81 which says, 'Open thy mouth wide and I will fill it.' He interpreted this as meaning that you should go into a pulpit without preparation, and that you would be given the matter which you were to utter. The poor fellow did this literally; the result was that he emptied his church, and was more or less useless as a preacher for some fifty years afterwards. The real tragedy was that he was a highly spiritual man and a very able man.

If therefore you do not write your sermon in full do not fall into any of these traps. Prepare as thoroughly as you can so that you will know in your mind what you want to say from beginning to end. I cannot emphasise this too strongly. If my experience is of any help or value I have to report that I have tended to make my notes fuller and fuller as I have gone on rather than shorter and shorter. Of course there are variations in all these matters.

While there are those two main methods—the fully written sermon and the preparation of notes for extempory preaching—it is also true that there are people who have used certain variations of these; and I see nothing wrong in that. Some men I have known have written their introduction fairly fully, and also the end of the sermon. Then in between they have relied upon their skeleton or notes. There is much to be said for that method, especially if you are changing from a fully written sermon to the extemporary method. It will help in this process of transition. Some write the introduction because they have found that having gone into the pulpit feeling that they had a sermon prepared in outline, and that they knew what they were going to say, they have suddenly found themselves beginning to stumble in the introduction. They simply could not get going, and this so upset them that the whole sermon was ruined. The way to correct that in this period of transition is to write out your introduction fully and perhaps the end of the sermon in exactly the same way.

* * *

We turn now to look at various matters that arise in the actual delivery of the sermon. Some men read their sermon in the pulpit from beginning to end. I do not want to be too dogmatic, but surely that must be wrong, that must be bad. I know that some notable instances can be cited from past history where men have done this and it has been greatly blessed; but you do not make rules out of exceptions. Surely preaching involves, as we saw in an earlier lecture, a direct contact between the people and the preacher, and an interplay of personalities and minds and hearts. There is the element of 'give and take'. It is good therefore that the preacher be looking at the people; and you cannot be looking at the people and reading a manuscript at the same time. Such reading is bad for you and bad for the people. You lose their attention and your grip on them, and they lose grip on you and what you are saying. Surely, by definition, preaching is speech addressed to people in a direct and personal manner. It is not something theoretical or an academic lecture; it implies a living contact. Anything that makes you lose that is bad in and of itself. I know that some preachers have been blessed as they have read their sermons;

there are exceptions to all the rules which can be laid down in these matters, but that does not affect the rule. There are others who while they do not read their sermons look out through one of the windows of the building while they are preaching to a congregation. That is no better, of course; you might as well be reading a manuscript. I have known men who have given the impression that they felt that this was a highly spiritual procedure—they were great mystics looking into some unseen depths!

But let me hasten to say that what many other preachers do, namely to memorise this written sermon, is to me almost as bad. Not quite perhaps; but it comes very near. It is a little better, because while you are reciting or declaiming you can look at the people. You have written your sermon; then you have read it through a number of times; and if you have a good memory you can easily memorise most of it. I have known many who do this. Though I agree that it is a little better, I still do not like it. My chief reason is that it binds the man, it interferes with the element of freedom. While reciting or declaiming you are really not making contact with the people. You are concentrating on what you have memorised and are trying to recall it; and to that extent it comes between you and the people whom you are addressing. The living element is lessened and the mechanical element comes in more. This is a very difficult matter, and many preachers have had to experiment and to change their procedure from time to time.

I always like to think that a distinction which can be drawn in the realm of secular speaking—political speaking if you like—has a validity in the realm of preaching also. There is a difference, is there not, between rhetoric and oratory. What is the difference? It is surely the difference that this point I am making brings out. The rhetorician is tied to his preparation, he is declaiming something which he has prepared very carefully. The most notable example of a rhetorician in recent history was the late Sir Winston Churchill. He is often called an orator; but he was not an orator, he was a rhetorician. His father, Lord Randolph was an orator, but Sir Winston never was. In his younger days he used to write every word of his speeches and then memorise and declaim them. Later on in life he used to read them; but in his younger days he used to recite what he had learned by heart. That such a procedure interferes with the vital contact and exchange between speaker and listeners can be illustrated in his case. His opponents, knowing that he was reciting and performing a feat of memory, would interrupt him. This would throw him off-balance and he would have to go back several sentences in his speech and recite them over again before he could continue. In other words because he was a rhetorician he was tied. The orator is always free and always owes a lot to his audience. In his case there is always a living exchange —a real transaction takes place.

All this is equally true in preaching. The preacher should be an orator rather than a rhetorician. There is always something lost in the memorising and reciting and declaiming of a sermon.

Another device that men often adopt, and I think there is much to be said for it, is to make full notes of the written sermon. Instead of memorising it, make notes of it. Having written it, and as a result having the gist of it in your mind, just make notes of it and then preach from those notes. This will secure much greater freedom than either of the two previous methods. That, again, is particularly good for a man who is in that stage of transition from writing to extemporary preaching. The great thing is freedom. I cannot over-emphasise this. It is of the very essence of the act of preaching—this freedom in your own mind and spirit, this being free to the influences of the Spirit upon you. If we believe in the Holy Spirit at all, we must believe that He is acting powerfully while we are engaged in this most serious and wonderful work. We must therefore be open to His influences.

Of course, this will lead to a number of possible consequences. It may well mean that your style is not quite so perfect, indeed from the strictly literary standpoint it may become bad. But you will be in good company. The pedants have always criticised the Apostle Paul for his anacolutha have they not? They point out how Paul starts a sentence and then gets so carried away by his theme that he forgets to finish it. That is freedom, freedom in the Spirit. He would not have done very well perhaps in the examination halls but the Spirit used him. I am not suggesting that you should not complete your sentences, but I am suggesting that you should be free. So when the Spirit lays hold of you and leads you out, allow yourself to be led. Do not be tied, do not be fettered.

No one should be discouraged by all this. There never has been a preacher that has not had to learn by experience. Do not be discouraged. If you find at first that you cannot preach without writing out your sermon fully, write it out fully. But experiment in the way I have indicated. Write one sermon and not the other; try these various modifications and variations. Above all do not be impatient with yourself. Do not be too downcast if you happen to have a very bad service and say that you will never again enter a pulpit without a fully written sermon lying on the desk before you. That is the voice of the devil. Do not listen to him; go on until you arrive at a stage where you know that you are free. I must not make too much of this, but there is a very real danger of our putting our faith in our sermon rather than in the Spirit. Our faith should not be in the sermon, it should be in the Holy Spirit Himself. So let us make sure of freedom first, last, everywhere, always; and then contact with the people.

We come now to certain matters which are common to both these types of preaching whether written sermons or extemporary preaching. I deal with these because people have often asked me about them and made comments and criticisms concerning them. I refer to the whole question of the use of stories and illustrations. This must have our attention. I assume that we are clear about the difference between the use of an illustration, and spiritualising a portion of Scripture. I am not advocating a wrong and a false spiritualising of Scripture; and I must not go too much into detail as I am not lecturing on homiletics, but I want to make it clear that there is a difference between spiritualising an Old Testament incident and using it simply as an illustration. The difference is this: You must make clear to the people, of course, exactly what you are doing. You must make it clear that what you are saying is, that as this particular thing happened in the realm of history so the same principle can or may be found in the spiritual realm.

Let me give an example. While lecturing on revivals once, I took the story of Isaac digging again 'the wells of water that had been digged by his father Abraham' and which the Philistines had stopped after the death of Abraham. Some people thought that in doing so I was spiritualising that Old Testament incident. They did so because they did not realise the difference between using a story like that as an illustration and spiritualising it. Had I been spiritualising it, it would have meant that I was asserting that Isaac was doing something spiritual on that occasion, whereas I had gone out of my way to say that I was simply using this story as an illustration and pointing out that what Isaac did in the matter of water—ordinary water essential to life and the well-being of the body—provides us with a picture of a principle which is of value in the spiritual realm in connection with revival. I was not saying that he did anything spiritual, but showing that as he did not waste his time sending out prospectors to find a new supply of water but simply re-dug the old wells because he knew there was water there, so it seemed to me to be the essence of wisdom in the spiritual realm, and in a time of difficulty and spiritual drought, not to waste our time in seeking for a new 'gospel', but to go back to the Book of Acts and every period of Revival in the history of the Church. Now that is not spiritualising that old incident. I could have gone for my illustrations or my stories to the realm of fiction, or to the realm of secular history; but I preferred on that occasion to take that Old Testament incident as my illustration. That is not spiritualising because I was not saying that what Isaac did led to a revival. But, of course, it is important that we should explain carefully what we are doing. Your congregations will generally understand this quite easily; it is only the 'experts' and pedants who are likely to misunderstand!

But, returning to stories and illustrations in general, what seems to me to be really bad is the kind of thing suggested by a book bearing the title, *The Craft of Sermon Illustration*. That kind of thing is to me an abomination. 'The Craft' does not come in to this realm at all.

That is prostitution again. I knew a preacher who always kept a little note-book in his pocket, and when he heard a good story he always pulled out his note-book and made notes of the story. Then, after he got home he wrote it out fully; and then he put this story into a certain file in a cabinet. It would be a good illustration for a certain theme. So he was always collecting stories and dividing and classifying them into various categories and filing them. Then when he came to prepare a sermon on a certain theme he would pull out the appropriate file and select the stories that he needed. He urged others to do the same.

To me, that kind of thing is not only professionalism at its worst, it is, as I say, the art of the harlot, because it pays too much attention to, and is too much concerned about, enticing people. What is even worse, of course, is when preachers repeat other preachers' stories and illustrations without acknowledgment; and even yet worse when they buy books of sermons mainly in order to find such stories.

Why am I opposed to this? It is because I feel that it makes an end in itself of the story or the illustration. These should never be an end in and of themselves. A too free use of them also panders to the carnality of the people who are listening. I have often noticed this. I remember preaching on one occasion in a certain place and how a minister who had been listening came to me at the close of the service and said, 'Thank you for your sermon. But you did not give us any illustrations this time.' That made me think and ask myself, 'What was that man listening for?' The previous time he had heard me, and I remembered the previous time, as it happened I had used more illustrations than I normally do. But here it seemed to me was a man who came to listen not so much for Truth as for illustrations. Is not this a serious perversion?

Stories and illustrations are only meant to illustrate truth, not to call attention to themselves. This whole business of illustrations and story-telling has been a particular curse during the last hundred years. I believe it is one of the factors that accounts for the decline in preaching because it helped to give the impression that preaching was an art, an end in itself. There have undoubtedly been many who really prepared a sermon simply in order to be able to use a great illustration that had occurred to them or which they had read somewhere. The illustration had become the first thing; you then find a text which is likely to cover this. In other words the heart of the matter had become the illustration. But that is the wrong order. The illustration is meant to illustrate truth, not to show itself, not to call attention to itself; it is a means of leading and helping people to see the truth that you are enunciating and proclaiming still more clearly. The rule therefore should always be that the truth must be pre-eminent and have great prominence, and illustrations must be used sparsely and carefully to that end alone. Our business is not to entertain people. People like stories, they like illustrations. I have never understood why, but people seem to like ministers who are always talking about their own families. I always find that very boring when I am listening, and I cannot understand a preacher who likes doing that. Surely there is a good deal of conceit about it. Why should people be more interested in the preacher's children than in those of other people? They have their own children and they could multiply such stories equally well themselves. The argument for this, generally, is that it introduces 'a personal touch'. I remember a Londoner telling me that he never failed to go to listen to a certain preacher whenever he visited London. This preacher used to come up from the Provinces once or twice a year. I met this man one day and he said, 'I was listening to Dr. So-and-so last Sunday; the great thing about him, you know, is that he always shares his sex life with us'! I was not quite sure whether he was suggesting that I should do likewise!

That is the thing certain people like, and that is actually what some preachers do; and you can well see how it can pander to that which is lowest and worst in many members of the congregation. It is sheer carnality, a kind of lust and desire to know personal details about people. But a preacher should go into a pulpit to enunciate and proclaim the Truth itself. This is what should be prominent, and everything else is but to minister to this end. Illustrations are just servants,

233

and you should use them sparsely and carefully. As the result of listening to preachers for many years, preaching myself, and discussing these matters, and considering them constantly, I am prepared to go so far as to say that if you use too many illustrations in your sermon your preaching will be ineffective. To do so always means loss of tension. There is the type of preacher who after saying a few words says, 'I remember'—then out comes the story. Then after a few more remarks again, 'I remember'. This means that the theme, the thrust of the Truth, is constantly being interrupted; it becomes staccato, and in the end you feel that you have been listening to a kind of after-dinner speaker or entertainer and not to a man proclaiming a grand and a glorious Truth. If such preachers become popular, and they frequently do, they are popular only in a bad sense, because they are really nothing but popular entertainers.

The only other thing I would say about stories and illustrations is that when you use them you should make sure of your facts. I remember when I was a young medical man listening to a sermon in which there was a great illustration which the preacher unfolded at some considerable length. His point was, the folly of the sinner in not paying attention to the first warnings of his conscience and so on. This was illustrated very elaborately by the story of a woman whom he had buried the week before. She had had a cancer in one breast, but by when she had gone to the doctor the secondary deposits had already spread to the spine and other parts of her body. It was now too late for a cure. What was the matter with this woman? 'Well,' said the preacher, 'the tragedy of this woman was she did not pay attention to that first twinge of pain.' To me, listening as a medical man, the whole thing was utterly ridiculous. The trouble with that sort of cancer is that it does not give you any pain until it has generally advanced to a considerable extent; it grows insidiously and quietly. The trouble with that poor woman was not that she had ignored pain, but probably had ignored a small lump which she may have felt. The great illustration was ruined as far as I was concerned because the man did not know his facts.

We can often fall into error in this way by using a scientific illustration without being quite sure of the accuracy of what we are saying, of our facts. Be careful of entering into realms about which you do not know much. You may have read something in a 'digest' or newspaper and think therefore that you know all about that particular subject; and you venture out on an illustration. Not infrequently the truth is that the man who wrote the article in the digest did not know much about it himself, and was more of a journalist than a scientist. You make it even worse, and so the man with scientific knowledge, who may be listening to you, begins to doubt the validity of the Truth that you are enunciating. He feels that you are not a careful man; and that if you handle your Scripture in the same way as you are handling the thing about which he knows, well then you are not a man to whom he is prepared to give much time and attention. So be careful about the facts if you do venture into this realm of stories and illustrations.

* * *

We must now give some consideration to the place of imagination in sermons and preaching. This is related of course to the former subject, and yet it is different. My feeling is that there is not as much danger with regard to the place of imagination in preaching today as there was at one time. We have all become so scientific that there is but little room left for imagination. This, to me is most regrettable, because imagination in preaching is most important and most helpful. I am very ready to agree that it can be dangerous; but imagination, let us not forget, is a gift of God. There would not be many poets were it not for the gift of imagination; and if you believe in winning all forms of culture for the Lord Jesus Christ do not despise the imagination. Why should imagination only be used by the non-Christian? No, imagination has a real place in preaching the Truth, because what it does is to make the Truth lively and living. Of course it can be over-done and then it becomes dangerous. Of course in this realm everything is dangerous as we have been seeing; but the use of the imagination can be particularly dangerous. This has always been to me one of the greatest problems in connection with preaching, maybe partly because of my nationality! What is the place of nationality in preaching, indeed the place of nationality and temperament in the Christian life as a whole, the place of nationality and temperament in ecclesiology; the place of nationality and temperament in theology? How easy it would be to digress at this point.

Whatever the actual explanation of why this has been a great problem to me, I am clear as to the essence of the problem. The danger is that imagination tends to run away with us and one can easily cross the line from which it has been helpful, to that point, once more, where it draws attention to itself and you have lost contact with the Truth which gave origin to it. In the end it is the imagination, and your statement of what you have seen with your imagination, that influences the people rather than the Truth.

It is not difficult to find notable examples of this from history. George Whitefield was obviously gifted with a great and exceptional imagination. Incidentally it seems quite clear from the reading of the history of preaching and the biographies of preachers, that the greatest preachers have generally been greatly gifted with imagination. It has been a part of their gift of oratory and power to influence people, gifts which are God-given. Whitefield clearly used his imagination freely, and I think that at times it is equally clear that it ran away with him. Take the famous occasion when Whitefield was preaching one day in the house of the Countess of Huntingdon in London to a very distinguished auditory amongst whom was the famous Lord Chesterfield. Chesterfield was an unbeliever, but he was interested in outstanding persons and particularly interested in good speaking. He had been persuaded to go to listen to Whitefield. The preacher on that occasion was using his famous illustration of a blind man walking along the edge of a cliff with his stick and his dog. At first the blind man was fairly far away from the edge, but he was getting nearer and nearer to it, and below there was a terrible drop which would mean certain death. Whitefield was illustrating the way in which the sinner goes on and on and gets nearer and nearer to the terrible abyss of the

Last Judgment and eternal perdition. In spite of all warnings the sinner goes on exactly as this poor blind man who having lost his stick, and the dog having run away, went on walking and got nearer and nearer to the abyss. Whitefield had been elaborating and painting this picture in most vivid colours for some time, in a most dramatic and imaginative manner, and with such effect, that at a given point Lord Chesterfield sprang to his feet shouting, 'By heavens! the beggar's gone!' What do we say about that? Had Whitefield crossed the line? What was it that influenced Chesterfield? This is where the problem arises.

But let me relate another authentic story. There was a preacher in Wales at the end of the eighteenth and the beginning of the nineteenth century called Robert Roberts. He also had this great gift of imagination—if anything even more so than Whitefield. He was preaching one day in a very crowded chapel, and again was dealing with this same point about the sinner not heeding warnings—enjoying himself and ignoring the intimations of the coming Judgment. To enforce this he used a vivid illustration. Some people staying at the seaside had gone walking along the beach. There were rocks leading out into the sea—a sort of promontory of rocks going well out. The tide was out so they had walked along to the very end of the little promontory, and having done so lay down on their backs basking in the sun. There they were enjoying themselves tremendously, sleeping and reading and so on. But they had not noticed that the tide had turned and was beginning to come in again very slowly. They paid no attention to this; but the tide continued to lap the rocks on both sides and slowly to encircle them and their promontory. The preacher worked this up graphically to the point at which the people 'came to themselves' and realised their predicament. There was still just enough time for them to get back on to the beach and to listen to the warning voices from the shore. Roberts so worked up this illustration with his powerful imagination, that when he used his equally powerful voice to represent the shouted warnings and appeals of the people on the shore to the others to escape immediately for their lives, it is recorded, and said to be literally true that the entire congregation rose to its feet and ran out of the chapel!

That cannot be explained away in terms of the Welsh temperament and the ignorance of people at that time. That kind of thing used to happen in the camp meetings in the U.S.A. and in England very often at exactly the same time, and even after that. The same thing is clearly seen in the ministry of Charles G. Finney. Here again was a man with a very powerful personality and imagination; and I believe that that explains what happened to many of his supposed converts.

My attitude to all this is that surely at this point we have crossed the line which divides the legitimate from the wrong use of the imagination. What was affecting the people I have been describing in those stories was surely not the Truth; it was this graphic delineation of a scene, it was the powerful and perhaps overwrought imagination of the preacher. The same thing can be done by films or dramatic plays. You remember the story of the lady who had gone to see a play in a London theatre on a winter's night. This was in the old days before motor-cars. Her coachman had driven her in her carriage and while she was enjoying the play for two and a half hours the coachman was sitting outside on the box of the coach with the horse in the shafts. There she had been in the theatre weeping and being profoundly moved at the suffering of some poor people depicted in the play. When she went out and found her poor coachman covered with snow and almost frozen to death she was not at all moved but took it all for granted as a part of the routine of her life. This is it. What is it that moves us? All I am trying to say is that our business is to make sure that what moves the people is the Truth and not our imagination.

As with most other matters, the use of imagination can become quite ridiculous and laughable. When you have a preacher who is not perhaps over-gifted with intelligence, but has a good imagination, it can become most amusing. I remember hearing of an old preacher— and this literally happened—who was once preaching on the parable of the Prodigal Son. The details of the parable as given in the Scripture was not enough for this preacher; he had to add to it. His imagination came in and eventually reached the depths of the ridiculous when he came to describe the condition of the foolish Prodigal Son in the far country during the famine, just before he came to himself. He pointed out how his money had all gone, how the food had all been consumed, and how he had now to fall back even on the husks that they were giving to the swine to eat. But even the supply of husks was beginning to fail, indeed eventually did fail, and not only was the poor Prodigal Son hungry and desperate, the swine were also desperate. 'There they were,' he said, 'the terrible hunger had made the swine so frantic that they were beginning to munch away at the legs of the poor boy's trousers'!

At that point the Truth has been forgotten and we are in the realm of fantasy, not to say comedy. There was a man carried away by his imagination. We must never allow that to happen. We are to make sure that everything we may have by way of gifts are always subordinate to the Truth. I hope to return to this again because I believe it is one of the biggest fights any true preacher ever has to wage. Where do you draw the line? I suggest that the preacher always knows himself when he is taking delight in the story or imagination itself rather than in what it is meant to illustrate. The moment that point is reached you must stop; because we are not concerned just to influence people or to move them; our desire must be that the Truth should influence them and move them.

* * *

With regard to the next section I really have to say very much the same thing; this is the place of eloquence or of oratory in preaching. I need say no more than that here, again, is something that can be of the greatest possible value, and has been, in the case of the men I have cited, and many others that I could quote. But, again, there is the great danger that we may cross the line and become interested in eloquence for its own sake, and become more interested in the way we say what we are saying than in the Truth itself, interested in the effect we produce rather than in the souls of the people we are addressing. Ultimately, of course, it becomes a matter of pride.

Is there a rule about this? The only rule I would lay down is that no man should ever try to be eloquent. I do not hesitate to say that, talking of course about preachers. It may be that statesmen and others have a right to try to be eloquent. I would lay it down as a rule that the preacher should never try to be eloquent; but if he finds himself becoming eloquent then it is of great value, and it can be used of God. Again I would refer to those eloquent flights of the great Apostle Paul in his epistles. He never set out to produce a literary masterpiece; he was not even concerned about literary form. He was not a literary man; but when the Truth took hold of him he became mightily eloquent. He tells us that the Corinthians said of him that 'his speech was contemptible'. That simply meant that he did not affect the rhetorical manner of the Greek rhetoricians; it did not mean that he could not be eloquent. What it did mean was that his eloquence was always spontaneous and inevitable—never contrived, never produced, never done to order. It became inevitable because of the grandeur of the Truth and the conception that had opened itself before his mind. When eloquence is so produced, I say that it is one of the best handmaidens of true preaching. The history of preaching demonstrates this again and again abundantly.

We turn now to another point in this list of the various things one has to consider in a sermon whether written or extemporary, namely the place of humour in preaching. Here again is a very difficult subject. What makes all these things difficult is that they are natural gifts, and the question that is raised is the use of natural gifts, or the place of the natural gifts, in this great work of preaching. The history of preaching and preachers shows that there have been tremendous variations. In the case of an outstandingly great preacher like Spurgeon there was a great deal of humour—some of us would say too much humour. You have heard of the lady who went to him and complained about the humour in his sermons. She was a great admirer of Mr. Spurgeon and derived great benefit from his preaching.

But she felt that there was too much humour in his sermons and told him so. Spurgeon was a very humble man and he said to her, 'Well, madam, you may very well be right; but if you knew the number of jokes I do not tell you, and the number of things that I refrain from saying you would give me more credit than you are giving me.' Now I believe that was true. He was a naturally humorous man, it bubbled out of him. But then take Whitefield, on whom Spurgeon modelled himself—he was never humorous. Whitefield was always tremendously serious. In the eighteenth century to which he belonged, there were other men like John Berridge of Everton in England, who, again, was one of these natural humorists. These men always trouble me because I feel that they tended to go too far, and allowed their humour to run away with them. I would not dare to say that there is no place for humour in preaching; but I do suggest that it should not be a very big place because of the nature of the work, and because of the character of the Truth with which we are dealing. The preacher is dealing with and concerned about souls and their destiny. He is standing between God and men and acting as an ambassador for Christ. I would have thought that as that is the overriding consideration, the most one can say for the place of humour is that it is only allowable if it is natural. The man who tries to be humorous is an abomination and should never be allowed to enter a pulpit. The same applies to the man who does it deliberately in order to ingratiate himself with the people. That this kind of thing has been expected of so-called 'professional evangelists' has always passed my comprehension.

All these things have got to be considered and must not be brushed aside. All these things can be handmaidens, can be of very great value; but we must always be careful in our use of them. We must be equally careful not to over-correct their abuse to such an extent as to become dull, colourless, and lifeless. As long as we forget ourselves, and remember the devil, we shall never go wrong.

My final word, and it is not inappropriate at this point, is the length of the sermon. Again I would say that we must not be mechanical, or too rigid either way. What determines the length of the sermon? First and foremost, the preacher. Time is a very relative thing, is it not? Ten minutes from some men seems like an age, while an hour from another passes like a few minutes. That is not simply my personal view, it is what congregations say. As it thus varies with the man, it is therefore ridiculous to lay down a flat rule with regard to the length for all preachers. The length of the sermon should also vary, I think, with the matter. Some things can be said in a short time, in a brief compass, and we should always handle them accordingly, and not feel that we have to spin it out so as to last for a given length of time. It also varies with the congregation. The capacity of congregations, as we have seen, varies tremendously. This therefore should come into our consideration of the length of the sermon, on condition that you remember all the qualifications I gave with regard to the place of the congregation in this whole matter. If some congregations were the arbiter in this matter every sermon would be of ten minutes duration only. The preacher must not pay heed to that type of 'worshipper' but make his own assessment of them. If you come to the conclusion that they are people who cannot take more than a given amount, give them that amount, and no more. You will be a bad teacher and a bad preacher if you fail to do this.

Are there any further rules that can be laid down concerning the length of the sermon? There is no need to say that ten minutes is ridiculously inadequate. How can anyone deal with any one of the themes of true preaching in minutes; it is just impossible. But then it is equally wrong to say that you must always preach for an hour. Am I imagining these things? I fear that I am not. The new interest in the Puritans, at any rate in Great Britain, has tended I fear to produce a number of young preachers who seem to think that you have not preached unless you have preached for an hour. That seems to be the big thing in their minds. They are thereby doing themselves and the Truth great harm. Their reason for preaching for an hour is that the Puritans did so. How ridiculous can we become!

No, there are no rules about this. But, to be really practical, I feel that we are in a kind of vicious circle at the moment concerning this question of the length of the sermon. The poor preacher is in this predicament; he does not want to offend the people who attend regularly by being too long. He knows that they do not like long sermons, and that they are tending to say that he is too long. The result of this, not infrequently, is that he makes his sermon so short that they, and others, begin to feel that it is not worth their while to go to listen to him at all. The time has long since arrived when we must break into this vicious circle. We must do so at the expense, perhaps, of offending certain people who come mechanically, or out of tradition or mere self-righteousness. We are commissioned by the Risen Lord, and not only by the people; our primary concern must be with the Truth and the people's need of it. We must not think primarily in terms of time nor allow the people to do so. Indeed it is a part of the preacher's business to deliver people from the bondage of time, and life in this world only. Let the Truth, the Message, dictate the amount of time, and, governed by that, and 'knowing the terror of the Lord' we shall truly 'persuade men' and be 'ready to give an account of the deeds done in the body' when 'we stand before the Judgment-Seat of Christ'. If, in addition, we can say honestly that 'the love of Christ constraineth us' we shall never go far astray in this, or any other respect.

CHAPTER THIRTEEN

What to Avoid

WE HAVE BY now considered the preparation of the sermon, and certain things common to the preparation of the sermon and the preparation of ourselves.

There is one further question which some may consider to be trivial but which, to me, has its importance. Should you announce beforehand the subject on which you are going to preach? It seems quite clear that most people seem to like this, and especially those churches which advertise their services; and so it has become the custom to announce the subject.

Once more I must record the fact that this is a practice of which I disapprove and which I have never followed. I say that for many reasons.

The first and the overriding reason is, that people should come to the house of God to worship God, and to listen to an exposition of the Word of His Truth, whatever it may be, whatever aspect, whatever portion is being considered. That should be our reason for attending, that should be uppermost in our minds, not some particular subject or question. It is wrong, therefore, because it is bad for the people. It encourages a pseudo-intellectualism. I call it that because I am sure that that is what it really is. It is a practice that began in the last century. As far as one can gather it was not done before that, and people used to come together to worship God and to listen to the exposition of the Scripture, or perhaps even to listen to a great preacher.

But towards the middle of the last century people began to regard themselves as now educated and intellectual and felt that they must have 'subjects'. It was a part of that great change which took place towards the middle of the last century which is known as Victorianism. It was to be found quite as much in the U.S.A. as in Britain and elsewhere. I have already referred to it in connection with the type of building and form of service. I commend, as being most important, a study of the subtle change that took place somewhere round about the middle of the last century. Prior to that the old idea was that of meeting together to worship God and to listen to the exposition of Scripture. Moreover, the people waited for the coming of the Holy Spirit upon the preacher and upon the whole service. But gradually a great change took place from that to a more man-centred type of service. We have seen how it worked out in evangelism. The interest in 'subjects' was a definite feature of this change. We were no longer simple people, and what was needed now was an 'address' or a lecture rather than to come under the power of the preaching of the Word. As people of understanding we wanted 'food for thought' or intellectual stimulus, and the affective element was neglected. We were interested in subjects, and the announcing of subjects encouraged this pseudo-intellectualism.

But it also encourages a too-theoretical approach to the Truth. We have seen how bad this is for the preacher himself; and if it is bad for him, it is very much worse for the people.

Another objection to it is that it has the tendency to isolate subjects from their context in the Scriptures; indeed ultimately it regards the Scriptures as but a collection of statements about particular subjects. So one atomises the Scripture and forgets the whole; and, surely, the whole is more important than the parts. This announcing of subjects is a bad practice therefore because it extracts these subjects and tends to isolate them from their context; tends, indeed, even to isolate them from one another. So one loses the sense of the wholeness of the biblical message and becomes interested in particular subjects and questions.

A still more important reason for opposing this practice is a more pastoral one. Why are people interested in 'subjects'? The answer is that they think they know what they need, and they only want to hear about the things in which they say they are 'tremendously interested'.

You must have gathered already that it is a part of my whole contention that they are not in a position, ultimately, to know what they need; and our experience of ourselves in the past, and experience as pastors of souls, teaches that so often their idea as to what they need is quite wrong. Of course the preacher may also be wrong in this respect, but this applies much more to the congregations. It is, I repeat, a part of our whole approach to this matter not to allow the pew to decide the theme of preaching and not to encourage them at all along this line; but rather to give them the whole truth, and to bring them to see that there are vital aspects of which they are ignorant and in which they are apparently not interested at all. They should be interested in the whole of truth and every aspect of it, and we must show them their need of this.

Or let me put it in this way. There is always the danger of becoming lop-sided and lacking in balance in the Christian life. Some people are tremendously keen, as they say, on prophecy; and they always want to know if you are going to preach on prophecy. If you are, they will be there; there will be no question about this. I have discovered this so many times. I remember the late Dr. G. Campbell Morgan, my predecessor, saying once jocularly to me, 'If you want an exceptionally large crowd announce that you are going to preach on prophecy; and you will get them.' There are such people; they have this lust after particular subjects—prophecy, holiness and so on. If therefore we announce our subjects we tend to increase this danger of a lop-sided, imbalanced Christian life.

But let me put this matter finally as a generalisation. It has often amazed me to notice how churches and preachers hold on to nine-teenth-century methods when they have long since bidden farewell to the great truths emphasised especially in the early part of that century. This habit and practice of announcing the subject, and of having a choir, and a children's address—all these things came in during the last century; they were not done before that time. It was all a part of that pseudo-intellectualism of the Victorians; and we are now experiencing a kind of hangover from this. I am calling attention to this because I feel that the urgent need today is to break free from these bad habits, this false respectability and intellectualism that was so characteristic of the end of the last century. These things have been dominating our services; and I feel that they detract from the preaching of the Gospel and the centrality of the preaching of the Gospel.

Instead of just perpetuating certain practices we must ask: Why should I do this? How did this custom ever start? As we do so we shall find that so many of these things which are regarded as essential were only introduced, and for wrong reasons, towards the middle of the last century. How different the state of our churches would be if we were all as concerned to be orthodox in our beliefs as we are to be orthodox in our conformity to 'the thing to do' and 'the done thing' in the churches.

It is essential today that something should be said about the whole question of radio and television preaching. I referred to it in the introduction to this series of lectures, but I have to bring it in again at this point because it is a live issue for most preachers today. With one or two exceptions, because of very special circumstances, this is something I have refused to do, because I held the view, and still hold it, that these ways of communicating truth have been inimical to true preaching. Discussions, and talks on different subjects, and interviews I place in a different category. Indeed I would go so far as to say that since about 1920 or so this has been one of the major factors militating against a belief in preaching. The argument on the other side is generally put in terms of the results that follow, and you will hear wonderful and thrilling stories of people accidentally turning on the radio and suddenly hearing a word which arrested them and led to their conversion. The same applies to television; it is always the argument from results.

This question needs to be examined carefully because there are many sides to it. My rooted objection to this modern method is very largely that the service is so controlled. In the nature of things it has to be. The broadcasting people have to draw up their programmes, and they are only given a certain amount of time, and that very little. From their standpoint this is quite all right, but, I argue that from the standpoint of preaching it is all wrong, because it militates against the freedom of the Spirit. If I have warned against the danger of allowing the congregation to dictate in this respect, how much more do we need to warn against allowing radio and television authorities to do the same thing? That they have to do so because of the exigencies of arranging programmes is irrelevant from our standpoint. Surely it is wrong at any time or in any circumstances to start in fetters and to be chained by any kind of time-limit.

I remember years ago having a discussion on this whole question with the then Religious Director of the British Broadcasting Corporation who had been good enough to invite me to preach on more than one occasion. The simple way in which I put my case to him was this. I said, 'What would happen to your programmes if the Holy Spirit suddenly descended upon the preacher and possessed him; what would happen to your programmes?' He could not answer me. The answer would be, of course, that the preacher would be turned off. But what a terrible thing to do. When preaching we are not to be in charge to that extent, and therefore it is wrong, it seems to me, to be hemmed in like this by these considerations of time and other proprieties. In addition, the Religious Director emphasised that they always had to have their eye partly on people who are in hospitals and institutions and in their homes, and that you have to have a certain number of hymns and prayers in the given time for their sakes. The result is, however, that the preaching is crowded out. They do not want too much preaching and, in any case, they would be disturbed if you should preach on certain aspects of the Truth, such as the question of death and judgment and so on.

Now from the standpoint of the authorities one can well understand this and sympathise with it; but from the standpoint of true preaching surely this is not legitimate. We need also to examine more closely this whole question of results. I would suggest that actually if you examined them very carefully you would find that the results are very few in number. The few are generally given great publicity, and we are never told very much about what happens to them afterwards. But even granting that they are genuine what we have to bear in mind is the difference between particular results and the whole trend of a method. This to me is a very important distinction. I am prepared to grant for the sake of argument that there are individual conversions, but when you come to evaluate a given method I suggest that you should do so in terms of its total effect upon the life of the Church, remote as well as immediate. Looking at it from the general and ultimate standpoint I do not think that there is any question but that the effect has been bad.

May I give just one illustration of what I mean? A few years ago I was preaching in a church in the U.S.A. where in the morning two services had to be held because of the number of people who attended, the one at nine-thirty and the other at eleven; and one was asked to repeat the service exactly. However, in the evening the service was broadcast. I was most interested to observe on the first Sunday I was there that having had two congregations in the morning—one say of about 1,400 people and the other of some 1,200 people—my total congregation at night was only about 400 which, I was told, was what was normally expected. I had a most interesting experience in that church. I was not familiar with their procedure in the evening broadcast services. The service began about seven forty-five p.m., and the song-leader was in charge. After a while a green light came on to say that we were 'on the air'. Then there was more singing, congregational, quartette, soloist and so on. I was instructed that when preaching I should keep my eye on the green light, and that when the red light appeared it was the sign that I was to end. Everything should be over by then, and I should really be pronouncing the Benediction when the red light appeared.

As the various types of singing continued I could see that my precious time was going and I began to feel rather anxious. The service was due to finish at eight fifty-five p.m. and I found to my dismay that I was not on my feet announcing my text until eight thirty-five, leaving me less than twenty minutes for my sermon, because we had to have a closing hymn and the Benediction before eight fifty-five p.m. I was in great trouble. I thought at first that it was my duty to cut down what I intended saying, to this space of time; and I began trying to do so. But, as it happened, I suddenly realised that I was being given exceptional freedom; so while I went on speaking there was a great debate going on within me: Should I be guided by this programme, or should I be guided by what seemed to me the influence of the power of the Holy Spirit upon me? I decided that I would be guilty of quenching the Spirit and of sin if I observed the rules and regulations of that church. So when I saw the red light coming on at eight fifty-five p.m. I took no notice whatsoever of it and went on preaching and finished eventually at nine twenty-five p.m.

The really important point of the story is the sequel. That was my first Sunday in that church. I had to leave that night to go to a conference in the country and return again for the following Sunday. There were three assistant ministers in that church, three very nice men. I apologised to them that first Sunday night for what I had done, and hoped they would not get into trouble! I told them to put all the blame on me. When I got back the following Sunday morning the three ministers were there to greet me. I said, 'I hope you have not had too bad a week.' They said, 'We have had a terrible week.' 'Well,' I said, 'I hope you explained that it was entirely my fault'; and added 'I hope you apologised on my behalf and explained that I was not accustomed to this kind of service and that I would try to make amends.' 'But,' they said, 'that was not the trouble we had at all.' 'What, I asked, was your trouble then?' 'Well,' they said, 'we have never had so many complaints about a service—never.' I asked, 'What were the complaints?' They said, 'Well, we received endless complaints on the telephone and in letters saying, "Why didn't you give that man more time to preach? We want to know how that sermon went on. What did it lead to, how did it end? Why did you have all that singing? We can have singing at other times. Why not give this man more time?"' The outcome was that on the second occasion I was given the time; they cut all preliminaries down to a minimum, and I was given about three-quarters of an hour for my sermon.

This seemed to me to point to an important principle. I told those men afterwards that if I were the minister of that church I would not broadcast the evening service on the radio, but that rather, I would advertise the church in these terms: 'The church which does not broadcast'. Why? Because that method, it seemed to me, would persuade the people to come out for the evening service. As long as they could sit at home and listen to it on the radio, why take the trouble to get your car out of the garage and struggle with the traffic and many other inconveniences? Broadcasting I fear has discouraged people from coming to the House of God and taught them bad habits. But even more serious is the harm it has done to the people's idea of the corporate life of the Church. Far too often they think of churches just as places where you sit and listen to a sermon; and now you can get this on the radio or on tapes and so on. So the whole notion of coming together, and sitting together round the Word, and listening to an exposition of it, is seriously damaged. The very facts and statistics demonstrate that during these last fifty years the life of the Church, as such, has deteriorated very seriously.

I suggest, here again, that it is for us to break into all this. The motives which have led men to use these media have of course been obvious. They thought that this was going to do good to their churches, and that people hearing them on the radio would then come and listen in the church. I suggest that it really has not worked out like that; and that you are likely to find in the future that God will revive His work in the Church, and that it is those who attend regularly who are the ones who are going to participate most of all in the blessing. That has always been God's way in the past. What is astonishing, once more, is that people do not want to do things in God's time-honoured way.

They are content with this detached attitude towards the Church. It is a fundamental failure to understand the true doctrine of the Christian Church—'the unity of the Spirit in the bond of peace', the gathering together of the people of God. 'Where two or three are gathered together in my Name, there am I in the midst.'

I have always opposed the idea of trying to force people to attend church services; what I am saying is that our preaching ought to fill them with a desire to do this. You should not have to whip them up to do it. Look at those people in Acts 2: 'Daily' you remember; 'from house to house,' they 'continued steadfastly' in these things. This idea that people should be content with attending just one service on a Sunday displays a failure to understand the true character of the Christian. He is like a 'newborn babe' desiring 'the sincere milk of the Word', and also desiring to be with his fellows, 'loving the brethren'. It seems to me to be indicative of a wrong view of the Church and of the individual Christian as a newborn babe. We have allowed these outside forces to influence us overmuch; and I suggest it is time for us to break into it all and to try to get back to the New Testament picture of the Church. With the advent of tape-recorders there is no longer any difficulty in making provision for the aged and sick members of the church.

* * *

We turn now to consider the things we have to avoid in preaching. We have been dealing with some of them already, but there are some further points. Starting with the preacher himself, what has he to avoid? First and foremost professionalism. That is the greatest of all dangers in the ministry. It is something preachers have to fight as long as they live. Professionalism is, to me, hateful anywhere, everywhere. I abominated it as much when I was practising medicine as I do now. There is a type of medical practitioner who is more professional than able. He has all the airs and graces, and knows all 'the things to do' and 'the things to say', but is often a bad doctor. The greater the doctor the less evidence there will be of this mere professionalism.

The same thing is infinitely more true in the realm of the Christian ministry.

Let me explain more explicitly what I mean. Nothing worse can happen to a preacher than that he should reach a stage in which his main reason for preaching on a Sunday morning is that he has been announced to do so. That means that preaching to him has just become his job. He has lost contact with what originally moved him and urged him; it is now a matter of routine. If such a man really asked himself honestly as he walks up the pulpit steps: 'Why am I doing this?' he would have to give as his answer, 'I have been announced to do this, therefore I must do it.' That is a confession of professionalism.

It comes out also in many ways during the service. Such a man is generally too formal; everything he does is too studied. That is always a sign of professionalism. To take an illustration from the realm of medicine, I remember a man who used to amuse those of us who were more concerned about learning medicine than acquiring a wonderful bedside manner. We were amused at the way in which this man used to apply his stethoscope to the patient's chest. The great flourish had nothing whatsoever to do with medicine. Actually he was not very good at interpreting what he had heard; but the airs and graces with which he applied the stethoscope were wonderful to behold. No doubt it had an effect on some people, especially those who were only suffering from some psychosomatic or psychological condition; but if you were really ill it did not help you.

Alas! this is sometimes seen in pulpits. It is pathetic at times to notice the stances and the studied character of almost everything that is done. There was a famous preacher in London who actually used to turn round a complete circle as the service went on, so that people would have the advantage of seeing the back of his head as well as his face! He obviously paid great attention to the cultivation and arranging of his hair. That literally happened, and people crowded to see this. Had I not seen it with my own eyes I would not have believed it. But that is sheer professionalism of the worst type. I have heard that another has his hair waved at least once a week and maintains an artificially produced tanned appearance of his skin.

In other words, the professional is a man who is always watching himself. At the same time he is always greatly interested in techniques. The man has gone round listening to others, picking up ideas, watching how other preachers do various things. Then he has tried to imitate them and to introduce what he has seen into his own 'technique'. I gather that something similar happens in the realm of acting in the theatre. There was a time when a man who was a born actor just went on and acted, learning as he went on. But I believe they have introduced something which is called 'the Method', and now they all tend to be doing the same thing. 'The Method!' It is no longer real acting in the old sense; it is the application of a method.

There are many other things that the preacher has to avoid. One is a display of knowledge. One of the besetting sins of preachers is to try to give the impression of wide reading and culture. I have emphasised the place and the value of reading, but if your chief reason for reading is to parade it and to make a display of your knowledge, it is obviously bad in every sense.

But perhaps the greatest danger of all is the danger of relying on your preparation. This is a very subtle matter, and I am sure that every true preacher will agree with me in this. The danger is that having finished your preparation, whatever that may be, and whenever it may be—on a Saturday evening or earlier—the danger now is to say: Well now I am ready for tomorrow. You have finished your preparation and feel that you have a good sermon, and so you tend to put your reliance on that. There is no greater danger connected with preaching than just that. You will be let down by it; you will be disappointed; and above all you will be less effective. It is a terrible temptation. That is why I have emphasised the preparation of the man himself so much; and I shall deal with it once more before we have finished. I just mention it at this point. Watch this. Watch it carefully, or you will find yourself falling into this trap.

Many a preacher in the pulpit relies on a good voice; many are proud of it and give a display of it. The preacher in many and varied ways is always fighting the devil. He is there with you and always out to trip you, he cares not how.

Let me try to sum it all up by answering the question, 'What advice would you give at this point?' Well, confessing that my only title to give such advice is that I am a great sinner who has fought this battle for so many years, I would put it like this. Watch your natural gifts and tendencies and idiosyncrasies. Watch them. What I mean is that they will tend to run away with you. It can all be summed up in a phrase—watch your strength. Not so much your weaknesses: it is your strength you have to watch, the things at which you excel, your natural gifts and aptitudes. They are the ones that are most likely to trip you because they are the ones that will tempt you to make a display and to pander to self. So watch these; and also your idiosyncrasies. We all have these, and we must watch them.

The preacher always has to guard himself against the terrible temptation to be a 'character'. People like a 'character', and if a man has certain elements in him that tend to make him a character—something out of the ordinary, something which people regard as attractive—he has to be careful. His danger is to pander to this and to play up to it; and in the end he is just calling attention to himself. Some men like to be quaint or odd or different, and to get people to talk about them. This is the danger, so beware of this; and, again, especially watch your strong points.

Let me put this in the form of a picture. I remember once hearing a man preach a sermon on Absalom, the point of which was that we should always keep a watchful eye on our strong points. I do not know that exegetically it was a sound point but it certainly impressed itself on me. You remember that Absalom was very proud of his hair. He used to pay great attention to it and to make his boast of it. But you remember that finally it was his undoing. He got caught up by his hair in some trees as he was going through a wood and so gave the opportunity to Joab to thrust a spear into him and kill him. The preacher's point was that this great strength of his—his hair—was his final undoing. I have remembered that sermon, showing thereby that sometimes even though a man does not always keep to the rules he gets his lesson home! All I am concerned to say is, watch your strength whatever it may be, your hair or anything else. Do not make a display of it.

The sum total of all this is that the greatest of all the temptations that assail a preacher is pride. Pride, because he is set up there almost on a pedestal. He is standing in a pulpit, he is above the people, all of whom are looking at him. He has this leading place in the Church, in the community; and so his greatest temptation is that of pride. Pride is probably the deadliest and the most subtle of all sins, and it can assume many forms; but as long as one realises this all is well. Though I have already said something about how to deal with it let me add a further word because it is so important. The best way of checking any tendency to pride—pride in your preaching or in anything else that you may do or may be—is to read on Sunday nights the biography of some great saint. It does not matter which, or to which century or branch of the Church he belonged as long as he was a saint. If you are tempted to think that you have done unusually well, and that nobody ever preached like that before, well just dip into Whitefield's Journals; and I guarantee that you will be cured in less than five minutes. Or take up a biography of David Brainerd or someone like that; and if that does not bring you to earth then I pronounce that you are just a professional and beyond hope. But that is the antidote; bring yourself down.

*   *   *

Those then are some of the special dangers confronting the preacher. But now with regard to the sermon. I bring that in here because when I was dealing with the preparation of the sermon I was anxious to do so in general. There are further special points or refinements in addition to what we have been saying. With regard to the sermon itself, therefore, beware of too much intellect. I put that first, particularly to those who are somewhat more gifted especially in the realm of intellect. I would not have to put it first to all men, but to some this has to come first.

I remember a bit of advice given to me in my first year as a preacher by an old preacher with whom I was preaching on one occasion. It was the custom in Wales at that time, on special occasions, to have two preachers who preached together in a service, the younger man first and the older one following. In those particular special services I found myself preaching alone in the afternoon service as the old man had preached alone in the morning service and then we both preached in the evening service. The old man was kind enough to listen to me in the afternoon, and it was the first time he had heard me trying to preach. As we were being driven in a car together to have some tea at the house of the minister of the church, the old preacher, who was exactly sixty years older than I was, very kindly and with a desire to help and to encourage me gave me a very serious warning. 'The great defect of that sermon this afternoon was this,' he said, 'that you were overtaxing your people, you were giving them too much.' He then went on to put it like this. He said, 'I will give you a rule; remember it as long as you live: Only one in twelve of your congregation is really intelligent.' Only one in twelve, that was his assessment—not mine! 'Remember that as long as you live; only one in twelve.' 'Remember that,' he said. 'They cannot take it; it is impossible for them to take it. You are only stunning them, and therefore you are not helping them.' And then he said, 'You watch what I shall be doing tonight. I shall really be saying one thing, but I shall say it in three different ways.' And that was precisely what he did, and most effectively. He was a very intellectual man, known as a great theologian, and the author of several excellent commentaries both in Welsh and English. But that is what he said. I am but repeating that excellent advice— 'Beware of too much intellect.' It is almost inevitable, is it not, that a young preacher should fall to this danger. He has had to spend so many years in studying and in reading and in discussing great questions with others, that he tends to assume that everybody is like that. The sooner he realises that this is not the case the better, and that the people listening to him are very different. They have not spent their time reading and studying and arguing; they are business people or professional people or people who work with their hands. Beware then of too much intellect.

Of course I would emphasise equally, beware of too little intellect. But that is not what needs to be emphasised today, speaking generally. However, there are preachers to whom it is necessary to say, beware of too much sentiment and emotion. The first type was lacking in this element and was too intellectual. But there are those preachers who are too emotional and sentimental. I have heard men who, having given out a text then proceed to tell a string of stories, generally most sentimental and often personal. That is bad.

Then there are those who need to be warned against mere exhortation. So often men seem to think that preaching is just an extended exhortation. They start exhorting the people at the beginning of their sermon; it is all application. They do not present the Truth first and then make the inevitable application. They spend the whole time 'getting at' their people, and slashing them and exhorting them, calling them to do this and that and forcing them.

On the other hand there are men who do not exhort at all. They have given their brilliant intellectual disquisition or exposition; and it is left at that. There is nothing to move anybody to tears or to action; no emotion, no feeling, no exhortation. All this is obviously wrong; so beware of too much of any of these emphases.

A most thorny problem is that of the place of polemics in a sermon and in preaching. The polemic element is obviously important, and it has its very definite place; it is good for the people. I am simply warning now against the danger of too much polemic. Again this will be the danger to the more intellectual type. The preacher has been struggling with rival theories and heresies and wrong interpretations, and so his mind is naturally full of this. But he must be careful not to have too much of this in his sermon. Why? Because the people—the bulk of the people to start with—are probably not interested, a large number of them do not even understand. Remember that—that there

are such people. There is definitely a place for polemics; all I am saying is that there must not be too much. There will be a certain number
of people in the congregation who are much too interested in polemics,
and it is very bad for them if there is too much in the sermon. They
are the people who will gladly travel miles in order to hear a slashing
attack on a man or on a theory. As you may know, preachers who are
always polemical generally get a good hearing—and generally a good
collection also. But this is a real snare.

I am very concerned about this because I have seen good men and
great preachers ruined in this way, and I have seen good ministries
ruined also. I once had a discussion with one such preacher whose
name I am not going to mention. He was one of the very greatest of
these polemical preachers. I had the privilege of spending a day with
him many years ago; and during our conversation we got on to this
theme. This happened as the result of his asking me the question, 'Do
you read Joseph Parker?' Parker was the famous minister of the City
Temple in London until about 1901. He published great volumes of
sermons called *The People's Bible*. I was asked, 'Do you read Joseph
Parker?' I replied, 'No, I read very little of Joseph Parker.' He was
amazed at this, and went on, 'Oh, I read Joseph Parker every Sunday
morning. I always read Joseph Parker before I go to church on
Sunday morning; he puts me right, you know. Old Parker,' he said,
'was wonderful. I cannot tell you how much I enjoy watching Parker
making mincemeat of those modernists and liberals of his age.' That
gave me my opportunity and I said, 'Well I must confess that that
does not appeal to me. What exactly did Joseph Parker achieve after
he had "made mincemeat" of those people?'

That set us off, and we had a great discussion which went on for the
whole day. I only remember three points in the discussion, and I
report them because I trust they will be of some help. I was suggesting
to this truly great preacher, who was known throughout the Christian
world, that he was ruining his great ministry with these tirades
every Sunday night in particular, either against some erroneous
liberal Protestant teaching or Roman Catholicism, and even at times

individual persons. These onslaughts were brilliantly done, but I was trying to suggest to him that it was ruining his ministry and appealing to him to return to more evangelical preaching. 'But,' he said, 'you are un-scriptural. Let me remind you that the Apostle Paul tells us in Galatians 2 that when Peter went astray he withstood him to the face.' He added, 'That is all I am doing. I am simply doing what Paul did; surely this is right?' To which I replied, 'Yes I know that Paul tells that he had done that, but,' I went on, 'I am interested in the result. I notice that the result of Paul's dealing with Peter, his attacking him to the face at Antioch, was that he persuaded Peter that he was wrong and won him to his position. I note that Peter later on in life in his Second Epistle expresses his great admiration of the Apostle Paul and his writings. Can you say the same about the people whom you attack?' At that he could but get up from his seat and walk away to the end of the garden in which we were sitting for a while. If you can win people to the Truth, and to see your position, by your polemics all is well. But be very careful that you do so, and that you do not end by antagonising them still more, and antagonising a number of others at the same time.

Then I remember that later on in the discussion he used another argument. He said, 'Look here; I will put this to you as a medical man. Here is a surgeon and there is a patient who has a growth in his system. If that growth is allowed to go on growing it will kill that man. There is only one hope for him, that growth has got to be removed by a surgical operation.' He said, 'The surgeon does not want to operate, but to save that man's life he has got to do it, he has got to get this cancer out of the man's system and body.' He then added, 'That is precisely my position. I do not want to do this sort of thing but I have to do it, this cancer has come into the body of the Church and it has got to be removed, and it has got to be extirpated.'

What was the reply to that? Well, one had to think quickly, but the reply, it seemed to me, was obvious. I said, 'There is such a thing as developing a "surgical mentality", or of becoming what is described as "knife-happy". The danger to the surgeon is to get into the habit of thinking only in terms of operations and to forget medical treatment.

That is a thing he has to be very wary of. If you are ever taken very seriously ill,' I said, 'never accept the verdict of a surgeon alone; always check his advice by your general practitioner or by some physician.' The surgeon tends to develop the surgical mentality and outlook, and, unconsciously, the moment he looks at a patient he tends to think in terms of operating. That is actual fact. So turning to my host I said, 'Do you tell me that you can say quite honestly that you are quite free from this surgical mentality? Can you say that you do not enjoy "operating" in this way?' Again he was in trouble for a short while.

I also remember the third great argument. He said, 'Well listen to this. This, surely, will prove the case to you. Every time I indulge in what you call one of these tirades of mine, every time I do this which you say is so harmful, do you know the result? The circulation of my weekly paper simply rockets up! What do you say to that?' 'Well,' I said, 'what I say to that is this. I have noticed always that whenever there are two dogs fighting that a crowd always gathers. There are people who always enjoy a fight so I am not surprised that the circulation of your paper goes up. If you attack various things and appeal for money to help you to do so, you will always get people to support you. But is is negative, it is destructive; it does not build up a church.' So be careful of too much polemics. This particular man with whom I had that discussion ended his life in comparative isolation, and his church, from having been a great church was greatly reduced in size and influence. People will gather together to hear such attacks; they appeal to the flesh and they enjoy it. But you cannot build up a church on polemics. You cannot build up a church on apologetics, still less on polemics. The preacher is called primarily to preach the positive Truth.

But, to be perfectly fair, let me say that you must be aware of too little polemics. There are some men who like to have the reputation of being nice men. It is claimed that they are 'never negative'; and they like to say that about themselves. 'Never negative', 'always positive'. That is humbug—sheer humbug and hypocrisy. The Scriptures have a pronounced polemical element in them; and it must be present in our preaching. We have to warn our people, we have to guide them. But you must now allow yourself to develop the idea that you are The defender of the Truth, and so spend your time always attacking people and points of view. That becomes negative. There is no life in it, and it will certainly ruin the life of your church.

Under this heading I would also say this. Beware of, and keep your eye carefully on, the use of irony. It has its place; but be careful with it. Most people completely misunderstand it because they do not realise that you are being ironical. They take you literally, and they are offended by it. So be careful with it. It can be used, sometimes it has to be used; but realise that, it is a dangerous weapon. Ridicule, I think, we should always avoid.

So the balance in this matter in the sermon is as Paul puts it in Philippians 1: 'We are set for the defence and the propagation of the Gospel.' It is not defence only. Do not become just a self-appointed guardian of the Faith, or a defender of the Faith. It must always be 'defence and the propagation'. Let there be this balance, and let there be more propagation than defence. Build up the people, give them a balanced message, preach 'the whole counsel of God' to them.

Lastly, care in the method of delivery. Many things arise in connection with the actual delivery of the sermon. I have known a man who never walked into his pulpit on Sunday morning; he always ran into it. He, the man I saw doing it, was imitating another man who used to do the same. The idea was, I imagine, to show how keen they were to preach the Truth. But as I see things it is just calling attention to self. But there is one thing that is even worse than running into the pulpit and that is the putting on of a smile when you have got there. You know the type of man who stands there and puts on a contrived smile, and then greets his congregation with the words, 'Good morning folks; nice to see you, how good of you to come.' Still worse if he proceeds to crack a joke or two just to put the people at ease.

I have heard it argued that this kind of thing can be justified in an evangelistic campaign in a public hall. I maintain that it is wrong, always, everywhere in connection with Christian work. Why is it wrong? Because the whole approach is wrong. It is not our service; the people do not come there to see us or please us. It is not like inviting people into our home as it were; it is not our service at all. They, and we, are there to worship God, and to meet with God; and what we must try to do is to show them that this is something entirely different from everything they do everywhere else. A minister in a church is not like a man inviting people into his home; he is not in charge here. He is just a servant himself; we are all there together to come into the presence of the living God. I cannot emphasise too much that we should go out of our way to show the difference between these two things. I would utterly condemn the practice of suggesting to the people that there is nothing strange or unusual about this, and of saying 'Good morning folks' and putting them at ease with a few jokes. If you want to do that sort of thing in your own home you are at liberty to do so; but a church is not your home, and you yourself are under God. We must emphasise this difference.

Let me enforce this point by putting it in a way which almost makes it quite ridiculous. I knew a deacon who, poor fellow, was anxious always to be nice and pleasant, as indeed he was. But he tended to carry this too far; and I began to notice that when I handed round the bread at the Communion Service to the deacons that this man, as he took his piece, always muttered beneath his breath, 'Thank you'. He did the same with the wine. I had to point out to him that it was wrong to say 'thank you' at such a time. If he were in my home as a guest and I handed him a plate of bread and butter I would expect him to say 'thank you', but not when he was taking bread at the Communion Service. But why the difference? At the Communion Table I am not giving him the bread, I am not giving him the wine; and he must not thank me in this way. Politeness, and the kind of behaviour that is correct on social occasions, is wrong here. The good man had never realised what was taking place. What is needed is a sense of God. This does not mean that you put on a false dignity and become pompous. I am talking about 'reverence and godly fear'.

Above all; do not put on a 'parsonic' voice. What a terrible thing that is, and yet how common. Young men develop this bad habit; they hear others and they begin to use the same affected parsonic unnatural voice. It offends people. Still worse is to put on a false appearance of piety—sanctimoniousness. What a horrible thing that is! According to a famous story Spurgeon once ridiculed this, rightly or wrongly, in the case of certain people whom he felt were somewhat guilty of this in his day. Adapting those words in Acts 1:11 he said, 'Ye men of . . . why stand ye there looking up into the heavens.' He was out to ridicule the type of person who looks upwards with a sanctimonious expression, persuading himself that he is very pious. He also said another very wise thing in the same connection. He said that whenever you see a man who has a reputation of looking very saintly, and who rather enjoys that reputation, you can be quite sure that he probably has a bad liver. I agree one hundred per cent! The New Testament tells us that when we are fasting 'to anoint the face with oil'; indeed to do everything you can not to give the impression that you are fasting. You must not call attention to yourself and what you are and what you are doing.

Another footnote—avoid chattiness and the so-called easy style. How unworthy all this is in connection with these things. Again: never be histrionic. Do not cultivate or practise gestures. Everything that is histrionic should be avoided.

What is the rule then? It is: be natural; forget yourself; be so absorbed in what you are doing and in the realisation of the presence of God, and in the glory and the greatness of the Truth that you are preaching, and the occasion that brings you together, that you are so taken up by all this that you forget yourself completely. That is the right condition; that is the only place of safety; that is the only way in which you can honour God. Self is the greatest enemy of the preacher, more so than in the case of any other man in society. And the only way to deal with self is to be so taken up with, and so enraptured by, the glory of what you are doing, that you forget yourself altogether.

CHAPTER FOURTEEN

Calling for Decisions

IN ORDER THAT we may be thoroughly practical and contemporary I must raise at this point the question of whether we should do anything to condition the meeting and the people for the reception of our message. The question of music arises here. After all, the preacher is the one who is in charge of the service and it is within his province therefore to control this. This can be a very thorny question at the present time, and I have known many ministers who have been in great trouble over the question of choirs and the singing of anthems, and perhaps quartets within the choirs. Sometimes churches have paid choirs and soloists who may not even be members of the church, or make any claim to being Christian. Then there is the matter of organ voluntaries. And, coming down to a more popular type, there is the endless chorus singing, and ultimately in some countries men who are known as 'song-leaders'. These are men whose special function it is to conduct the singing and to do what they can to get the people into the right mood and condition for the reception of the message.

How do we evaluate all this? What is our attitude towards it? My first comment is that here again we have something which falls into the same category as some of the things we have already considered. It is something which we have inherited from Victorianism. Nothing is needed more urgently than an analysis of the innovations in the realm of religious worship in the nineteenth century—to me in this respect a devastating century. The sooner we forget the nineteenth century and go back to the eighteenth, and even further to the seventeenth and sixteenth, the better. The nineteenth century and its mentality and outlook is responsible for most of our troubles and problems today. It was then that a fatal turn took place in so many respects, as we have been seeing, and very prominent among the changes introduced was the place given to music in various forms. Quite frequently, and especially in the non-episcopal churches, they did not even have an organ before that time. Many of the leaders were actively opposed to organs and tried to justify their attitude from Scripture; in the same way many of them were opposed to the singing of anything but psalms. I am not concerned to evaluate the rival interpretations of the relevant scriptures, or to argue as to the antiquity of hymn singing; my point is that while hymn singing became popular at the end of the seventeenth and particularly in the eighteenth century, that the entirely new emphasis on music which came in about the middle of the last century was a part of that respectability, and pseudo-intellectualism which I have already described.

But, more particularly, there is a very real danger, often, of a kind of 'organist tyranny'. This arises because the organist is in a position where he or she can exercise considerable control. With a powerful instrument they can control the rate at which a hymn is sung, and the effect will vary completely according to whether he takes it too quickly, or too slowly. Many a preacher has had great trouble in his ministry with a difficult organist, and especially with the type that is more interested in music than in Truth. One should be very careful therefore in appointing an organist to make sure that he is a Christian. And if you have choirs you should insist upon the same with every member of the choir. The first desideratum should not be the voice, but the Christian character, the love of the Truth, and a delight in singing it. That is the way to avoid organist tyranny and the sister-trouble choir tyranny. There was an expression which used to be heard frequently in my home country, Wales. It had reference not so much to choirs as to congregational singing; it was known as 'the demon of the singing'. What it meant was that this question of singing caused more quarrelling and divisions in churches than practically anything else, that singing gave the devil more frequent opportunities of hindering and disrupting the work than any other activity in Church life. But quite apart from that, music in its various forms raises the whole problem of the element of entertainment insinuating itself and leading people to come to the services to listen to the music rather than to worship.

I contend that we can lay it down as a fairly general rule that the greater the amount of attention that has been paid to this aspect of worship—namely the type of building, and the ceremonial, and the singing, and the music—the greater the emphasis on that, the less spirituality you are likely to have; and a lower spiritual temperature and spiritual understanding and desire can be expected. But I would go further and ask a question, for I feel it is time we began to ask this question. As I have said previously in another connection, we must break into certain bad habits that have settled into the life of our churches and which have become a tyranny. I have referred to the set-form, and to the people who are ready to play about with the Truth and try to modify it, but who resist any change in the service and this rigid set-form. So I suggest that it is time we asked the question: Why is any of this accent on music necessary? Why does it have any place at all? Let us face this question; and surely as we do so we must come to the conclusion that what we should seek and aim at is a congregation of people singing the praises of God together; and that the real function of an organ is to accompany that. It is to be accompaniment; it is not to dictate; and it must never be allowed to do so. It must always be subservient. I would go so far as to say that the preacher generally should choose the tunes as well as the hymns, because sometimes there can be a contradiction between the two. Some tunes virtually contradict the message of the hymn though the metre may be correct. So the preacher has the right to be in charge of these matters; and he must not surrender this right.

You may not be prepared to agree when I suggest that we should abolish choirs altogether, but surely all must agree that the ideal is that all the people should be lifting up their voices in praise, worship and adoration and rejoicing as they do so. I trust that you will also agree that deliberate attempts at 'conditioning' the people are surely thoroughly bad. I hope to deal with this in the next section, so for the moment I content myself with saying that this attempt to 'condition' the people, to soften them up, as it were, actually militates against the true preaching of the Gospel. This is not mere imagination or theory. I remember being in a very famous religious conference in which the invariable routine in every meeting, and for all the speakers, was as follows. You were asked to be on the platform at a given time. Then there followed literally forty minutes of singing conducted by the song-leader, interspersed with supposedly humorous remarks by the said gentleman. There was no reading of the Scripture, the briefest possible prayer; and then you were 'put on' to speak.

That is an example of what I mean by the entertainment element. I have not given a detailed description of the form the singing took. I recall that there was an organ solo, a xylophone solo, and then a group of people—I even remember the name—The Eureka Jubilee Singers, who more or less acted what they were singing. All that went on for forty minutes. I confess that I found it very difficult to preach after that. I also felt compelled to modify my messages to deal with that situation with which I was confronted. I felt that the 'programme', the set pattern, dominated the situation, and one became a part of an entertainment. That is why we have to be so careful. So I would say as a general rule: Keep the music in its place. It is a handmaiden, a servant, and it must not be allowed to dominate or to control in any sense.

I mention another matter that sounds trivial—and yet some people have paid great attention to this. It is as to whether you should manipulate the lights in the building in which you are preaching so as to make the preaching more effective. Some have different coloured lights installed and as the sermon goes on the lights are gradually put out until at the end, in one particular case of which I am thinking, there was no light on except an illuminated red cross suspended above the preacher's head. All this is just psychological conditioning, and it is being justified in terms of making it easier for people to believe and to accept the Truth. We can leave it at that, and simply say that the question that really arises here is one's view of the work and the power of the Holy Spirit. How impossible it is to fit all that into the New Testament Church and its spiritual worship.

But that leads on quite naturally to another question, a bigger one, and that is the whole question of whether at the close of the sermon which the preacher has preached in the ways we have been considering, he should appeal for decisions there and then. Various terms such as 'altar call', and 'enquiry room', 'penitent form', 'anxious seat' have been used to describe this procedure.

This is a subject which has gained considerable prominence at the present time, and therefore we must deal with it. In any case it is a problem that faces every preacher. I have often had to face this problem. People have at various times come to me at the close of a service and have chided me, indeed sometimes reprimanded me, because I have not made an appeal for immediate decisions. Some of them would go so far as to say that I had been guilty of sin, that an opportunity had been created by my own preaching but that I had not taken advantage of it. They have said, 'I am quite sure that if you had only made an appeal you would have had a great response'—that kind of argument.

In addition to that I have been told by a number of ministers within the last ten years or so that they have been told by people at the end of a service that they had not preached the Gospel, simply because they had not made an appeal. This had happened to them in a morning service as well as an evening service. This had happened to them, not in evangelistic services only, but also in other services which were plainly not meant to have a primary evangelistic intent. But they were charged with not having preached the Gospel because there was no 'appeal'. I once met three men, three ministers, who had virtually been given a call to minister in certain churches, and who were on the verge of accepting, when someone suddenly asked the question: Did they give an 'altar call' at the end of every sermon? And because these three particular men had said that they did not do so, they had not received the call, the decision was reversed. This has become a very acute problem as the result of certain things that have been happening since the end of the Second World War.

Once more it is important that we should be clear about the history of this question. The historical approach is always helpful. So many do not seem to be aware of the fact that all this, like so many other things only came into the life of the Church during the last century. It came in fairly early in that century, earlier than some of the things I have mentioned, actually in the twenties; and it came in with Charles G. Finney. It was he who introduced the 'anxious seat', this 'new measure' which called on people to take a decision there and then. It was an essential part of his method and approach and thinking; and it led to great controversy at the time. It is a most important controversy, and a very interesting and fascinating one. I commend it as a subject for reading. The two great protagonists in the debate were W. H. Nettleton and Finney. Nettleton was a preacher who was greatly used in preaching services. He travelled extensively and was constantly invited to preach in other men's churches. He never made an 'altar call' or an appeal for immediate decision, but he was greatly used, and large numbers of people were converted under his ministry and added to the churches. He was a Calvinist in doctrine and he put his beliefs into practice in this matter. But then Finney came upon the scene with his direct appeal to the will for decision there and then. This led to a great controversy between the two views, and many ministers found themselves in great difficulties as between the two. There is a very fascinating account of this in the autobiography of Dr. Lyman Beecher, the father of Dr Henry Ward Beecher. He had been a great friend of Nettleton, and, at first, sided with him: but eventually he went over to the side of Finney. Dr. Charles Hodge and others of the Princeton men were actively engaged in the discussion, and also J. W. Nevin, the founder of the Mercersberg Theology.

That is the history of the origin of this practice, and it is important that we should know it. It is not an accident that it came in with Finney, because ultimately this is a matter of theology. At the same time it is not only a theological question; and we must never forget that an Arminian like John Wesley and others did not use this method.

Perhaps the best way in which I can stimulate thought, and give some little help in this matter, is to make the blunt statement that I have not followed this practice in my ministry. And let me give some of the reasons which have influenced me in that respect. I shall not attempt to state them in any exact systematic order, but here is roughly the order. The first is that it is wrong, surely, to put direct pressure on the will. Let me explain that. Man consists of mind, affections and will; and my contention is that you should not put direct pressure on the will. The will should always be approached primarily through the mind, the intellect, and then through the affections. The action of the will should be determined by those influences. My scriptural warrant for saying that is Paul's Epistle to the Romans chapter 6, verse 17, where the Apostle says: 'God be thanked that ye were the servants of sin, but ye have obeyed from the heart that form of doctrine which was delivered you.'

Observe the order in that statement. They have 'obeyed', yes; but how? 'From the heart'. What was it made them do this, what was it moved their hearts? It was this 'form of teaching' that had been delivered to them. What had been delivered or preached to them was the Truth, and Truth is addressed primarily to the mind. As the mind grasps it, and understands it, the affections are kindled and moved, and so in turn the will is persuaded and obedience is the outcome. In other words the obedience is not the result of direct pressure on the will, it is the result of an enlightened mind and a softened heart. To me this is a crucial point.

Let me work out the importance of this idea. In a previous lecture I ventured to suggest that even the great Whitefield at times fell into the error of making a direct attack upon the emotions or the imagination, and we reprobated any attempt to do that deliberately. We have here another aspect of exactly the same principle. As it is wrong to make a direct attack upon the emotions, so it is equally wrong to make a direct attack upon the will. In preaching we are to present the Truth, and, clearly, this is something first and foremost for the mind. The moment we depart from this order, and this rule, and make these direct approaches to either of the other elements we are asking for trouble; and we are likely to get it.

In the second place I argue that too much pressure on the will— there is inevitably an element of this in all preaching, but I say too much pressure —or too direct pressure, is dangerous, because in the end it may produce a condition in which what has determined the response of the man who 'comes forward' is not so much the Truth itself as, perhaps, the personality of the evangelist, or some vague general fear, or some other kind of psychological influence. This reminds us once more of the place of music in a preaching service. We can become drunk on music—there is no question about that. Music can have the effect of creating an emotional state in which the mind is no longer functioning as it should be, and no longer discriminating. I have known people to sing themselves into a state of intoxication without realising what they were doing. The important point is that we should realise that the effect produced in such a case is not produced by the Truth but by one or other of these various factors.

I came across a notable illustration of this very point a few years ago. I am simply going to repeat something that was reported in the Press, so I am not divulging anything secret or betraying any confidence. A certain evangelist in Britain had been asked to conduct a programme of hymn singing on a Sunday night on the radio. The programme was a regular Sunday programme lasting for half an hour. Different churches are asked to do this week by week. On this particular occasion this well-known evangelist was taking this programme in the Albert Hall in London. It had been planned as usual, months ahead of time. About a week or so before the programme was actually due to take place, another evangelist arrived in London; and on hearing this the British evangelist invited him to preach before the half-hour broadcast of hymn singing. He did so. This visiting evangelist was told that he must stop at a given time because at that moment they would be 'on the air' for the broadcast of the hymn singing. So he preached and finished promptly on time, and then immediately, they were on the air for the half-hour hymn singing. When that had finished, and they were no longer 'on the air', the visiting evangelist made his customary 'altar call' giving an invitation to people to come forward. He was interviewed by the Press the next day and, amongst other questions, he was asked whether he was satisfied with the result of his appeal. He replied at once that he was not, that he was disappointed, and that the number was much smaller than he had been accustomed to in London as well as in other places. Then he was asked the obvious question by one of the journalists—To what, then, did he attribute the fact that the response was comparatively small on this occasion? Without any hesitation the evangelist answered that it was quite simple, that unfortunately the half-hour of hymn singing had come in between the end of his sermon and the giving of the appeal. That, he said, was the explanation. If only he had been allowed to give his appeal immediately at the end of the sermon the result would have been altogether greater.

Is not that an illuminating and instructive story? Does it not prove that sometimes at any rate what produces the results is clearly not the Truth, or the work of the Spirit? Here was the preacher himself admitting that the 'results' could not even stand up to the test of half an hour's hymn singing, admitting that half an hour of hymn singing can do away with the effect of a sermon whatever that might have been, and so the result had been disappointing. It is a striking illustration of the fact that direct pressure on the will can produce 'results', but that that may have no real relationship to the Truth.

My third argument is that the preaching of the Word and the call for decision should not be separated in our thinking. That calls for further explanation. It was a great principle emphasised in the Reformed teaching that began in the sixteenth century, that the sacraments should never be separated from the preaching of the Word. The Roman Catholics had been guilty of that separation, with the result that the sacraments had been divorced from the Word and had become entities in and of themselves. The effect and the results in the people were produced, not by the preaching of the Truth, but, according to that teaching, by the action of the sacrament acting *ex opere operato*. Protestant teaching condemned that and stressed that the sacrament should never be separated from the preaching, that that was the only way to avoid semi-magical notions and spurious experiences.

My contention is that the same principle applies to this matter of calling for decisions, and that the tendency increasingly has been to put more and more emphasis on the 'appeal' and the taking of a decision, and to regard it as something in and of itself. I remember being in an evangelistic meeting in which I, and others, felt that on that occasion the Gospel had not really been preached. It had been mentioned, but it certainly had not been conveyed, it had not been preached; but to my amazement a large number of people went forward in response to the appeal at the end. The question that arose immediately was, what accounted for this? I was discussing this question the following day with a friend. He said, 'There is no difficulty about that, 'these results have nothing to do with the preaching.' So I asked, 'Well, what is it, what was happening?' He replied, 'This is God answering the prayers of the thousands of people who are praying for these results throughout the world; it is not the preaching.' My contention is that there should be no such disjunction between the 'appeal' and the preaching, any more than there should be between the sacraments and preaching.

My fourth point is that this method surely carries in it the implication that sinners have an inherent power of decision and of self-conversion. But that cannot be reconciled with scriptural teaching such as 1 Corinthians 2:14, 'The natural man receiveth not the things of the Spirit of God: for they are foolishness unto him: neither can he know them, because they are spiritually discerned,' and Ephesians 2:1, 'You hath He quickened, who were dead in trespasses and sins,' and many other statements.

As my fifth point I suggest that there is an implication here that the evangelist somehow is in a position to manipulate the Holy Spirit and

His work. The evangelist has but to appear and to make his appeal and the results follow inevitably. If there were an occasional failure, an occasional meeting with little or no response, the problem would not arise; but so often today the organisers are able to predict the number of 'results'.

Most would agree with my sixth point which is that this method tends to produce a superficial conviction of sin, if any at all. People often respond because they have the impression that by doing so they will receive certain benefits. I remember hearing of a man who was regarded as one of the 'star converts' of a campaign. He was interviewed and asked why he had gone forward in the campaign the previous year. His answer was that the evangelist had said, 'If you do not want to "miss the boat" you had better come forward.' He said that he did not want to 'miss the boat' so he had gone forward; and all the interviewer could get out of him was that he somehow felt that he was now 'on the boat'. He was not clear about what this meant, nor what it was, and nothing had seemed to happen to him during the subsequent year. But there it was: it can be as superficial as that.

Or take another illustration out of my own experience. In the church where I ministered in South Wales I used to stand at the main door of the church at the close of the service on Sunday night, and shake hands with people as they went out. The incident to which I am referring concerns a man who used to come to our service every Sunday night. He was a tradesman but also a heavy drinker. He got drunk regularly every Saturday night, but he was also regularly seated in the gallery of our church every Sunday night. On the particular night to which I am referring I happened to notice while preaching that this man was obviously being affected. I could see that he was weeping copiously, and I was anxious to know what was happening to him. At the end of the service I went and stood at the door. After a while I saw this man coming, and immediately I was in a real mental conflict. Should I, in view of what I had seen, say a word to him and ask him to make his decision that night, or should I not? Would I be interfering with the work of the Spirit if I did so? Hurriedly I decided that I would not ask him to stay behind, so I just greeted him as usual and he went out. His face revealed that he had been crying copiously, and he could scarcely look at me. The following evening I was walking to the prayer-meeting in the church, and, going over a railway bridge, I saw this same man coming to meet me. He came across the road to me and said, 'You know, doctor, if you had asked me to stay behind last night I would have done so.' 'Well,' I said, 'I am asking you now, come with me now.' 'Oh no,' he replied, 'but if you had asked me last night I would have done so.' 'My dear friend,' I said, 'if what happened to you last night does not last for twenty-four hours I am not interested in it. If you are not as ready to come with me now as you were last night you have not got the right, the true thing. Whatever affected you last night was only temporary and passing, you still do not see your real need of Christ.'

That is the kind of thing that may happen even when an appeal is not made. But when an appeal is made it is greatly exaggerated and so you get spurious conversions. As I have reminded you even John Wesley, the great Arminian, did not make appeals to people to 'come forward'. What you find so often in his Journals is something like this: 'Preached at such and such a place. Many seemed to be deeply affected, but God alone knows how deeply.' Surely that is very significant and important. He had spiritual understanding and knew that many factors can affect us. What he was concerned about was not immediate visible results but the work of the Holy Spirit in regeneration. A knowledge of the human heart, of psychology, should teach us to avoid anything that increases the possibility of spurious results.

Another argument—the seventh—is that by doing this you are encouraging people to think that their act of going forward somehow saves them. This is something that must be done there and then, and it is this act that really saves them. That was the case with the man who felt that he was now 'on the boat' because he had gone forward though he had no understanding.

But, as I have already suggested, is not this practice based ultimately on a distrust of the Holy Spirit and His power and His work? Does it not imply that the Holy Spirit needs to be helped and aided and supplemented, that the work has to be hastened, that we cannot leave it in the hands of the Spirit? I cannot see how that conclusion can be evaded.

Or, to put it in yet another way—as a ninth point—does it not raise the whole question of the doctrine of Regeneration? This, to me, is the most serious thing of all. What I mean is this, and it covers this point and the previous one, that as this work is the work of the Holy Spirit, and His work alone, no one else can do it. The true work of conviction of sin, and regeneration, and the giving of the gift of faith and new life is solely the work of the Holy Spirit. And as it is His work it is always a thorough work; and it is always a work that will show itself. It always has done so. You see it in a most dramatic form on the Day of Pentecost in Jerusalem as recorded in Acts 2. Even while Peter was preaching, people cried out under conviction of sin. 'Men and brethren, what shall we do?' Peter was preaching in the power of the Spirit. He was expounding the Scriptures and applying them. He did not employ any techniques and there was no interval between the sermon and the appeal. Indeed Peter was not even allowed to finish his sermon. The mighty work of conviction was going on, and it showed itself, as it invariably does show itself.

I remember reading an account of a Revival in the Congo in a book called *This is that,* and in particular one of the chapters written by a man whom I knew personally. He had been a missionary in the heart of Africa for twenty years and had at practically every service made appeals to people to come forward in response to his message. Very few had responded, and he was almost broken-hearted. He pressed them and pleaded with them, he did everything he could in the customary evangelistic manner; but he could not get a response. Then on one occasion he had to go away to a distant part of the district of which he was in charge. While he was away a Revival broke out in the central area of his district. His wife sent him a message giving an account of it. At first he did not like this. He was not pleased to hear about it because it had happened while he was not there—such is the pride of which we all tend to be guilty. However, he hurried back with the intention of controlling what he felt was an outburst of emotionalism or some kind of 'wild fire'. Having returned he gathered the people together into the chapel and began to preach to them. To his utter astonishment and before he was halfway through his sermon, people began to walk forward under deep conviction of sin. What he had failed to get them to do for twenty years they were now doing spontaneously. Why? Because the Holy Spirit was doing the work. His work always shows itself. It must do so of necessity, and always has done so. This surely needs no demonstration or argument. The work of God always shows itself whether in nature and creation or in the souls of men.

I have had many experiences along this line. I shall be saying something later about the romance of the work of the preacher and the minister; and this is one aspect of it. I remember how during the depths of the Second World War when everything was about as discouraging as it could be—bombing had scattered our congregation and so on—and I was facing great discouragement. I suddenly received a letter from the Dutch East Indies, now known as Indonesia. It was from a Dutch soldier who wrote saying that his conscience had been pricking him and, at last, had driven him to write to tell me what had happened to him eighteen months before. He explained how he had come to England with the Dutch Free Army and while stationed in London had attended our services for some time. While doing so he had been convinced of the fact that he had never been a Christian at all though he had thought he was. He had then passed through a dark period of conviction of sin and hopelessness, but, eventually, he had seen the Truth and had been rejoicing in it ever since. He had never come to tell me about this for various reasons, but was now doing so in this letter.

My reaction to that is this. What does it matter whether I know or not? It matters of course from the standpoint of one's encouragement in the work, but it does not matter from the standpoint of the work itself. The work had been done, and the work had showed itself, and it had been showing itself in the man's life before he ever wrote to me about it. That is what really matters.

Thank God, I find that experience being repeated at the present time. Having retired from a pastoral charge and travelling round, and having more time, I find people in various parts of Great Britain coming to tell me that they had been converted while listening to my preaching. I knew nothing at all about it, but it had happened years ago. I was preaching in the chapel of a certain preacher just eighteen months ago. While introducing me to the congregation he gave a short account of his spiritual life, and to my utter amazement I heard that I had played a vital part in it. This man who was a well-qualified professional man had left this profession and had become the pastor of that church. He told the people of how he was walking aimlessly along a street in London on a hot summer's evening in the month of June, and how hearing the sound of singing coming out of Westminster Chapel he had gone in and had stayed through the service. 'I went out,' he said, 'a new man, born again, regenerated.' He was completely ignorant of these things before, indeed had tended to despise and dismiss them. That was the first I had heard of that, though it had happened in 1964, but what does it matter? The important point is that because it is the Spirit who does the work it is a real work, it is a solid work; and it will declare itself.

I go on to assert as my tenth point that no sinner ever really 'decides for Christ'. That term 'decide' has always seemed to me to be quite wrong. I have often heard people use expressions which have disturbed me, and made me feel very unhappy. They have generally done so in ignorance and with the best intentions. I can think of an old man who often used the following expression: 'You know, friends, I decided for Christ forty years ago, and I have never regretted it.' What a terrible thing to say! 'Never regretted it!' But that is the kind of thing people say who have been brought up under this teaching and approach. A sinner does not 'decide' for Christ; the sinner 'flies' to Christ in utter helplessness and despair saying—

Foul, I to the fountain fly,
Wash me, Saviour, or I die.

No man truly comes to Christ unless he flies to Him as his only refuge
and hope, his only way of escape from the accusations of conscience
and the condemnation of God's holy law. Nothing else is satisfactory.
If a man says that having thought about the matter and having considered all sides he has on the whole decided for Christ, and if he has
done so without any emotion or feeling, I cannot regard him as a man
who has been regenerated. The convicted sinner no more 'decides' for
Christ than the poor drowning man 'decides' to take hold of that rope
that is thrown to him and suddenly provides him with the only means
of escape. The term is entirely inappropriate.

But then one is confronted by the argument of 'results'. 'Look what
happens,' people say. This is an argument, it seems to me, that can be
answered in many ways. One is that as Protestants we should not use
the Jesuitical argument of the end justifying the means. That is what
that argument really means. But we must go further and examine the
results and the claims that are made. What percentage of these
'decisions' last? I have heard evangelists say that they never expect
more than one-tenth to hold. They say that openly. What was it then
that influenced the others? And if it be said that it is only the tenth
that matters because they are the result of the work of the Spirit, then
I reply that this would have happened in the absence of an 'altar
call'.

Going yet further, it is important that we should differentiate between immediate and remote results. Let us grant for the sake of
argument that there may be a number of immediate results. You still
have to consider the remote effects and results of this procedure—the
effect upon the life of the local church, and upon the life of churches
in general. In spite of all we have been told of phenomenal and
staggering results during the past twenty years it can scarcely be dis-
puted that the general level of true spirituality in the life of our
churches has undergone a serious decline. That is the remote effect,

and it is the exact opposite of what has always happened at a time of spiritual Revival and awakening.

Moreover, I find in ministers' meetings, and in private conversation with many ministers, that in general, ministers find that their problems have increased rather than decreased in recent years. I have already mentioned the case of men who cannot even get a call from certain churches because of this. I have spoken of others who are criticised by their members because they do not make this 'call' at every service. The practice seems to have introduced a new kind of mentality, a carnality expressing itself as an unhealthy interest in numbers. It has led also to a desire for excitement, and to an impatience almost with the message because they are waiting for the 'call' at the end and the seeing of the results. All this is surely very serious.

Another element comes in at this point. As I said earlier it is a fact to say that the men who organise this kind of activity are able to predict with extraordinary accuracy the number of responses and results they are likely to get. They have even put this in print before the campaign starts, and they are generally not very far off the mark in their estimations. This is something that is quite unthinkable in connection with the work of the Holy Spirit. You never know what the Holy Spirit is going to do. 'The wind bloweth where it listeth.' You cannot predict, you cannot anticipate. The greatest preachers and saints have often had hard, barren services in which nothing has happened, and they have deplored that. Even in times of Revival there have been days and meetings when nothing has happened; and then perhaps the next day there has been overwhelming power. So the very fact that you can more or less anticipate and state beforehand what is likely to happen is indicative that this does not conform to what has always characterised the work of the Spirit. I trust that it is quite clear in all this that I am in no way querying the motives or the sincerity of those who use this method, or the fact that there have been genuine converts; I am concerned simply to show why I have not used it myself.

What, then, you ask, should one do? I would put it like this. The appeal must be in the Truth itself, and in the message. As you preach your sermon you should be applying it all the time, and especially, of course, at the end, when you come to the final application and to the climax. But the appeal is a part of the message; it should be so inevitably. The sermon should lead men to see that this is the only thing to do. The appeal should be implicit throughout the whole body of the sermon, and in all that you are doing. I would say, without hesitation, that a distinct and separate and special appeal at the end after a break, and after a hymn, should only be made when one is conscious of some overwhelming injunction of the Spirit of God to do so. If ever I feel that, I do it; but it is only then. And even then the way in which I do it is not to ask people to come forward; I just make it known that I am ready to see them at the end of the service or at any other time. Indeed I believe that the minister should always make an announcement in some shape or form that he is available to talk to anybody who wants to talk to him about their soul and its eternal destiny. This can be put on a card in every seat—which is what I did—or you can do it in some other way. Make yourself available, let it be known that you are available, and so you will find that people who have come under conviction of sin will come to speak to you because they are unhappy. Not infrequently they may be afraid to go home as they are. I have known people to go halfway home and then come back again to the church to see me because they could not endure the sense of conviction and unhappiness; the agony was too great.

Or, if they have found salvation and are rejoicing in it, they will want to come to tell you about it. They will do so in their own time; let them do so. Do not force these things. This is the work of the Holy Spirit of God. His work is a thorough work, it is a lasting work; and so we must not yield to this over-anxiety about results. I am not saying it is dishonest, I say it is mistaken. We must learn to trust the Spirit and to rely upon His infallible work.

CHAPTER FIFTEEN

The Pitfalls and the Romance

THERE ARE STILL a number of odd matters to which I must refer. One is the question of repeating the same sermon. There is no very great problem here, but I have found that some Christian people are surprised that a preacher should repeat a sermon. They seem to think that it is almost sinful to do so; so we must just look at this matter.

When I say repeating a sermon I obviously am not thinking of repeating the same sermon in the same church and to the same people. I am referring to using a sermon which you have preached in your own church elsewhere when you are invited to preach on vacation or on some special occasion. With regard to preaching the same sermon in the same church I find it very difficult to understand how anyone could possibly do that. Personally I should be too self-conscious to do it. But there are men who have done this. An organist once told me that he had heard a certain preacher preach his famous sermon on 'Balaam and his ass' seven times in the church where he was organist; and he could recite certain parts of it verbatim. I need say no more about that. I have also been told of a well-known preacher in the U.S.A. who used to repeat one particular sermon every year when he was a minister in Philadelphia. All the members of the church knew that he was going to do this and they used to look forward to it. I have also known this to be done by request. People have asked the minister to preach a particular sermon at different times and he has done so repeatedly. I have nothing to say in favour of that; indeed I could say a great deal against it.

But what of preaching the same sermon in another church or other churches? Is there a principle involved here? As far as I know the history of this matter from reading and conversations, there is only one man who seems to have taken exception to this, and that was Charles Haddon Spurgeon. So we have a duty to pay some attention to this question.

Spurgeon did not approve of repeating sermons; he always tried to prepare a fresh sermon for every occasion. Yet it is very interesting to read of what happened on the occasion when he first visited Scotland and preached in Edinburgh. He adhered to his usual method and preached a new sermon though he knew that he would be preaching to a large and curious congregation. It fell completely flat and was a complete failure, and so Spurgeon sent an urgent message to his home in London asking them to send up the notes of a sermon he had preached in the Tabernacle on the previous Sunday! So Spurgeon had to fall back on this in a moment of crisis and of difficulty.

But apart from the one case of Spurgeon, as far as I am aware, the whole tendency of other great preachers has been to repeat their sermons. Whitefield, of course, did this constantly, as did John Wesley. You have only to read their Journals to discover this. They record that they preached a sermon on such and such a text, and that they preached it again elsewhere many times. I was interested to notice recently in one of the volumes of the Diaries of Benjamin Franklin that are being re-published, that he claimed that he could always tell when Whitefield was preaching a fresh sermon. He could tell immediately, just by listening and observing the preacher, whether it was a new sermon or whether it was one with which Whitefield was familiar through frequent repetition. There was not the same ease and freedom in the case of the new sermon. The preacher was more careful, and particularly because he was an extemporary preacher. There was a great Welsh preacher who died in 1921 who used to say quite definitely and deliberately that he felt he had never really preached a sermon properly until he had preached it at least twenty times! While I can well understand what he meant, I am not quite happy about it. In that particular case I feel that there was a tendency for him to become a rhetorician or dramatic reciter.

In this connection I also remember a very good answer that was once given by another great old preacher to someone who went to him and complained that he had just been listening to him preaching that sermon for the third time. It was not in the same place, but in different places. The listener was one of those people who follow preachers round from place to place; and they can be a nuisance! When this man made his complaint the wily old preacher looked at him and asked, 'Have you put it into practice yet?' The listener hesitated to say that he had. 'All right,' said the preacher, 'I will go on preaching it until you do.'

That is a satisfactory answer as far as it goes; but is there a real justification for this practice? I believe there is, and I would defend it in this way. A sermon, after all, is not just a statement of truth or a statement of a number of truths. It is not, as we have defined it, only an exposition of a passage: it is more than that. If it were only an exposition, and stopped at that, I would be ready to grant that the case against repeating it is a good one. But if you accept the definition of a sermon as being a message and a burden, and as an entity, a complete message in itself, having a particular form and shape, well then I think there is a great deal to be said for repeating the same sermon in various places. My main reason for saying that, and this is surely the experience of every preacher, is that some messages are given to the preacher in a very special way. I have already referred to that. Some sermons come to the preacher with an unusual clarity; he seems to have been given the very order in which the points are to be presented; it all seems to be a direct gift from God. Moreover, he finds that this message is honoured and used by the Spirit perhaps to the conversion of someone or as a means of special blessing to others. There is no question about this; every preacher will testify to it. So I ask, Why should such a sermon not be repeated? Surely it should be the preacher's concern always to give the best that he has, the very best that he has. It is therefore surely legitimate for him to select his best sermon and to preach it to the people.

There is a further argument. Taking the view that I have been advocating of sermons and preaching, you will find that sermons grow and develop as the result of being preached. You do not see everything when you are preparing in your study; you will see further aspects while you are preaching, and so your sermon will grow and develop. This is a most interesting and fascinating matter. Again I am speaking out of my own experience and from what I have known of others. I remember a preacher telling me once of how he was filled with alarm on one occasion. This man was a great admirer of another preacher. He himself was a good preacher, but he was not an outstanding and popular preacher like the other man. But being a good and a humble man he was a sincere admirer of the other preacher. On one occasion he was attending a great Synod; and it was the custom that the last day in these Synods should be devoted to preaching. The great preachers were always invited to preach on such occasions. My friend's great hero got up to preach, and, said my friend, 'To my dismay I heard him give out a particular text. I really began to feel miserable and ill because,' he said, 'I had heard him preach on that text in my own church about three months before in some special meetings. I had felt on that occasion that that sermon was not up to his usual standard, so when I heard him giving out this text on this great occasion I felt dismayed and anxious about his reputation. But,' he said, 'I need not have been disturbed. That sermon of his had grown and developed almost out of recognition. I could still recognise the bare scaffolding but it had now become a truly great sermon which he preached with great power. The extraordinary thing about the old man,' he added, 'is that his sermons grow; they develop in a most amazing manner.' He contrasted that with his own, saying, 'Mine don't.' He himself prepared so meticulously and carefully, writing every word, that in a sense his sermons could not grow. The other preacher did not, and so his sermons could grow and develop. The result is that though such a man is, basically preaching the same sermon, in many other senses it is not the same sermon; it becomes a better sermon, and a fuller and a greater sermon.

Not only that; but once more the whole question of the relationship between the sermon and the preaching arises. As I have confessed already, it is very difficult to define this; but it is very true to experience to say that as you become more familiar with your sermon it will greatly add to the effectiveness of your preaching of that sermon. There is less sense of strain, and you are not concentrating to the same extent on trying to remember what you have to say. You have attained to a measure of freedom because you are now familiar with the material in a way that you could not be when you preached it for the first time. So, for all these reasons I would say that to preach the same sermon when you feel that there is something exceptional about it as far as you are concerned, when you feel that it has a real message in it, and when it has been blessed and used of God, is thoroughly legitimate. Indeed to do so is to benefit the people who will be listening to you.

But someone may ask, 'How often, then, should you repeat this one sermon?' Here, again, is a somewhat difficult question. My distinguished and famous predecessor, Dr. G. Campbell Morgan, was quite unashamed about this. I remember listening to him on one occasion; and this is how he began. He said, 'We are told that confession is good for the soul. So I might as well tell you now before we start, that I am this morning preaching this sermon for the one hundred and nineteenth time.'

How many times should you repeat the same sermon? All I would say about it is this, that it is not a question of figures or mere statistics. Dr. Campbell Morgan was very careful to put down on the envelope in which he kept his notes the number of times he had preached the sermon, and where he had done so. That was good. But as to the number, it is not a mechanical matter; and there is only one rule it seems to me. Stop preaching that sermon when it ceases to grip you, when it ceases to move you, when it ceases to be a means of blessing to you yourself. Stop then; because from there on your preaching of it will be mechanical and, indeed, can even become a 'performance'. Nothing is worse than that.

I once heard a man at a big Bible conference in the U.S.A. repeat a sermon at the request of many people. He had a great sermon on the Lord Jesus Christ which was worked out in terms of the letters of the alphabet starting with 'A' and going through to 'Z'. Naturally it was a somewhat long sermon. As I listened to that sermon I must confess that the effect it had upon me was not to bring me to see the glory of the Lord or to be grateful; I felt it was a performance that came very near to being blasphemous. He rushed through it. He had to do so in order to get through in time. He had to leave the conference immediately afterwards, and so it was galloped through. Great and glorious truths were jostled out mechanically. Many of the people had heard the sermon many times before and they clearly thought that it was wonderful. It was certainly clever, a clever sermon, a kind of acrostic; but to me it was a sheer performance which sent people away not admiring and worshipping the Lord, but admiring the preacher's memory and cleverness. We should never give a performance; we cannot reprobate this too strongly.

I would also issue certain further warnings. If you repeat a sermon in this way there are certain things you have got to avoid. There is the story of a very well-known preacher—as well-known in the U.S.A. as in Britain—who prepared his sermons very carefully, writing them out fully, and who generally read them while preaching but in a very unobtrusive manner. He was particularly interested in words and fine shades of meaning. He was famous for this. The story goes, and it is said to be true, that on one occasion a certain commercial traveller was visiting the town where this man then ministered, and on the Sunday morning he went to listen to the famous preacher. He felt that he had heard the greatest sermon he had ever heard in his life. What impressed him particularly was something that happened halfway through the sermon. The great preacher stopped dramatically and said, 'Now, what is the word I want here?' Then he mentioned a word. 'No; that comes near to it but it is not quite right.' Then he took another word: 'No, not quite right.' Then, very dramatically, 'Ah, here it is, just the word which brings out the exact shade of meaning.' The visitor thought that this was marvellous. He had never heard anything like it. The following weekend this same commercial traveller was in an entirely different part of the country. He looked at the Saturday evening paper to see who was preaching in the town next day, and to his great joy and delight he saw that this great preacher was due at the Anniversary Services in a certain church. There was of course no question as to where he should go next morning. He went to that church, and when the time came for the sermon the text was given out and proved to be the same text as on the previous Sunday. He was a bit taken aback, but he thought it was well worth hearing again. Halfway through the sermon there was the same dramatic pause, and the question 'What is the word I want' etc. The man was disgusted, and got up and went out, saying he would never listen to that preacher again.

So, if you do repeat a sermon, avoid doing that sort of thing. That is what has done such great harm to preaching; it is dishonest. The speaker knew the word when he asked his question, and yet was out to give the impression that it had suddenly come to him.

I have much greater sympathy with an old preacher whom I actually knew myself, a good old man who had done faithful service in his local church for many years. He was not much of a preacher, but he was given the great honour, when he was well on in life, of being asked to preach at what was called a quarterly association. This was the height of the ambition of many a preacher, and certainly the greatest honour that could come to them. This great honour had at last come to the old man, and, as was the custom on those occasions, he was one of two preachers. So the two preachers were together in the pulpit. During the singing of the hymns the other preacher noticed that this old man was scrutinising the congregation and looking carefully at each person in the various pews. So he whispered to him during one of the hymns, 'What are you doing? Are you looking to see if there is anybody here who has heard your sermon before?' 'No,' said the old man, 'I am looking to see if there is anybody here who has not heard it before!' If your sermon has been heard before by many people, don't preach it again.

I well remember the last time I heard a certain well-known preacher. When he gave out his text, the minister sitting next to me in the congregation nudged me and said, 'We are in for an outing tonight.' I said, 'Yes, I know we are.' 'What,' he said, 'have you heard it as well?' 'I have,' I replied. 'I have heard him preach it three times in what once was his own church; and I have also read it several times in the paper which he edits.' The fact was that most people present on that occasion—it was a conference consisting of ministers and deacons from all parts of the country—had already heard this sermon, and read it probably more than once.

Why do men do this sort of thing? Let us be fair about this. Do not rush too readily and too easily to condemn these men lest you find yourselves in trouble one day, and your own words will come back to you. There are many reasons for this. One is laziness, of course. That is never an excuse and it must not be used as an argument. But, sometimes, it is sheer panic. I gathered from the man I have mentioned that on that particular occasion it was a kind of panic. He told some of us at the close of the service that he had prepared a special sermon for this great occasion. But then he had not felt very well over the weekend, and the result was that when he went up into the pulpit he had lost his confidence in the new sermon, and in a moment of panic had fallen back upon the old masterpiece. Unfortunately he was very often guilty of doing that very thing. Of course we cannot exclude an element of pride in this whole matter. A man may be more concerned about his own reputation as a preacher than about conveying Truth to the people. It is a subtle matter; and we must never allow pride to take charge. So if you do repeat certain sermons keep a record of what you are doing otherwise you will almost certainly find yourself in trouble.

I close this section with another story about this selfsame man to whom I have been referring, and who failed to keep such a record. I was talking one day to the minister of a large church in a big provincial city. We were talking about this particular preacher and he said, 'Yes, I had him down at my Anniversary a few years back. He preached on the text, "Thou therefore, my son, endure hardness, as a good soldier of Jesus Christ." We all thought it was the greatest thing we had ever heard. So, when next year the question arose as to whom we should have as our Anniversary preacher there was no discussion; we agreed unanimously that we must have the same man. We wrote to him and he accepted the invitation and came down the second year. On the great day he stood up to preach and gave out his text—"Thou therefore, my son, endure hardness, as a good soldier of Jesus Christ." Well, it was still very good, and we enjoyed it very much, though we were a little disappointed. When we came to decide on our Anniversary preacher for the next year there was a good deal of discussion. Some wanted the same man but others were opposed in view of what he had done. However, after much discussion, it was decided to give him another chance—we all make mistakes sometimes and so we must not condemn him for one slip. So down he came the third year and gave out his text: "Thou therefore, my son, endure hardness, as a good soldier of Jesus Christ." At that point,' said my friend, 'we really did begin to feel that we were "enduring", so we have not asked him again!' The lesson is: Keep a record.

*   *   *

We turn now to something which I regard as extremely interesting, namely the character of sermons. What I mean by this is that each sermon tends to have a character of its own. This is a most mysterious matter. You have prepared the sermon, you have composed it, yet it seems to have a character of its own. I was interested to learn during a long and fascinating conversation I had with a novelist recently that he found exactly the same thing with the characters in his novels. 'I have great trouble with them,' he said. He could not keep some of them in their place; he felt that they were tending to handle him. Though they were his own creations, they had such character and individuality and personality that they were controlling him, instead of his controlling them. It is exactly the same with sermons. How to explain it I do not know, but it is a very definite fact. Some sermons virtually preach themselves and you have very little to do; they preach themselves and they never let you down.

Alas, this is only true of some; there are others—and I cannot explain the difference between them—which require very careful handling; and if you fail to handle them carefully they will half kill you. I have known sermons that have almost exhausted me in the introduction, and it has taken me a long time to get to know them and understand them so that I can handle them correctly, instead of their handling me and running away with me. Many a time I have known sermons that have so carried me away in the introduction that when I came to what was really important, and especially to the climax, I found I was already tired out and exhausted and could not do justice to the matter.

There is a very definite character to every sermon; and you have to get to know your sermon. This is a point of great value. I remember an old preacher—he was at the end of his life when I was very young— who always compared sermons to horses. He had ridden many horses in his youth as a countryman, and invariably in talking about sermons and preaching he would make use of the analogy of horse riding. I remember his saying on one occasion after a bad service, 'That old sermon threw me, I had a feeling that it would; and there was I lying on the ground.' The sermon had 'thrown him' as if it were a horse. There is great point in all this; so my advice is, get to know your sermons. You will then get to know the right sermon for any particular occasion, and also the right sermon for any particular physical state or condition you may be in yourself. All these factors come in and are of very great importance. To speak like this may sound most unspiritual to some; but I assure you that it is of great practical importance. We are still 'in the flesh' and 'have this treasure in earthen vessels'. Any consideration that helps to make preaching more effective is not to be despised.

The Pitfalls and the Romance

I hesitated about making any reference at all to the next point—preaching other people's sermons. I feel that I must mention it because I am assured that it is a not uncommon practice. I have but one comment to make about this—it is utterly dishonest unless you acknowledge what you are doing. I never have understood how a man can live with himself, who preaches other men's sermons without acknowledgment. He receives the praise and the thanks of people, and yet knows that it is not due to him. He is a thief and a robber; he is a great sinner. But, as I say, the amazing thing to me is that he can possibly live with himself.

There are some odd aspects to this matter which are of interest. There is, for example, the famous story about Spurgeon and one of the students in his college that was brought to him to be reprimanded on one occasion. This was the story. This young man had been preaching in different churches on Sundays, and reports concerning his preaching had been coming back to the college. Some said that his preaching was very good, but adverse criticisms began to come in to the effect that this young man was repeatedly preaching a sermon of Mr. Spurgeon's. The Principal of the college had of course to deal with this; so he sent for the young man. He said to him 'I hear that you are going round and preaching one of Mr. Spurgeon's sermons. Is this true?' The young man replied, 'No, sir, it is not true.' The Principal pressed him but he still persisted in saying that it was not true. This went on for some time so at last the Principal felt that the only thing to do was to take the young man to Mr. Spurgeon himself. So they went together and the case was put before Mr. Spurgeon. 'Well now,' said Mr. Spurgeon, 'you need not be frightened. If you are honest you will not be punished. We are all sinners, but we do want to get at the facts. You have been preaching a sermon on such and such a text?' 'Yes, sir.' 'And you have divided up the subject as follows?' 'Yes, sir.' 'And you say that you have not been preaching my sermon?' 'That is so, sir.'

This questioning went for some time, until at last Mr. Spurgeon was beginning to feel somewhat impatient; so he said to the young

293

man, 'Well, are you saying, then, that it is your sermon?' 'Oh no, sir' said the young man. 'Well, then, whose sermon is it?' 'It is a sermon of William Jay of Bath, sir' said the student. Jay was a famous preacher in Bath in the early part of the last century and some of his sermons had been printed in two volumes. 'Wait a minute,' said Spurgeon, and turning to his library, he pulled out one of the volumes and there was the sermon, the exact sermon—the same text, the same headings, the same everything! What had happened? The fact was that Mr. Spurgeon had also preached William Jay's sermon and had actually put it into print with other sermons of his. Mr. Spurgeon's only explanation was that it was many years since he had read the two volumes of Jay's sermons and that he had forgotten all about it. He could say quite honestly that he was not aware of the fact that when he had preached that sermon he was preaching one of the sermons of William Jay. It had registered unconsciously in his memory. The student was absolved of the charge of preaching one of Mr. Spurgeon's sermons, but was still guilty of theft!

There is another very good story which I repeat for the comfort of any preacher in need, or any man in a state of desperation—lay-preachers particularly. It is another story about Spurgeon who, as is known, was given to fits of depression. He suffered from gout, and that condition is often accompanied by an element of depression. During one of these attacks Spurgeon was so depressed that he felt he could not preach, indeed that he was not fit to preach. So he refused to preach in the Tabernacle the following Sunday and went off to the country to his old home in Essex. On the Sunday morning he slipped into a seat at the back of the little chapel where he had attended as a boy. A lay-preacher was preaching that morning, and the poor man proceeded to preach one of Mr. Spurgeon's printed sermons. The moment the good man had finished Spurgeon rushed on to him with tears streaming down his face, and thanked him profusely. The poor man said, 'Mr Spurgeon I don't know how to face you, I have just been preaching one of your sermons.' 'I don't care whose sermon it is,' said Mr. Spurgeon, 'all I know is that your preaching this morning has convinced me that I am a child of God, that I am saved by grace, that all my sins are forgiven, that I am called to the ministry; and I am ready to go back to preach again.' His own sermon through the lips and the mouth and the tongue of the lay-preacher had done that for him. That is, I think, about the only justification for this sort of thing.

But let me warn you to be careful. I crossed the Atlantic in 1937 with the dear old saint and evangelist Mel Trotter of Grand Rapids. After a life of sin and shame he had been converted in a glorious manner and had become the superintendent of a great Rescue Mission Hall and work. He told me the following story with great relish. He had been working very hard one week, speaking, organising the work and counselling many people in trouble. He was not a studious man, and he had not had time to prepare properly for the Sunday. He had prepared his Sunday evening sermon, but he simply could not think of anything for the morning service. He had had to go to bed on the Saturday night in that unhappy state, without a Sunday morning sermon. So he got up very early on the Sunday morning, but still nothing would come, and he did not know what to do. At last in desperation he decided that he would have to preach one of his friend Dr. G. Campbell Morgan's sermons. So he went into the pulpit and conducted the service in the usual manner—hymn, scripture reading, prayer, etc. As they were just finishing the hymn before the sermon Mel Trotter saw a door at the back of the building opening, and to his utter dismay in walked Campbell Morgan and sat at the back! There was nothing to be done, and Mel Trotter preached the sermon. At the close of the service Campbell Morgan went on to him and thanked him warmly for the sermon. 'What, man,' said Mel Trotter 'do you not recognise one of your own children simply because it has my suit on it?'

In the year 1936 on the second Sunday in August we were as a family on holiday in the west of Wales. The only church there was the Anglican church, so we went there with the farmer and his wife with whom we were staying. When eventually the vicar went up into the pulpit to preach his sermon and gave out his text, my wife nudged me because that was actually the first text on which I had ever preached in Westminster Chapel on the occasion of my first visit there on the last Sunday in 1935. Because of that, I suppose, and because I was a stranger to London pulpits, that sermon of mine had been printed in two or three religious journals and papers; and my wife having read these knew this sermon fairly well. The vicar gave out that text and then began to preach. I regret to say that he attempted to preach my sermon; and there was I listening to him. He did not know me, and had never seen me before. I did my best to avoid meeting him during the following week but our farmer host brought him into our room one day and introduced us. Though I was not impressed by the way in which he handled my sermon I had to award him full marks for the way in which he handled the situation! Without any apparent embarrassment he looked me straight in the eye and said, 'I am glad to meet you, as I have often heard of you. If I had only known that you were here I would have asked you to read the lessons in the service.' 'Verily they have their reward'; and I did not betray him. But that is what may happen to you if you preach another man's sermon.

My wife has a story which illustrates another possible danger. Two preachers came on two successive Sundays to preach in the chapel of which she was a member, and preached the identical sermon. The question was, which of them was the author? The probable answer was—neither. The probability is that they had both borrowed it or rather, stolen it. But that is how you are caught out. A further comment—changing the text is not enough! Any discriminating listener will always be able to detect what you are doing.

To add a few of your own illustrations or stories does not cover it either. I knew a man who said that his method was to read a Spurgeon sermon three or four times a few days before the Sunday and then preach it. 'You see,' he said, 'I am not really preaching Spurgeon's sermon; it has just passed through my mind!' So we try to rationalise our sins, but succeed only in showing the kind of mind we have.

Just one further word about this. If you must preach somebody else's sermon, if you are really in desperation on some occasion and feel there is nothing else to do for the sake of your people, avoid doing what a poor preacher I knew once in South Wales did. I am probably stating the literal truth when I say that he had probably never been outside Wales at all, not even to England, let alone anywhere else. This man one Sunday morning read out his text and then began his sermon with these words: 'As I stood the other day at the head of the Wyoming Valley . . .'! In other words, learn what to leave out. If the clergyman who preached my sermon had had a little sense he would not have started with my first sentence. He actually did. I still remember it, because he fixed it in my mind. It was, 'A very good subject for discussion in a church fellowship meeting . . .' The vicar never held a church fellowship meeting. I did, and so I naturally introduced my subject in that way. Avoid things like that if you feel at any time that you must preach someone else's sermon. But to put yourself altogether in the right, tell the people about your indebtedness to the other man.

*   *   *

Now let us hurry on to something much more important—the romance of preaching! There is nothing like it. It is the greatest work in the world, the most thrilling, the most exciting, the most rewarding, and the most wonderful. I know of nothing comparable to the feeling one has as one walks up the steps of one's pulpit with a fresh sermon on a Sunday morning or a Sunday evening, especially when you feel that you have a message from God and are longing to give it to the people. This is something that one cannot describe. Repeating your best sermon elsewhere never quite gives you that. That is why I am such an advocate of a regular and a longish ministry in the same place. That is something, I fear, I shall never know again having retired from the pastoral ministry. But there is nothing to equal that. You can have a very happy time while preaching elsewhere, but this special experience which results from the relationship between you and the people, and your preparation, and many other factors are peculiar to the regular ministry in one church.

Another aspect of this romantic element is the endless possibilities of a service. Or, if you prefer it, the uncertain element in a service. There is something glorious even about the uncertainty; because if you are a true preacher you really do not know what is going to happen when you enter a pulpit. If you are a lecturer, as I have explained, you do know; but if you are a preacher you certainly do not. And you will have most amazing experiences. You may enter the pulpit feeling really well, confident in your preparation and anticipating a good service, only to have a bad service. There is something wonderful even in that because it shows at any rate that you are not the sole person in control. You tended to think you were, but you have discovered that you are not, and you are reminded that you are 'under God'.

But conversely, and thank God for this, you may enter the pulpit feeling ill, feeling nervous, conscious of inadequate preparation for various reasons; and suddenly all is well, even physically. The effect of preaching on one's own health is quite remarkable. Those who have read the Journals of Whitefield will have noticed that he often referred to that. He had not been feeling well—probably it was his heart troubling him, or his excessive corpulence in his later years—and you find in his Journal, or in a letter to somebody a statement like this, 'I shall not be right again until I have had a good pulpit sweat'. And it did put him right so frequently—'a good pulpit sweat'. I have often said that the only Turkish baths I have had have been in pulpits. This is something that literally happens, one is completely reinvigorated and restored to health and strength by preaching, and you scarcely know yourself. I know nothing else that does this. However weak and jaded you may be when you enter your pulpit you may come out an entirely different man.

I want to add one qualification to this, and once more it is a point that has interested me very much throughout the years. There were times when I could tell on a Saturday what was going to happen on the Sunday. Note that I say 'times'; it is certainly not the regular experience. When you yourself are gripped and moved in the preparation you will generally find that the same happens in the preaching. I emphasise that it is when you are gripped and moved, not when you have composed well. It is when you have been stirred in this way, when the message you are preparing comes with power to you, and does something to you, that it is likely to do the same to the people. Whenever I was so gripped and moved in my study, I generally knew what was going to happen on the Sunday; and it generally did happen.

Under this heading of romance I mention once more what I was referring to earlier when I talked about the theme developing while you are preaching. That again is a most thrilling and wonderful experience which fills one with a sense of amazement. It is quite extraordinary, and one seems to have no control over it; it just happens. I have often found when I have gone into the pulpit with a prepared sermon, that while I have been preaching, my first point alone has developed into a whole sermon. Many times I have gone out of the pulpit realising that I had a series of sermons which I had not seen before. As the first point had become a complete sermon I could see that the same would happen to the others and so I would have a series. I had not seen this in my preparation, but while preaching, it had all opened out before me.

Is not this truly romantic? As long as this kind of thing happens to you you will never be short of matter, you will never be looking desperately for a sermon. In fact you will reach the stage in which you will be longing for the next Sunday to come and looking forward to it eagerly. I am speaking out of sheer experience, and to the glory of God. What one had never thought of, or even imagined, suddenly happens in the pulpit while one is actually preaching, and one is left with a sense of amazement, gratitude and unspeakable joy. There is nothing like it.

Then there is, as it were, the other side to that kind of experience. There have been times when I have felt that I have been restrained from preaching the whole of my prepared sermon. I have been led to develop and work out the sermon in a modified way, so that I have had to readjust my planned series. Or sometimes—and I am thinking especially of one particular occasion—I have gone out of the pulpit having only preached half my prepared sermon. I could not quite understand this on that particular occasion to which I am referring. But, however, it had happened, and so, in a sense, I was ready for the next Sunday morning. The next Sunday morning came and I preached the remainder of my original sermon, which had now become a sermon in and of itself. I found that I was given unusual liberty. A man came to me at the end and told me that there was a visitor there who would like to see me. He seemed to him to be a minister. Eventually I saw this minister whose home was thousands of miles away. He was so moved that he could scarcely speak. What had happened? Why was he so moved and affected? This man was quite certain that God had brought him there all that distance in order to hear that particular sermon. I have referred to this in the Foreword of a little book called *Faith on Trial*; but it is worth repeating. I am sure that that man was right. But this is what astounded me. If I had not been dealt with on the previous Sunday in the way I have described, and restrained from preaching all my sermon, I would have preached on the previous Sunday what this man had just heard. But I had been restrained, I was only allowed to preach half my sermon the previous Sunday; the second half had been kept back. As I have said, I was a little disturbed about this but now it was perfectly clear to me. We do not control the situation; this is of God. This is where the romance comes in; you have no idea what you are doing. I had never heard of this man and knew nothing at all about him, but what he had heard that morning might well have been prepared specially for him. What I had planned for the morning in my original planning would not have suited his case at all. Is there anything comparable to this? Is there anything as romantic as this? This is the sort of thing that happens to a preacher, and the more you experience it the more amazed will you be at it, and thank God that you have been called to such a glorious ministry.

Someone may ask on the practical level: What do you do, then, when you suddenly find while preaching that this is happening to you? You will find that you have to think very quickly, and see to it that you round off this sermon you are actually preaching, and which has developed while you were preaching. You have to make it an entity in itself. You will have to re-arrange it in certain ways and make certain additions and elaborations and so bring it to a conclusion and climax. You must not leave it unfinished but work it out to its own logical end and conclusion and application. All this obviously implies the element of freedom while preaching; and the ability to do it grows with experience.

Another element in this romance of preaching is that you never know who is going to be listening to you, and you never know what is going to happen to those who are listening to you. It may be the turning point in somebody's life. Thank God it is so not infrequently. 'The fools who came to scoff remained to pray.' Men who may have come in to the service in a state of utter hopelessness go out rejoicing—converted, regenerated, new men and women. Their entire life has been changed, and you have been involved in this and played a part in it. Is there anything in the world that compares with this? There is nothing—nothing at all. This is the most wonderful thing that can ever happen to a human being. You are standing there between a soul and God. Eternal matters have been dealt with, and eternal destinies have been determined.

Another very frequent experience is that people will come to you at the close of a service and say: 'Do you know, this is astonishing; if you had known my, or our, position you could not have preached more directly to it.' It was the very thing they needed. Some problem, some perplexity, some difficulty, some tragedy had been oppressing them, and you have been given the very words that were necessary. I have a friend, a very fine pastor in another country, who had been persecuted to such an extent that he had had to leave. He and his family had intended settling in another country. But they were passing through London and so happened to come to our service on a Sunday morning.

I had never heard of them and knew nothing about them; but I was led to say something which spoke directly to them. It was just a part of the exposition of the text and a general application of it. This man turned to his wife at the end, and she turned to him, and they said to each other, 'That's our answer.' The answer was that they were not to go to settle in the new country then; they were to go back to their own country where they had received such terrible persecution to face it out, and to battle it out. They did so, and they were honoured in doing so. I knew nothing about this until they told me several years afterwards. Such experiences lead to 'thoughts that do often lie too deep for tears'.

Let me end this section by telling you what is perhaps the most striking example of all this that I have ever been privileged to know. This is something that actually happened during a prayer and not a sermon. I knew a poor man who had been converted from a terrible life of sin and who had become a fine Christian. That was when I was in South Wales. But, afterwards, unfortunately, for various reasons this poor fellow had become a backslider and had fallen very deeply into sin. He had run away from his wife and children to live with another woman of a very poor type. They had come to London and there they had lived in sin. He had squandered his money, and he had actually gone home and told his wife a lie in order to get further money out of her. The house in which they lived was in their joint names, but he got this changed and put into his name. Then he sold it in order to get the money. He had thus gone very very far into the 'far country', he had sinned terribly. But now the money had finished and the woman had deserted him. He was so utterly miserable and ashamed that he had solemnly decided to commit suicide, feeling that in his deep state of repentance God would forgive him. But he could not forgive himself, and he felt that he had no right ever to approach his family again. So he solemnly decided to walk to Westminster Bridge and throw himself into the Thames. He was actually on the way to do this. Just as the poor soul arrived at the bridge, Big Ben struck half-past six—six-thirty. Suddenly a thought flashed into his mind and he said to himself, 'He (referring to me) will now be just entering his pulpit for his evening service.' So he decided that he would come and listen to me once more before he put an end to his life. He made his way to Westminster Chapel in about six minutes, got in through the front door, walked up the stairs and was just entering the gallery when he heard these words, 'God have mercy upon the backslider'. I uttered that petition in my prayer and they were literally the first words he heard. Everything was put right immediately, and he was not only restored but became an elder in a church in a suburb of London and rendered excellent service for a number of years.*

What does it mean? It means that we are in the hands of God, and therefore anything can happen. 'With God nothing is impossible.' 'Ask great things of God,' as William Carey said, and go on to 'expect great things from God', and He will lead you on from surprise to surprise. There is no romance comparable to that of the work of the preacher. It is a road along which there are many Bethels, and one is constantly driven to remember Francis Thompson's words, 'Turn but a stone and start a wing.'

* In the time between the delivery of these lectures and their publication he died a glorious and triumphant death.

CHAPTER SIXTEEN

'Demonstration of the Spirit and of the Power'

I HAVE KEPT and reserved to this last lecture what is after all the greatest essential in connection with preaching, and that is the unction and the anointing of the Holy Spirit. It may seem odd to some that I keep the most important thing of all to the end instead of starting with it. My reason for doing so is that I believe that if we do, or attempt to do, all I have been saying first, then the unction will come upon it. I have already pointed out that some men fall into the error of relying upon the unction only, and neglect to do all they can by way of preparation. The right way to look upon the unction of the Spirit is to think of it as that which comes upon the preparation. There is an Old Testament incident which provides a ready illustration to show this relationship. It is the story of Elijah facing the false prophets of Israel on Mount Carmel. We are told that Elijah built an altar, then cut wood and put it on the altar, and that then he killed a bullock and cut it in pieces and put the pieces on the wood. Then, having done all that, he prayed for the fire to descend; and the fire fell. That is the order.

There are many other examples of the same thing. One of the most notable is in connection with the account of the erection of the Tabernacle in the wilderness in Exodus 40. We are told how Moses first did in detail everything that God had told him to do, and that it was only after he had done it all that the glory of the Lord came down upon the Tabernacle. That is my reason for reserving what is beyond doubt the most important factor of all, in connection with preaching, to the end. 'God helps those who help themselves' is true in this connection as in many others. Careful preparation, and the unction of the Holy Spirit, must never be regarded as alternatives but as complementary to each other.

We all tend to go to extremes; some rely only on their own preparation and look for nothing more; others, as I say, tend to despise preparation and trust to the unction, the anointing and the inspiration of the Spirit alone. But there must be no 'either/or' here; it is always 'both/and'. These two things must go together.

What is meant by this 'unction or anointing' of the Spirit? The best way of approach is to show from the Scriptures first of all what is meant by this. But before we do that let me put a question to all preachers. Do you always look for and seek this unction, this anointing before preaching? Has this been your greatest concern? There is no more thorough and revealing test to apply to a preacher.

What is this? It is the Holy Spirit falling upon the preacher in a special manner. It is an access of power. It is God giving power, and enabling, through the Spirit, to the preacher in order that he may do this work in a manner that lifts it up beyond the efforts and endeavours of man to a position in which the preacher is being used by the Spirit and becomes the channel through whom the Spirit works. This is seen very plainly and clearly in the Scriptures.

I propose therefore to look first at the scriptural teaching, then to view the subject from the historical standpoint, and finally to make some comments. It is quite clear in the Scriptures that all the Old Testament prophets are illustrations of this anointing, but I propose to confine our attention to the New Testament. We start with John the Baptist, because he is the forerunner of the Saviour. In Luke 1 we are told that a message was given to his father Zacharias to this effect:

For he shall be great in the sight of the Lord, and shall drink neither wine nor strong drink; and he shall be filled with the Holy Ghost, even from his mother's womb. And many of the children of Israel shall he turn to the Lord their God. And he shall go before him in the spirit and power of Elias, to turn the hearts of the fathers to the children, and the disobedient to the wisdom of the just (verses 15–17).

That is an excellent summary of the position of the prophets of the Old Testament. Those men were aware of an afflatus which came upon them; the Spirit took hold of them and they were given a message, and the power to deliver it. It is the great characteristic of the prophets, and John was the last of the prophets. So we are told about him that he was endued in this very special way with the Holy Ghost and His power to do his work. And when you read the accounts of his ministry this becomes obvious. He spoke in such a manner that people came under powerful conviction. The preaching of John the Baptist convicted even Pharisees—that is the surest proof of the power of a ministry. But John was well aware of the merely preliminary character of his ministry and always emphasised that it was but preparatory—'I am not the Christ,' he says. 'One mightier than I cometh, the latchet of whose shoes I am not worthy to unloose.' 'I indeed baptise you with water; . . . he shall baptise you with the Holy Ghost and with fire' (Luke 3:15–17). There was something further to come, something altogether greater.

Next we must observe what happened in the case of our Lord Himself. This is a point which is very often missed. I refer to the way in which the Holy Ghost descended upon Him as He was coming up out of the river Jordan after John the Baptist had baptised Him. The Spirit came upon Him in the form of a dove. He Himself explained afterwards what this meant, when He spoke in the Synagogue in His home town of Nazareth as recorded in Luke 4:18 ff. 'The Spirit of the Lord is upon me, because He hath anointed me to preach the gospel to the poor . . . ' What I am concerned to emphasise is that He says that what had happened to Him there at Jordan was that He was anointed by the Spirit to preach this Gospel of salvation, 'to preach the acceptable year of the Lord'.

This is a most striking statement. It throws great light, of course, upon the whole meaning and purpose of the Incarnation; but what is significant is that even our Lord Himself, the Son of God, could not have exercised His ministry as a man on earth if He had not received this special, peculiar 'anointing' of the Holy Spirit to perform His task. It is true even of Him.

Then—and I am but selecting what I regard as the most important passages which deal with this matter—we come to the Book of the Acts of the Apostles, and in Acts 1:8 we read, 'But ye shall receive power, after that the Holy Ghost is come upon you: and ye shall be witnesses unto Me both in Jerusalem, and in all Judaea, and in Samaria, and unto the uttermost part of the earth.' That, of course, should be linked up always with the last chapter of the Gospel according to St. Luke, where we have an account of what our Lord said to the assembled disciples in the upper room. He said He was sending them out.

Thus it is written, and thus it behoved Christ to suffer, and to rise from the dead the third day: And that repentance and remission of sins should be preached in His name among all nations, beginning at Jerusalem. And ye are witnesses of these things. And, behold, I send the promise of my Father upon you: but tarry ye in the city of Jerusalem until ye be endued with power from on high.

That leads on to Acts 1:8, and to the fulfilment of that, as recorded in Acts 2.

The significance of this, as I see it, is that here we have men whom, you would have thought, were in a perfect position and condition already to act as preachers. They had been with our Lord for three years, they had heard all His discourses and instructions, they had seen all His miracles, they had had the benefit of being with Him, looking into His face and, having personal conversation and communion with Him. Three of them had witnessed His Transfiguration, all of them had witnessed the Crucifixion and the burial, and above all they were all witnesses of the fact of His physical resurrection. You would have thought these men therefore were now in a perfect position to go out to preach; but according to our Lord's teaching they were not. They seem to have all the necessary knowledge, but that knowledge is not sufficient, something further is needed, is indeed essential. The knowledge indeed is vital for you cannot be witnesses without it, but to be effective witnesses you need the power and the unction and the demonstration of the Spirit in addition. Now if this was necessary for these men, how much more is it necessary for all others who try to preach these things?

We read of the Spirit coming upon those men assembled on the Day of Pentecost at Jerusalem; and at once you see the difference that made to them. The Peter who in a craven spirit had denied his Lord, in order to save his own life, is now filled with boldness and great assurance. He is able to expound the Scriptures in an authoritative manner and to speak with such mighty effect that three thousand people are converted under his preaching. This was the inauguration, as it were, of the Christian Church as we know her in this dispensation of the Spirit, and that is the graphic picture we are given of how it began.

Here I must call attention to a further point which I feel we also tend to miss. This 'accession of power', or if you prefer it, this 'effusion of power' upon Christian preachers is not something 'once for all'; it can be repeated, and repeated many many times.

Let me adduce some examples of this. There on the Day of Pentecost we have seen the apostles filled with this power, and seen also that the real object of 'the baptism with the Spirit' is to enable men to witness to Christ and His salvation with power. The Baptism with the Holy Spirit is not regeneration—the apostles were already regenerate—and it is not given primarily to promote sanctification; it is a baptism of power, or a baptism of fire, a baptism to enable one to witness. The old preachers used to make a great deal of this. They would ask about a man, 'Has he received his baptism of fire?' That was the great question. It is not regeneration or sanctification; this is power, power to witness.

The Apostles received this on the Day of Pentecost and Peter immediately witnessed in a most powerful manner; and he and John again witnessed after the healing of the impotent man, and did so in their preaching in the Temple. But look again at Acts 4:7. Here are Peter and John on trial before the Sanhedrin, and charges are brought against them: 'When they had set them in the midst, they asked, By what power, or by what name have ye done this?' But notice what the record goes on to say: 'Then Peter, filled with the Holy Ghost, said unto them, Ye rulers of the people . . .'

How do you interpret that? Why does it say, 'Then Peter, filled with the Holy Spirit?' You might argue, 'But was he not filled with the Holy Ghost on the Day of Pentecost as the other men were?' Of course he was. What then is the point of repeating it here? There is only one adequate explanation of this. It is not just a reminder of the fact that he had been baptised with the Spirit on the Day of Pentecost. There is no purpose in the use of this expression unless it means that he received a fresh accession of power. He was in a critical position. Here he was on trial with John, indeed the Gospel and the entire Christian Church were on trial, and he needed some new, fresh power to witness positively and to confute the persecutors—some new, fresh power, and it is given him. So the expression is used, 'Peter filled with the Holy Ghost'. This was another filling for this special task.

There is yet a further example of this in that same fourth chapter of Acts in verse 31. There were all the members of the Church praying, in fear, at the threatening of the authorities who were trying to exterminate the Church. Then this is what happened, 'And when they had prayed, the place was shaken where they were assembled together; and they were all filled with the Holy Ghost'—the same people again. They had all been filled with the Holy Ghost on the Day of Pentecost, and Peter and John on subsequent occasions also; but here the entire company is filled again with the Holy Ghost. It is obvious, therefore, that this is something which can be repeated many times.

Then going on to Acts 6 we have an account of how the first deacons were appointed. Notice the qualifications which are stressed in verses

3 and 5: 'Wherefore, brethren, look ye out among you seven men of honest report, full of the Holy Ghost and wisdom.' This is not true of everybody, but it is true of some—'whom we may appoint over this business'. And then in verse 5: 'And the saying pleased the whole multitude and they chose Stephen, a man full of faith and of the Holy Ghost'. 'But,' you say, 'were they not all filled with the Holy Ghost?' Not in this sense. There is something special here, there is something peculiar, there is something additional; and they were told to look out for that. In every case it is exactly the same point.

Then there is another example in Acts 7:55—the picture of Stephen just before he was stoned to death. This is not only memorable but of great importance—verse 54: 'When they heard these things'—these were his accusers, the members of the Sanhedrin—'they were cut to the heart, and they gnashed on him with their teeth. But he, being full of the Holy Ghost, looked up stedfastly into heaven, and saw the glory of God, and Jesus standing on the right hand of God.' This is again, obviously, a special endowment. It is once more a man in a great crisis; and the Spirit comes upon him in an exceptional manner and enables him to face the crisis and to give a powerful witness.

One further example must suffice—in connection with the Apostle Paul who came later into the Church. It is in Acts 13:9. The Apostle Paul with Barnabas had arrived at a country where there was a deputy of the name of Sergius Paulus who desired to hear the Word of God. 'But Elymas the sorcerer withstood them, seeking to turn away the deputy from the faith.' Then verse 9: 'Then Saul, (who is also called Paul), filled with the Holy Ghost, set his eyes on him.' When the record says there, 'filled with the Holy Ghost', it is not referring back to the fact that he was filled with the Holy Ghost in connection with his conversion and as the result of his meeting with Ananias. It would be ridiculous to repeat this if it had happened once and for all. This is again a special enduement of power, a special crisis, a special occasion, and he was given this special power for this special occasion.

I would go further and suggest that this always happened to the Apostles whenever they worked a miracle or whenever they had some very special situation to deal with. The significance of that comes out in this way. There is a great difference between the miracles worked by the Apostles and the 'miracles' it is claimed certain men perform today. One big difference is this, that you never find the Apostles announcing beforehand that they are going to hold a Healing Service in a few days' time. Why not? Because they never knew when it was going to happen. They did not decide, and it was not within their control: what invariably happened rather was this. There was Paul for instance dealing with this man—you find the same thing in the case of the man at Lystra recorded in the fourteenth chapter—and suddenly he was given a commission to heal him. Paul knew nothing about this until he was impelled by the Spirit and given the power; and so did it. So the first difference between the so-called miracle workers today and the Apostles is that the Apostles could never predict or foretell or announce the working of miracles, and never did so.

There is a second difference also. The Apostles, you notice in the Book of Acts, never failed. It was never a case of making an experiment; there was no tentative element. They knew. They were given a commission, so they spoke with authority. They issued a command, and there was no failure; and there can be no failure when this is the position. That is clearly the general picture given in the Book of the Acts of the Apostles.

But there is something yet more direct and specific even than all this, namely the great statement of the Apostle Paul in 1 Corinthians 2, the crucial statement in which he describes his own preaching at Corinth. 'And I was with you in weakness, and in fear, and in much trembling. And my speech and my preaching was not with enticing words of man's wisdom, but in demonstration of the Spirit and of power: That your faith should not stand in the wisdom of men, but in the power of God' (verses 3–5). That is the vital and controlling statement with respect to this entire matter. Here is a man who was greatly gifted, who had exceptional natural powers; but he deliberately determined not to use them in a carnal manner. He 'determined not to know any thing among them, save Jesus Christ, and Him crucified';

he then deliberately eschewed the manner of the Greek rhetoricians, both as to content and style, with which he was so familiar. As he says later to these same Corinthians he became 'a fool for Christ's sake', in order that it might be clear that the power was not his but God's, and that their whole position should not be based upon 'the wisdom of men but upon the power of God'.

Coming from Paul of all men this, I think, is most striking. He reminds the Corinthians of this once more in the fourth chapter in verses 18–20. Some of the members in the church at Corinth were talking a great deal, criticising the Apostle Paul, and expressing their opinions freely on him and his teaching. So he challenges them and says, 'Now some are puffed up, as though I would not come to you. But I will come to you shortly, if the Lord will, and will know, not the speech of them which are puffed up, but the power. For the kingdom of God is not in word, but in power.' There is no text, perhaps, of which we need to be reminded so much at the present time as just that. There is certainly no lack of words; but is there much evidence of power in our preaching? 'The kingdom of God is not in word, but in power.' 'That,' says the Apostle, 'is the test'; and it is still the test of true preaching.

We find later that he repeats much the same thing in 2 Corinthians 4. Talking about his own ministry he says, 'As we have received mercy, we faint not; But have renounced the hidden things of dishonesty, not walking in craftiness, nor handling the word of God deceitfully; but by manifestation of the truth commending ourselves to every man's conscience in the sight of God.' He goes on to the moving statement in verse 6, 'God, who commanded the light to shine out of darkness, hath shined in our hearts, to give the light of the knowledge of the glory of God in the face of Jesus Christ.' And then immediately, 'But we have this treasure in earthen vessels, that the excellency of the power may be of God, and not of us'. It is always the same, he is always anxious to emphasise this utter dependence upon the power of the Spirit. The same is found again in 2 Corinthians 10:3 –5: 'For though we walk in the flesh, we do not war after the flesh:

For the weapons of our warfare are not carnal, but mighty through God to the pulling down of strong holds; Casting down imaginations, and every high thing that exalteth itself against the knowledge of God, and bringing into captivity every thought to the obedience of Christ.' It is always the same point, 'not carnal', 'mighty through God'. It is a spiritual power. Indeed, the same emphasis is to be found in that extraordinary statement in 2 Corinthians 12 where he tells us of how he had been 'lifted up into the third heaven, and had heard things which cannot be uttered'. And how then 'the thorn in the flesh' had come and he prayed three times for its removal; but the thorn was not removed. He was perplexed by this at first, but he had come to understand its meaning when God had said to him, 'My grace is sufficient for thee: for my strength is made perfect in weakness.' He is now able to say therefore, 'Most gladly therefore will I rather glory in my infirmities, that the power of Christ may rest upon me . . . for when I am weak, then am I strong.'

Another statement of this which never fails to move me is found at the end of Colossians in chapter 1. 'Whom we preach, warning every man, and teaching every man in all wisdom; that we may present every man perfect in Christ Jesus: Whereunto I also labour, striving according to His working, which worketh in me mightily.' That is always Paul's testimony. He was doing his utmost, but what really counts is 'His working, which worketh in me mightily'. That is what is meant by 'unction'. A still more precise definition even than that is found in 1 Thessalonians 1:5: 'For our gospel came not unto you in word only, but also in power, and in the Holy Ghost, and in much assurance.' The Apostle is reminding the Thessalonians of how the Gospel had come to them. He had had to leave them in order that he might preach elsewhere, and he writes this letter to them, which many think was his first letter to a church. It is a most important chapter indeed as the definitive and controlling statement concerning preaching and evangelism. He reminds them that the Gospel had 'come' to them; 'not in word only'. It had come 'in word', and he reminds them of the content of the word in verses 9 and 10, but it was 'not in word only, but also . . .' It is this 'also', this addition of the power of the Holy Ghost that ultimately makes preaching effective. This is what produces converts and creates Churches, and builds up Churches— 'power', 'Holy Ghost', and 'much assurance'.

Peter teaches precisely the same truth in reminding the Christians to whom he wrote in his First Epistle of how they had become Christians, and of the character of the Gospel message. He says, referring to the prophets of the Old Testament, 'Unto whom it was revealed, that not unto themselves, but unto us they did minister the things, which are now reported unto you by them that have preached the gospel unto you with the Holy Ghost sent down from heaven; which things the angels desire to look into.' That is how the Gospel is preached says—'with the Holy Ghost sent down from heaven'.

My last quotation comes from the last book of the Bible, the Book of Revelation. It is the statement by John about himself in the first chapter, verse 10: 'I was in the Spirit on the Lord's day, and heard behind me a great voice.' How do we interpret that? Does it mean that John, being a Christian, was always 'in the Spirit'? If that was the case why does he trouble to say so? This, clearly, was not his ordinary usual state and condition; it was something quite exceptional. He says, There was I on that Isle of Patmos on the Lord's day and suddenly I found myself 'in the Spirit'. It was a visitation of the Spirit of God. And it was as the result of this that he was given his great vision, the messages to the Churches and his understanding of the future course of history.

That is the clear and unmistakable scriptural evidence and testimony with regard to preaching. But it may well be that your position is, 'Yes, we accept that and we are in no difficulty about that. But all that ended with the Apostolic age, therefore it has nothing to do with us.' My reply is that the Scriptures are also meant to apply to us today, and that if you confine all this to the Apostolic era you are leaving very little for us at the present time. In any case how do you decide what was meant for them only, and what is for us also? On what grounds do you do that; what are your canons of judgment? I suggest that there are none save prejudice. The whole Scripture is for us. In the New Testament we have a picture of the Church, and it is relevant to the Church at all times and in all ages.

Thank God, the history of the Church proves the rightness of this contention. The evidence for this is abundant. The long history of the Church shows repeatedly that what we find in the New Testament has characterised the Church always in periods of revival and reformation. This is why I have always maintained that next to the reading of the Bible itself, to read the history of revivals is one of the most encouraging things that one can ever do. Take the situation with which we are confronted today. Look at the task, look at the state of the world, look at the modern mentality. Without believing in and knowing something of the power of the Spirit, it is a heart-breaking task. I certainly could not go on for another day but for this. If I felt that it was all left to us, and our learning and our scholarship and our organisations, I would be of all men the most miserable and hopeless. The situation would be completely hopeless. But that is not the case. What we read of in the New Testament is equally possible and open to us today; and it is our only hope. But we must realise this. If we do not, we shall spend our time in 'shallows and in miseries'; and we shall achieve nothing.

What then is the evidence of history? We could well start from the Protestant Reformation. There is ample evidence at that time of the mighty working of the Spirit. There was that great experience that Luther himself describes when the whole room seemed to be filled with light. That undoubtedly is the key to the understanding of his extraordinary preaching. We are so interested in Luther the theologian that we tend to forget Luther the preacher. Luther was a mighty preacher. The same is true of John Calvin also.

But there were two men in England who were quite outstanding in this respect. One was Hugh Latimer, whose preaching at St. Paul's Cross in London was obviously attended with very great unction and the power of the Holy Spirit. This again is something we tend to forget. We are rightly interested in the great theological upheaval at the time of the Protestant Reformation; but let us never forget that it was also a popular movement. It was not confined to the learned and the professors; it came down to the people because there were these great preachers who were anointed with the Spirit.

There was a man called John Bradford who obviously was a very great preacher in this same sense. He was one of the early Protestant martyrs. The same was true of other countries also at that time. There was a mighty preacher in Scotland at the end of the sixteenth century called Robert Bruce. A little book concerning him has recently been republished. In that book you can read the account of what happened on one occasion when he was at a conference of ministers in Edinburgh. At that time things were very bad indeed and most discouraging. The ministers were talking to one another and conferring, but they were all very depressed. The more they talked the more depressed they became—as is not unusual in general assemblies and other religious conferences. Robert Bruce tried to get them to pray, and they were trying to pray. However it was clear to Bruce that they were but 'trying to pray', and he did not regard that as praying. So he was 'stirred in his spirit', as Paul was at Athens, and said that he was going to 'knock' the Holy Spirit into them. So he began to thump the table with his fists; and he certainly achieved something. They then really did begin to pray 'in the Spirit' and they were lifted up out of their depression to the heights and given great assurance from God that He was still with them and that He would 'never leave them, nor forsake them'. They went back to their work re-invigorated and with a new hope and confidence.

But come to what is in many ways my favourite illustration. It concerns John Livingstone who lived at the beginning of the seventeenth century in Scotland. John Livingstone was also a very able man as most of those men were. Those early Reformed ministers in Scotland were a succession of tremendous men from the standpoint of ability, learning and knowledge; but the thing that characterised them above everything else was their knowledge and experience of this spiritual power and unction.

John Livingstone, as I say, was a very fine scholar and a great preacher. He had had to escape to Northern Ireland on account of persecution, and while there had had some experiences of a Revival. But his great day came in 1630. There was a Communion season at a place called Kirk O' Shotts, just off the road between Glasgow and Edinburgh. These Communion seasons would last many days and were characterised by much preaching by several visiting preachers. On this particular occasion they had all felt from the beginning right through to the Sunday evening that there was something unusual. So the brethren decided to have an additional preaching service on the Monday, and they asked John Livingstone to preach. Now Livingstone was a very modest and humble and godly man, and so was fearful of the great responsibility of preaching on such an occasion. So he spent most of the night struggling in prayer. He went out into the countryside and there continued praying. Many of the people were praying also. But he was in a great agony of soul, and he could find no peace until in the early hours of Monday morning God gave him a message and at the same time gave him an assurance also that his preaching would be attended with great power. So John Livingstone preached on that famous Monday morning, and as the result of that one sermon 500 people were added to the churches in that locality. It was a tremendous day, an overwhelming experience of the outpouring of the Spirit of God upon an assembled congregation. The remainder of his life's story is equally significant and important. John Livingstone lived many years after that but he never had such an experience again. He always looked back to it, and he always longed for it; but it was actually never repeated in his experience.

Similar spiritual experiences are described in the lives of preachers in the U.S.A. I derived great benefit a few years back from reading the Journals of Cotton Mather, the author of *Magnalia Christi Americana*. Those journals, and his history of religion in America, have many illustrations of the power of the Holy Spirit. There is nothing more important for preaching, as I have said, than the reading of Church history and biographies. There are remarkable descriptions in Cotton Mather's own Journal of these 'visitations' as he would call them, of the Spirit of God and the effect they had upon his preaching. Again I emphasise the fact that Cotton Mather was a very able and scholarly man, and not just an ignorant, credulous and excitable preacher. All those Mathers were able men; and he had the still abler Cotton influence in his blood as well. He was a grandson of both John Cotton, perhaps the most scholarly of the first American preachers, and also Richard Mather. No man could have a better pedigree, a better ancestry from the standpoint of intellect and ability; yet nothing is more striking about this man than his realisation that he could really do nothing without this unction and power of the Holy Spirit, and his sense of utter dependence upon it.

'Time fails me,' like the author of the Epistle to the Hebrews, to speak about Jonathan Edwards and David Brainerd. Their biographies are available, both old and new, and should be compulsory reading for all preachers. Then there was Gilbert Tennant and other members of that notable family. Gilbert Tennant was used for a period like a flaming sword, and then the power seems to have left him, and for the remainder of his ministry in Philadelphia he was a comparatively 'ordinary' preacher.

Once more there is the story of George Whitefield and the Wesleys. John Wesley is an important man in this whole argument for several reasons. One of these, and the most important in many ways, is that if ever there was a typical scholarly man it was John Wesley. He was also a typical Englishman, which means that he was not emotional by nature. The Englishman we are told is phlegmatic and does not get excited; he is not easily moved, and is not mercurial like the Celts and the Latin races—though this does not appear to be true in the realm of football! Now John Wesley was the most typical Englishman conceivable, pedantic, precise, and exact. His upbringing had been very strict and rigorous and disciplined, and after an excellent academic career as a student he had become a fellow of a college in Oxford. He was exact in his exegesis, precise in statement, with every word in order, and moreover he was a very devout and religious man. He gave his spare time to visiting the prisoners in jails; he would even go with some of them to their execution. He gave of his money to feed the poor. Even all this did not satisfy him; he gave up his position at Oxford and crossed the Atlantic to preach the Gospel in Georgia to the poor slaves and others. But he was quite useless, a complete failure, and he came to the conclusion that he needed the Gospel quite as much as the poor slaves in Georgia. And he did. There was no power in his ministry. In addition he was not clear about the way of salvation, and this was brought home to him in a storm in mid-Atlantic, when he observed the difference between himself and some Moravian brethren face to face with death. So he returned to England.

Having got back to England he was first of all put right on the doctrine of justification by faith only. He came to see it clearly in March 1738, but still he was a failure as a preacher, indeed he began to feel that he should not preach. He said to the Moravian Brother, Peter Bohler who had helped him into this understanding of justification by faith, 'I see it clearly with my head but I do not feel it, and I had better stop preaching until I feel it.' 'No,' said Peter Bohler in that immortal answer, 'Do not stop preaching it, but go on preaching it until you do feel it.' You remember what happened. On the twenty-fourth of May, 1738, he had that climactic experience. In a little meeting in Aldersgate Street in London, a number of people had met together to study the Scriptures and to build one another up in the faith. On that particular night a man had been appointed to read the Preface to Luther's Commentary on the Epistle to the Romans—not the Commentary but the Preface. Here was this man reading that Preface to Luther's Commentary on Romans, and as he was reading Wesley says that his heart 'was strangely warmed' and he suddenly felt that God had forgiven his sins—even his. As he felt this warmth something began to melt within him; and it was from that moment this man began to preach with a new power and was greatly used by God. All this is but confirmatory of what we find in the Scriptures. You can have knowledge, and you can be meticulous in your preparation; but without the unction of the Holy Spirit you will have no power, and your preaching will not be effective.

Whitefield tells us that he was aware, actually in his Ordination Service, of the power coming down upon him. He knew it. He was thrilled with the sense of power. The very first Sunday after his ordination he preached in his home-town of Gloucester, and it was an amazing service. It was so remarkable that people wrote to the Bishop —Bishop Benson—complaining against Whitefield, and asserting that as the result of his sermon fifteen people had become insane. The Bishop was not only a wise man but a good man; so he replied saying that he wished all his clergy could produce some effect on people, for most of them had no effect at all. He was glad to hear of a man who had some effect. Of course these people had not become insane; what had happened was that they had come under terrifying and powerful conviction of sin. People at that time, even as many medical doctors and others today, were very ready to make the diagnosis of 'religious mania'; but what actually happens is that the person, or persons, concerned have been brought under tremendous conviction of sin by the Holy Spirit of God. The subsequent Journals of Whitefield, and the various biographies of him, contain endless accounts of his awareness of the Spirit of God coming upon him while he preached, and also at other times.

In my native country of Wales there were two remarkable men in the eighteenth century, Howel Harris and Daniel Rowlands. Their lives are equally eloquent in this respect. Howel Harris was a young schoolmaster. He was convicted of sin at Easter-time in 1735, and was in great trouble of soul until Whit Sunday when he was given assurance that his sins were forgiven and he began to rejoice in this fact. However, three weeks later as he was sitting in the tower of a church reading the Scriptures, praying and meditating, he says, 'God began to pour out His Spirit upon me.' He describes how it came in 'wave upon wave' until he could scarcely contain it physically, and tells how he was filled with the love of God shed abroad in his heart. Now it was from that moment that Harris began to feel the impulse to evangelise his heathen neighbours. At first he used to visit the sick, and he would read good books to them. He did not utter a word of his own, he just read out of books to them. But there was such unction and power attending his reading of these books that people were convicted of sin and converted. This went on for some time. He felt that he was so unworthy that he was unfit to be a preacher, so though he felt he was somewhat dishonest in doing so, he went on reading out of the books but began also to interpose some of his own remarks as the thoughts came to him, still keeping his eyes on the book. He continued like that for a while. Eventually he began openly to exhort the people, and great crowds gathered to listen to him. This man was the pioneer, in a sense, of a movement that shook the whole country and brought into being the denomination known as the Welsh Calvinistic Methodist, or present-day Presbyterian, Church of Wales. That is how it happened; it was the direct result of this special anointing and unction of the Holy Spirit. He would lose this at times for a while, and he would grieve; then it would come back again. He went on like that until he died in 1773. The same thing was true of many of his contemporaries and especially of the great Daniel Rowlands whose private journals were unfortunately lost.

You will find the same thing in the biography, written by Andrew Bonar, of the greatly used preacher W. H. Nettleton to whom I have referred previously.

In other words you find exactly the same type of experience in very different types of men. Most of the men I have mentioned so far were very able men. But in addition you have a man like D. L. Moody who was not an able man but was nevertheless greatly used of God. This was the direct outcome and result of an experience he had while walking down Wall Street in New York City one afternoon. Moody had been the pastor of a church in Chicago before that, and a successful pastor. He had certainly been doing good work, but that pales into insignificance when you compare it with what he was afterwards enabled to do.

But let me take a final illustration. There was a great Revival in the U.S.A. in 1857 which spread over to Northern Ireland in 1858 and to Wales in 1859. Revivals have generally happened simultaneously in a number of countries. This was true in the eighteenth century as well as the nineteenth, a most interesting fact in itself. But I am thinking in particular of the man who was most used of God in Wales in that Revival, whose name was David Morgan, and particularly of one aspect of his amazing story. There was a Welshman in the U.S.A. at the time, a Humphrey Jones, who came powerfully under the influence of the Revival. Having entered into this new life, and being filled with the Spirit of joy and rejoicing,he said to himself, 'I wish my people at home could experience this'. This became such a burden to him that he went home to Wales. Having arrived he just began to tell the people of his home county about what he had seen and experienced. He went round and spoke in the chapels, and the ministers and people would listen to him. David Morgan had listened on a number of occasions to Humphrey Jones, and gradually became interested and began to feel a longing for Revival. One night Humphrey Jones was speaking with exceptional power and David Morgan was profoundly affected. He said later, 'I went to bed that night just David Morgan as usual. I woke up the next morning feeling like a lion, feeling that I was filled with the power of the Holy Ghost.' At that time he had been a minister for a number of years. He was always a good man, not outstanding—in fact just an ordinary preacher. Nothing much happened as the result of his preaching. But he woke up that next morning feeling like a lion, and began to preach with such power that people were convicted and converted in large numbers followed by rejoicing; and additions to the churches followed. This went on for over two years; wherever this man went tremendous results took place.

Among the many stories of conversions under Morgan's ministry none is more striking than that of T. C. Edwards, the author of a well-known Commentary on the First Epistle to the Corinthians, which can still be found on the shelves of second-hand bookshops. Thomas Charles Edwards was an undoubted genius. His father Lewis Edwards was the Principal of the first Theological College in the Welsh Calvinistic Methodist Church, and his mother was a grand daughter of the famous Thomas Charles who, to a great extent was responsible for the founding of the British and Foreign Bible Society. T. C. Edwards, at that time a student, was home on vacation and heard that this David Morgan and another preacher were going to preach in his home town. He decided to go to listen, and subsequently described how he went to the meeting with his mind full of philosophical difficulties and perplexities. His faith had been shaken by his reading of philosophy and he was in trouble. He did not quite know where he stood, and he said that he went in that mood just out of curiosity to see and hear what these two simple preachers would have to say. He had heard a great deal about the enthusiasm and excitement connected with the Revival and he heartily disapproved of it.

But this is what happened. He had a red silk handkerchief in his pocket as was the habit of such young men in those days; and all he knew was this, that at the end of the meeting the red silk handkerchief was torn to shreds on the floor of the pew in which he was sitting in the gallery. He was quite unaware of the fact that he had done this but the fact was that his entire life was changed, his philosophical doubts were dispersed, all his uncertainties vanished like the morning mist, and this great scholar was filled with the power of the Holy Spirit and became an outstanding preacher. He became the first Principal of the University College at Aberystwyth and eventually followed his father as President of the Theological College. Sir William Robertson Nicol, the first editor of a famous religious weekly known as *The British Weekly*, and an acute judge of men and preachers, said that of all the great preachers he had known T. C. Edwards was the only one whom he could visualise as the founder of a new denomination—such was his dynamic power.

Such was the type of ministry exercised by David Morgan for about two years. What was the end of his story? Years later he said, 'I went to bed one night still feeling like a lion, filled with this strange power that I had enjoyed for the two years. I woke up the next morning and found that I had become David Morgan once more.' He lived for about fifteen years afterwards during which he exercised a most ordinary ministry.

The power came, and the power was withdrawn. Such is the lordship of the Spirit! You cannot command this blessing, you cannot order it; it is entirely the gift of God. The examples I have given from the Scriptures indicate this. 'Peter, filled with the Spirit.' The Spirit filled him. He did the same to David Morgan; and then in His own inscrutable wisdom and sovereignty He took it from him. Revivals are not meant to be permanent. But at the same time I maintain that all of us who are preachers should be seeking this power every time we preach.

How do we recognise this when it happens? Let me try to answer. The first indication is in the preacher's own consciousness. 'Our gospel came not unto you in word only', says Paul, 'but also in power and the Holy Ghost, and much assurance'. Who knew the assurance? Paul himself. He knew something was happening, he was aware of it. You cannot be filled with the Spirit without knowing it. He had 'much assurance'. He knew he was clothed with power and authority. How does one know it? It gives clarity of thought, clarity of speech, ease of utterance, a great sense of authority and confidence as you are preaching, an awareness of a power not your own thrilling through the whole of your being, and an indescribable sense of joy. You are a man 'possessed', you are taken hold of, and taken up. I like to put it like this—and I know of nothing on earth that is comparable to this feeling —that when this happens you have a feeling that you are not actually doing the preaching, you are looking on. You are looking on at yourself in amazement as this is happening. It is not your effort; you are just the instrument, the channel, the vehicle: and the Spirit is using you, and you are looking on in great enjoyment and astonishment. There is nothing that is in any way comparable to this. That is what the preacher himself is aware of.

What about the people? They sense it at once; they can tell the difference immediately. They are gripped, they become serious, they are convicted, they are moved, they are humbled. Some are convicted of sin, others are lifted up to the heavens, anything may happen to any one of them. They know at once that something quite unusual and exceptional is happening. As a result they begin to delight in the things of God and they want more and more teaching. They are like the people in the Book of the Acts of the Apostles, they want 'to continue steadfastly in the apostles' doctrine, and fellowship, and breaking of bread and in prayers'.

What then are we to do about this? There is only one obvious conclusion. Seek Him! Seek Him! What can we do without Him? Seek Him! Seek Him always. But go beyond seeking Him; expect Him. Do you expect anything to happen when you get up to preach in a pulpit? Or do you just say to yourself, 'Well, I have prepared my address, I am going to give them this address; some of them will appreciate it and some will not?' Are you expecting it to be the turning point in someone's life? Are you expecting anyone to have a climactic experience? That is what preaching is meant to do. That is what you find in the Bible and in the subsequent history of the Church. Seek this power, expect this power, yearn for this power; and when the power comes, yield to Him. Do not resist. Forget all about your sermon if necessary. Let Him loose you, let Him manifest His power in you and through you. I am certain, as I have said several times before, that nothing but a return of this power of the Spirit on our preaching is going to avail us anything. This makes true preaching, and it is the greatest need of all today—never more so. Nothing can substitute for this. But, given this, you will have a people who will be anxious and ready to be taught and instructed, and led ever further and more deeply into 'the Truth as it is in Christ Jesus'. This 'unction', this 'anointing', is the supreme thing. Seek it until you have it; be content with nothing less. Go on until you can say, 'And my speech and my preaching was not with enticing words of man's wisdom, but in demonstration of the Spirit and of power.' He is still able to do 'exceeding abundantly above all that we can ask or think'.